Praise for **Athene Palace:**

"*Athene Palace* . . . is a textured miniature painting in words or Romanian manners, as seen from the lobby of the Athene Palace Hotel in Bucharest during the fascist revolution of 1940–41."—Robert D. Kaplan, from "A Reader's Guide to the Balkans," *New York Times*, 1993

"The most vivid report, long or short, I have ever seen on Rumania comes out this morning under the title of *Athene Palace*. It is brilliantly written and mercilessly barbed. . . . She writes throughout with a sharp and witty pen and with a knowledge of men and events by no means bounded by her seven months in Bucharest. An unusually skillful and readable book."—Ralph Thompson, *New York Times*, 1942

"The Countess Waldeck takes current history out of the funeral parlor and puts it into the Grand Hotel. Her book is as perversely engrossing, gossipy and gamy as a clandestine conversation in the lobby. Her Grand Hotel is the Athene Palace in Bucharest, 'the last cosmopolitan stage on which post-World-War Europe and the new-order Europe made a joint appearance.' Theme of her book is the murder of a nation—Rumania."—*Time*, February 16, 1942

"For once, the publisher's blurb does not exaggerate. This book really is 'brilliantly written' and 'perversely intelligent.' . . . The author was in Bucharest from June 1940 until January 1941, and from the vantage point of the Athene Palace, the 'grand hotel' of Bucharest, she witnessed at close quarters the incredible happenings on the Rumanian political scene during those seven months. That scene and those happenings are described with great gusto, insight and a good dose of amusing malice."—*International Affairs Review Supplement*, 1943

"The writer . . . lived at the Hotel Athenée-Palace from June, 1940, until January, 1941. Allowing for the fact that she was an American newspaper correspondent there is . . . excellent description and shrewd observation. . . . The writer's account of the worst of the anti-Jewish excesses bears the mark of truth."—*Times Literary Supplement*, April 10, 1943, Sir Alec Walter George Randall

BIOGRAPHICAL NOTE

Rosie Goldschmidt Waldeck (August 24, 1898–August 8, 1982), born Rosa Goldschmidt in Mannheim, Germany, was the author of several works, including *Prelude to the Past: The Autobiography of a Woman* and *Athene Palace*. Waldeck was born Jewish but later became a Catholic in April of 1939 and gained American citizenship. Born into a banking family, she received a doctorate in sociology in 1920 from the University of Heidelberg where she studied under Alfred Weber. From the 1930s, she was based in the United States. From June 1940 to January 1941, she was a correspondent in Bucharest for American and Canadian publications. Living in the Athene Palace Hotel, she used her experiences during this time as the foundation for her novel, *Athene Palace*. The surname Waldeck comes from her third husband, the German count Armin Wolrad Widekind Bela Erich Maria Gottschalk Graf von Waldeck.

Athene Palace

ATHENE PALACE

HITLER'S "NEW ORDER" COMES TO RUMANIA

R. G. WALDECK

With a new Foreword by
ROBERT D. KAPLAN

THE UNIVERSITY OF CHICAGO PRESS
Chicago and London

The University of Chicago Press, Chicago 60637
Originally published in 1942
University of Chicago Press edition 2013
Printed in the United States of America

22 21 20 19 18 17 16 15 14 13   1 2 3 4 5

ISBN-13: 978-0-226-08633-0 (paper)
ISBN-13: 978-0-226-08647-7 (e-book)
DOI: 10.7208/chicago/9780226086477.001.0001

Library of Congress Cataloging-in-Publication Data

Waldeck, R. G. (Rosie Goldschmidt), 1898–1982.
    Athene Palace : Hitler's 'New Order' comes to Rumania / R. G. Waldeck ; with
a new foreword by Robert D. Kaplan.
        pages ; cm
    ISBN 978-0-226-08633-0 (paperback : alkaline paper) —
ISBN 978-0-226-08647-7 (e-book) 1. Romania—History—1914–1944.
2. Romania—Politics and government—1914–1944. 3. World War, 1939–1945—
Romania. I. Kaplan, Robert D., 1952– II. Title.
    DR266.5.W35 2013
    949.8'02—dc23

                                                                    2013011193

⊗ This paper meets the requirements of ANSI/NISO Z39.48-1992
(Permanence of Paper).

Contents

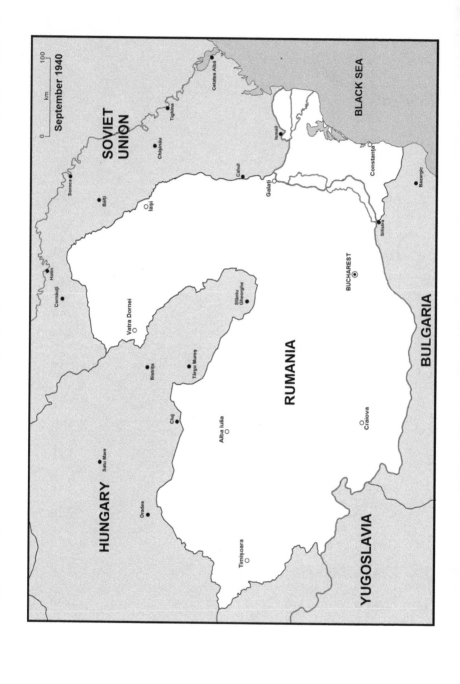

ACKNOWLEDGMENT

In a book which in any way deals with totalitarian politics and conditions, it is not polite for the author to acknowledge his sources. Therefore, I can only express my anonymous gratitude to the people in Bucharest and Transylvania whose conversations provided so important a part of my material.

I can, however, express my most sincere gratitude to those in America whose advice has proved of the greatest assistance in writing the book, first among them Allen Churchill, whose inexhaustible patience and warm encouragement have meant most to me and the book. Another who has been kind enough to give me assistance on many points is Mr. Jacob Rosenthal, secretary of the United Rumanian Jews of America, to whom I am also greatly indebted.

To anticipate any protests by purists, the author wishes to go on record as being aware that the name of Bucharest's Grand Hotel is really spelled Athénée Palace, and has been shorn of one "e" and of accents for no other reasons than simplicity and readability.

R. G. W.

FOREWORD
Robert D. Kaplan

In August 1984, I was in Bucharest reporting on perhaps the most repressive state in Communist Europe. Nicolae Ceaușescu's totalitarian regime had turned Romania into a grainy, black-and-white prison yard where the sense of paranoia was so overpowering, so intimidating, that it seemed the country had no past and no future. It wasn't true that the satellite states of the Soviet bloc were all of a kind. Traveling by rail from Budapest, Hungary, to Bucharest in those years, one saw that the quality of the houses and other construction immediately deteriorated and the lights went dim as the train car passed into Romania. The toilet paper in the restroom disappeared at the first stop when Romanian officials boarded the train to stamp passports and register typewriters—so controlling was the regime. Romania in the 1980s, as I can attest from several trips there during that decade, was a European country where Stalinism lived on, unbowed.

In the Romania of 1984, the Second World War seemed not decades but centuries removed. After all, the Cold War, which in Eastern Europe had been a fact of life for four decades already, appeared likely to go on for many more. But so it was that on that, my fifth, visit to Romania since 1973, I met an American diplomat and area specialist, Ernest H. Latham Jr., who had made it his passion to collect the memoirs and other writings of visitors to Romania prior to the onslaught of the Communist ice age. Latham told me that I absolutely had to read *Athene Palace* by R. G. Waldeck, published in 1942, an account of the Nazi takeover of Romania as seen from the vantage point of one magazine correspondent staying at the Athene Palace Hotel in Bucharest from June 1940 to January 1941. It would open my eyes to "another Romania," he said: one with a pre-Communist past and, therefore, with a post-Communist future.

At the time, when one thought of a book on World War II Romania, it was the British author Olivia Manning's 1960 work, *Balkan Trilogy*, which came to mind. But Latham counseled me that while Manning's treatment of Romania was on the scale of an epic, Waldeck's *Athene Palace* was something even better: an obscure and sparkling little jewel that within the confines of one hotel and the streets around it provided an intimate study of Romanian manners.

Waldeck's story seems so much more recent in the second decade of the twenty-first century than it did when I first read it in 1984. Then the pre-Communist past did not seem quite real. Now her descriptions of the Romanians, with their intrigues and subterfuges and sensual elegance, appear almost contemporary, mirroring as they do the corruption and infighting that mark Romanian politics in 2013, as well as all the new and elegant cafes, coffee shops, and other aesthetic paraphernalia that today help to define Bucharest, a city now almost a quarter century removed from the demise of Ceauşescu's Communism.

Waldeck suggests a people fated by geography to live amid clashing empires—Austrian and Turkish, German and Russian—a people who have thus cultivated survival nearly as an art form. Some Romanians of Waldeck's narrative, ingratiating themselves in certain instances with the Nazis, were acting according to a historical pattern. For here was yet another advancing empire, more powerful than they were, and so the trick was how to both benefit from and endure under the new order.

Thus did Waldeck partly reveal for me the logic of Ceau-şescu's rule. Under Ceauşescu, the secret police, the *Securitatae*, was so overwhelming in its influence on the society that it was said that "one half of the country spied on the other half." This, of course, was apocryphal, even as it captured a reality that few disputed: a significant portion of the country had found a way to survive by working with the regime. And while Ceauşescu may have made himself convenient to the West with his so-called maverick foreign policy, his police state was, ultimately, a product of Soviet—make that *Russian*—imperialism. As a correspondent during the Cold War, I was witnessing but another chapter in Romanian endurance.

What made the country so hard to write about was this: precisely because of the freeze-frame, Communist-induced poverty, even urban Romanians had been reduced to a veritable, backbreakingly poor peasantry, and so were robbed of their individuality. One saw them en masse, in other words, dehumanized. But Waldeck's account, which I read during the darkest period of Ceauşescu's rule, illuminated for me their individuality, allowing me to see Romania and its people slightly differently on my subsequent visits.

Waldeck paints glittering characters in rapid brushstrokes. Even the worst of these Romanians for the most part were not inherently evil people, and some were quite brave. It is easy to condemn ordinary, nonheroic individuals as cowardly in extraordinary historical circumstances that call for equally extraordinary forms of personal and communal resistance. But keep in mind the period that she writes about: the arrival of Nazi power following the West's essential abandonment of Central and Eastern Europe, as symbolized by the 1938

Munich Pact. She arrived at the grand hotel across the plaza from King Carol II's palace on the very day the German army marched unopposed into Paris. During Waldeck's six months in Bucharest, the Holocaust still lay in the future as something few could have imagined, even while the West was already a lost hope. Indeed, it would be another year before the United States entered the war.

As for Waldeck herself, she was born in 1898 as a Jew in Germany, becoming a naturalized American in 1939. She was thus one of those multilingual cosmopolitan journalists from an exotic background (by the professional standards of her era), which so enrich the journalistic community of our own day. Just as we have native Arab speakers employed by American news organizations in order to report on extremist groups in the Middle East, there was an American correspondent, Rosie Waldeck, whose first language was German, interviewing Nazi officers at the Athene Palace Hotel in Bucharest. It was an extraordinary situation in its own way. Bucharest in the second half of 1940 was perhaps the only other city in Europe aside from Lisbon where Nazis, American newspaper correspondents, and diplomats and spies from the West, the Axis Powers, and the Soviet Union could all sit at the same bar and restaurant tables and take each other's measure.

Soon, as Waldeck intimates, the whole canvas would go dark. Hitler's new order descended on Romania in full force, leaving no breathing space for observers like her from the outside. Waldeck, therefore, captures a precious interregnum, when the Germans were infiltrating Romania but before they held all the levers of power. She captures the moment, not as dry history but as a delicious cocktail of intrigues inside an extraordinary hotel. The book reads almost like a screenplay dashed off by a very knowing mind: that is, by a socially sophisticated woman who is nobody's fool. Here is a dark nightmare suffused with humanism because of its very concentration on individual characters. A short book, yet a feast.

Robert D. Kaplan is the author of *Balkan Ghosts* and many other books. He has been a foreign correspondent for the *Atlantic* for nearly three decades.

Athene Palace

Shall I be accused of
approving these things
because I describe them?
STENDHAL

When will it be recognized in Europe that peoples have only that degree of liberty in and among themselves which their courage wrests from their cowardice?

STENDHAL

1—RUMANIAN SCENE

I came to the Athene Palace the day Paris fell, in the summer of 1940. The Square before the hotel was still and hot that day, the only comfortable spot it offered being the short shadow cast by the canopy over the Athene Palace entrance. There was a patch of lawn before the hotel, bordered with gigantic red gladiolas, but all around this bit of vegetation was a vast expanse of asphalt, with nothing growing on it but a beautiful bronze horse with a bronze rider, high on a red-granite base. The rider was Carol I, founder of the present Rumanian dynasty. Facing as they did, horse and rider seemed about to jump over the gate right into the present Carol's palace.

The Athene Palace lined the width of the Piazza Atheneului, Bucharest's magic square that opens on the most glamorous artery of the Near East, the Calea Victoriei. Imagine the White House, the Waldorf Astoria, Carnegie Hall, Colony Restaurant, and the Lincoln Memorial, all standing together around a smallish square blossoming out on an avenue which is a cross between Broadway and

11

Pennsylvania and Fifth Avenues, and you understand what the Piazza Atheneului means to Rumania. Here was the heart of Bucharest topographically, artistically, intellectually, politically—and, if you like, morally.

At the left of the hotel, on the long side of the Piazza, was an ugly building designed along classical lines in a dirty yellow. This was the Athene, the concert hall that gave the Square and the hotel their name and where Georges Enesco, Rumania's beloved maestro, conducted his concerts. Next to the Athene was smart Cina's Restaurant with its lovely garden, the rendezvous of Bucharest's real and café society.

Only a stone's throw away, at the right of the hotel where the Piazza merged with the Calea Victoriei, King Carol's white palace began. One says "began" because the palace, looking very new and unfinished all the way, sprawled on and on up the Calea Victoriei, Rumania's road of destiny on which the Turkish conquerors had descended upon the city from the South and the German conquerors from the North, and which had witnessed all the passing glories and miseries of the country.

Built in 1910 and styled originally after the fashionable Paris hotels, the Meurice and the Ritz, the Athene Palace had two years ago been scraped clean of its caryatides and turrets and its façade streamlined into white smoothness with all the shutters painted a brilliant blue. The entrance hall, too, with its modernistic desk and gleaming showcases of glass and aluminum, had the same forcibly functional look. Even in the mirrored green salon with its low sofas and tables, a modern decorator had tried his hand; but for the rest you did not find much streamlining inside the hotel. You were apt to live in a pseudo-Louis XV room hung with blue brocades, and the restaurant was red and gold and white in the manner of the French restaurants of the second Empire. In the large darkish lobby where you spent most of your days, rows of yellow marble pillars formed three naves as in a church.

When the revolving door first discharged me into the cool entrance hall of the Athene Palace, I felt little beyond the traveling journalist's curiosity for the most famous hostelry of the Balkans. Landing in Naples in May, I had travelled leisurely through an Italy more poignantly beautiful than ever on the eve of her disastrous folly. I had spent a fortnight in Jugoslavia, where the abandon with which every racial group and political- and court-faction was busy hating every other racial group and political- and court-faction was bewildering in view of the pressing danger from outside. Rumania was meant to be merely the next short stage on a long journey around the war. Such at least had been the plan with which I had set out from America for Europe, and I could not know that here at this odd, elegant Grand Hotel I would get the perfect close-up of the Nazis' conquest and colonization of Europe; a close-up which, though it covered only a slab of Europe, lost nothing of its significance by its size—a blood test is taken from only a drop of blood.

When I came to the Athene Palace on that hot June afternoon in 1940, I was an American who had felt, and still did feel against my will, that Hitler might not only win the war but could win the peace and organize Europe if he did. When I left the Athene Palace on an icy morning at the end of January 1941, I was convinced that under no circumstances could Hitler win the peace or organize Europe.

Hitler's recent military victories had little to do with my earlier conviction that he could win the war *and* the peace. It went farther back than that, back to a night in March 1936, in Berlin. Hitler's troops had just marched into the Rhineland and I saw high German officials tremble in their boots for fear of the consequences. One of them confided to me that each German troop commander who marched carried a sealed order telling him to retreat from the Rhineland area—the second the French and English made a warlike move, Hitler would have given the sign to open that order. This was, I felt, the last moment when a strong stand on the part of France and England could have blown away the nightmare of Hitlerism. It would not even have been necessary to fight. But the democracies let the moment pass.

From then on everything I saw on my travels across the European continent seemed to confirm this conviction. The statesmen of the democracies, vacillating, weak, petty, betrayed the principles they were supposedly living by; failed in every effort to present a united front to dictatorship; ignored every opportunity of finding generous and imaginative solutions for the emergencies created by the cruelty of totalitarian revolution; failed especially to provide a program which appealed to the European peoples.

These European peoples themselves had become increasingly indifferent to democracy, which was advertised to them in intellectual terms of freedom of thought and freedom of speech, but which in terms of their daily experience meant chiefly freedom to starve. I saw that not more than ten percent of the people on the European continent cared for individual freedom or were vitally enough interested in it to fight for its preservation. As to the remaining ninety percent, they were partly unaware of the real nature of Hitler's menacing shadow, partly indifferent to it, and partly ready to take a chance on the Führer.

Facing this torn-up, stagnant world was the German nation powerfully united in the one purpose of conquest, a purpose which appealed to the people's most intimate dreams. Added to this was the amazing phenomenon of the German leaders, who deceived and lied all the time but who could afford to be cruelly sincere when it was a question of the sacrifices they demanded from the people and of the necessity to fight; leaders frightfully imaginative and bold in planning and organizing, so much so that the rest of the world still pooh-poohed the feasibility of their plans when they were already carried out. Hitler's revolution, it seemed to me, was the answer to what Ortega y Gasset called "the formidable cry rising like the howling of innumerable dogs asking someone or something to take command, to impose an occupation, a duty." Hitler, I felt, could take Europe from the democracies like candy from a baby.

Not that any of this afforded me pleasure! I had nothing to gain and everything to lose from the victory of an order of which antisemitism was an integral part. Besides, it was hard for an intellectual, vitally interested in freedom of thought and speech, to find that so few people in Europe were similarly interested. I viewed my diagnosis of Europe with the agonized fascination that a doctor turns on the X-ray plate of his own deadly cancer, always hoping that the diagnosis will prove wrong, yet in a detached, scientific way interested in the progress of the illness as such. I never found, in these years studded with surrender and defeat, anything that seemed to disprove my diagnosis—until I came to the Athene Palace. Then, at close quarters, I saw the Nazis conquer and impose their new European order.

Rumania in 1940 was both an easy conquest and a fertile place to establish a new order. Here the Nazis found a bloodstained corrupt regime, despised by everyone except the few people who profited by it. Here the Germans found an upper class indifferent or pro-Nazi. Here they found a deep-seated popular antisemitism. Here they found a fascist movement which, decimated though it was, had the halo of martyrdom. Here they found four-fifths of the people, eleven million out of fourteen—peasants, humble, starving, inarticulate, abjectly poor—who had never enjoyed any of the privileges of democracy. It would seem that, if the Nazis could establish their new order anywhere in Europe, Rumania was the place of places. Yet even under such ideal circumstances, the Germans succeeded only partially in establishing their order, and then only because they were able to enforce it at any moment by military might.

All this I watched during my seven months at the Athene Palace. And that is why I became convinced that Hitler, even if he should win Europe, would not be able to win the peace and establish his New Order.

Toward evening of the day I came to the Athene Palace a light breeze relieved the glaring heat. The sinking sun put a rose sheen on the whiteness of King Carol's palace, and brought life to the bronze Carol I in the Square. Cars began to come out then, and people. At one point in the Square each car hit a bump in the asphalt, jumped high, then wobbled amusingly as it settled down.

This was the hour of the "Korso," the slow nightly stroll up and down the Calea Victoriei which was dear to the hearts of Bucharestians. It was the bourgeoisie of Bucharest which made the Korso, looking as the bourgeoisie looks in most Southeastern capitals of Europe. The women were mostly hatless, with dark curls swept up over highly made-up, strong-featured, large-eyed faces. Voluptuous bodies balanced gingerly on the exaggerated cothurns of cork which served as shoes. These were Western women, but about them hung the flavor of the harem. They were an attractive mixture beside whom their men were disappointing. Rumanian men pride themselves that they descend from the bastards whom dashing Roman conquerors begot with the native Dacian ladies. But since the Roman colonization under Emperor Trajan torrents of barbaric populations successively descended upon Rumania: Goths and Ostrogoths, Sarmates and Huns, Tartars and Bulgars, Finno-Hungarians and Mongols, and finally the Turks had conquered the country, one after the other. All left their mark on the Rumanian men, flattening out their hard tribune's profiles and grafting all kinds of un-Latin features upon them. I knew that there were handsome Rumanians, but the average product as it appeared that night on the Square was pasty-faced and paunchy.

Collectively these people seemed a pleasant crowd, but as I watched them from my window on the first floor of the Athene Palace—couple by couple, person by person— I saw that they were tense and did not smile. For this day had given them a bolt from the blue, sudden, unexpected,

devastating. Yesterday ten out of their twelve daily newspapers—the remaining two were said to be paid by Dr.
Goebbels—had expressed the confidence of the past year:
pro-Ally bulletins, pro-Ally editorials, and articles by Allied military experts were prominent and, as for the last
nine months, all of them scoffed at the ability of an ill-fed,
ill-trained German horde to attack mighty France. German victories in Poland, Norway, Holland, and Belgium
were called military stupidity on the part of these small
countries, and the work of treasonable fifth columns. . . .
But the French! They would just have to say "Assez" and
the Nazis would be licked.

Then today, under the pressure of hard facts, the Rumanian press had for the first time told the truth; all
regular editions and one-page extras gave information of
a new sort. It could not be said any longer that papers
predicting French defeat were supported by Goebbels.
Goebbels was not everywhere; Goebbels could not have
planted in every paper the story that Hitler had demanded the surrender of Paris to save it from destruction.
Or that the French had declared Paris an open city. Nor
could the radio be guilty of deception when it carried
Reynaud's appeal to America. . . .

Night was falling on the Square with a suddenness
which was reminiscent of the Orient. The bold outlines
of the bronze rider faded into the dusk. Though the
people were blotted out by the night and I could not see
their faces or hear their voices, I knew that they were
talking of France—loved, admired France—now beaten
and crushed. Paris deserted, open to the victorious Germans. Roads to the south crammed with millions of
peoples following the government in senseless flight. No

other people in Europe had had such a passion for France as the Rumanians; France was tied up with every great hour of Rumania's short independence. The Rumanian horizon had always been filled with France; there had been no place in it for anyone else, not even for England.

The bond began when the Moldavian and Walachian Principalities, under the belated influence of the liberal ideas of the French Revolution, shook off the yoke of their Turkish masters and the Greek phanariotes and turned to what they called Europe—but which really was France. From then on, sons of Rumanian princes and boyards were sent off ,to Paris to learn the ways of the great world and young Walachian liberals were sent to the same place to learn the means of revolution. And when they returned to Bucharest the former continued to make love, and the latter to make politics, like the French. Malicious Bucharestians called these young dandies "Bonjouristes," for they spoke French rather than Rumanian and were always yearning for Paris. Yet it was from their passion for France that was born the real independence of Rumania.

There is one story which the Rumanians like to tell caricaturing their newness on the European scene. It is about Jon Bratianu, who fled to Paris after the revolution of 1848 failed in the Principalities. Jon Bratianu went around Paris trying to interest the Paris liberals in his idea of "the miracle of a Danubian France, as astounding as the miracle of the Canadian France in the middle of foreign oppressors." But willing as the Paris liberals were to get enthusiastic, they were hazy about these remote regions. Monsieur Bastide, then French foreign minister, receiving the young Bratianu in audience, cut into his

eloquent exposition of his political program by asking:
"Pardon, monsieur, what is the capital of your country?"

"Bucharest, Excellency."

"Ah, Buchara? Buchara, you say? Please, monsieur, go
on!"

Nobody guessed then that this handsome, somber refugee
would become the first statesman of the new Rumania
and the progenitor of a line of prime ministers, the most
spectacular of whom would bring Rumania into the first
world war on the side of France. Jon Bratianu went back
to Bucharest in 1856. There, with the support of the
French Consul in Yassy against complicated Russian intrigues, he created the Union of the Danubian Principalities. The new Rumania, though nominally still under
the rule of the Sublime Porte, embarked on her existence
as a European nation armed with the Code Napoleon, a
French Group Theatre, and the novels of Dumas père.

France had even been responsible for Rumania's Hohenzollern dynasty. When Jon Bratianu found that no Rumanian Prince had enough authority to rule the country
(there were always so many other princes who were jealous
of him and wanted his job), he went to Napoleon III for
advice, and Napoleon III made Bratianu offer the Rumanian throne to Carol I, the profoundly Teutonic
Hohenzollern whose grandmother was Stephanie Beau-
harnais, adopted daughter of Napoleon I. Napoleon III
had given shrewd advice. The beak-nosed spartan, who
used to keep an eye on his watch when he paid his rare
visits to the room of his erratic poetess-queen Carmen
Sylva, made an excellent ruler for Rumania. His long
reign brought the country final independence from the
Turks in 1877 and international recognition as a king-

dom in 1881. From then on the foreign minister of France was well aware that it was not Buchara but Bucharest.

Carol I died in September 1914, heartbroken by the refusal of the Crown Council to enter the war on the side of Germany. (Rumor had it that the old man committed suicide.) For though the Rumanians liked and respected their German king and for forty years had belonged to the Triple Alliance, their passion for France was stronger than dynastic loyalties. Two years after the old king's death, years filled with bitter political quarrels between interventionists and neutralists, Jon Bratianu's son and Queen Marie brought Rumania into the war on the side of France. Rumania was terribly beaten, but she had fought on the winning side and reaped enormous spoils for her loyalty.

All this spelled France to the Rumanians—and today France was falling. Every Rumanian down on the Square this night felt that the fall of France signified a turning point in the existence of his own country, and that it would be a turning point for the worse. Henceforth nobody could doubt that Hitler's army, which beat the Grande Armée in less than a month, could beat any other army in Europe, the Rumanian included, in a few days. This was no pleasant outlook for a country rich in oil, a product which Hitler could find nowhere else so near and which he needed for this war.

But there was another aspect to the situation which worried the Bucharestians on the Square even more. This was the painful realization that without France the Great Rumania could not survive. Owing to her enormous gains in the last war at the expense of three of her neighbors—Rumania had added 60,198 square miles with a popula-

tion of 11,957,000 people to her pre-world war area of
53,698 square miles and 7,234,900 people—Rumania today
was surrounded by enemies. For never in the past twenty
years had Hungary, Bulgaria, and Russia renounced their
claims on their lost provinces. From time to time Russian statesmen wept gentle tears over their unhappy brethren in Bessarabia, and Bulgarian statesmen did the same
over their unhappy brethren in Dobrudscha. And worst
of all were the Hungarians, whose skillful clamor for
Transylvania had ended up by affecting the whole world
in their favor. Yet none of this was very serious as long
as France was strong enough to keep the have-nots off
Great Rumania. But now that the Nazis had punched
France out of existence, the three could pounce on Rumania. In all probability they would pounce together.
In all probability they would also have Hitler's permission: Hitler had always said that this was a war to get the
have-nots back what was theirs. . . . There was many a
Rumanian today, doing his Korso before the Athene Palace
who, maybe for the first time in his life, found it most
uncomfortable that his country belonged to the haves.

It had grown dark. A lonely woeful horn blowing the
Zapfenstreich gave the sign to Bucharestians that it was
time for dinner. A few minutes later the Square was
empty.

At the right King Carol's sprawling white palace was
outlined by a festoon of lights. Its left wing was unfinished,
hiding behind a high straw screen; its annexes were still
in raw brick and roofless. Shortly before the war Carol
had decided to tear down most of the center of the town
to add a few wings and annexes to his palace, which act

made a very bad impression on the citizens, who felt that this was not the moment to spend the people's money on better and bigger royal palaces. Nor did this impression improve when, owing to the architect's miscalculations, the left wing, already completed, had to be pulled down again. Then Carol decided to hide the rebuilding from the world by putting up a huge straw screen.

On this evening the whole palace was dark except for a few brightly lighted windows on the third floor. Every Bucharestian in sight of these particular windows knew the King was working late that night. And every Bucharestian went home feeling pleased to think that his King was at his job, and feeling even more pleased to think that his King was not in the Avenue Vulpache at Madame Lupescu's, where he was said to spend most of his evenings.

Strictly speaking, the lighted windows were those of Ernest Urdareanu, the court minister. The King's study was at the back of the palace facing the park. But as the two rooms were connected, and Carol was constantly going back and forth, the popular interpretation of the lighted windows was not far off the mark.

What Hitler was to the Germans, Mussolini to the Italians, Stalin to the Russians, King Carol II of Rumania was to the Rumanians. Only more so. For Carol was not the head of a party dictatorship, as the other dictators were, but had ruled as a personal dictator ever since 1938, when he had abolished the Constitution and the old party system. True, there were a chamber of deputies and a senate, and some sort of single party had been formed, called the National Front. But all this had no importance. The regime in Rumania was a one-man show, and the one man was Carol, the third Hohenzollern King of

Rumania, and the first Hohenzollern King born in the country—if one omits the short episode when his baby son Michael was King in his stead, while Carol was in exile with Lupescu.

I could visualize Carol that night, sitting at his large eighteenth-century table which was loaded with photos, cigaret boxes, flower vases, but which left enough space for all kinds of sharpened pencils, notebooks and other working utensils, all of which were methodically arranged. Tall, slender, and immaculate in his Bond Street clothes, Carol would be sitting back in his chair, a nervous hand holding the eternal long black cigaret holder. His beautiful blond hair with its natural wave was still rich and silky like a child's. There was about the slightly puffed-up face and the stormy gray-green eyes a strong resemblance to Czar Alexander II, his great-grandfather. It was odd that this Hohenzollern, who had in his veins all the noblest blood of Europe, should look most of all like a Romanoff.

I could see Carol, tired from a long day, his royal affability spent. He had had many audiences that day, with his prime minister, Tartarescu, and with his new foreign minister, Gigurtu, and he had received several gentlemen of the Crown Council. Now at last he was alone with Ernest Urdareanu, the all-powerful court marshal.

Fantastic stories about Urdareanu made the rounds of Bucharest—you heard them all at the Athene Palace. All tried to solve the riddle of the extraordinary power which this minor officer had, from 1936 on, gained over the King and through him over the country. The most fantastic story had it that the King had married Lupescu off to his Urdareanu. While it was almost impossible to get through

the thick curtain of gossip and rumor to the true facts of
Ernest Urdareanu's extraordinary career, it was certain
that Lupescu had put him into the Palace. There had been
a time when Carol talked too much and too freely to all
comers and had even talked about Lupescu. This Madame
did not like, so she put Urdareanu in to keep an eye over
the too-voluble King and to shroud the throne in the
secrecy becoming to thrones. The result was that Urdareanu became the strongest single influence in Carol's
reign. Prime Ministers and cabinets came and went often,
but Ernest Urdareanu was always there, firmly between the
King and the outside world. No letters or telephone calls
reached the King unless approved by Urdareanu. The King
received in audience only persons whom Urdareanu approved, and even these were received in Urdareanu's presence. Even His British Majesty's minister, ponderous Sir
Reginald Hoare, and the Führer's stiff and polite envoy,
Dr. Fabrizius, had to count heavily on the good will of the
all-powerful court minister.

Urdareanu was about 45, a swarthy little man of flashy
elegance, with a silver plate in his skull, who was said
to use powder and rouge. He lunched almost daily at
Lupescu's house, which was next to his own. Young
Michael detested him and behind his father's back called
him "Murdareanu," which was the Rumanian for dirt.
Urdareanu was the best-hated man in Rumania. People believed him corrupt to his bones. The great wealth which
he had amassed in a very few years strengthened this
belief. He sat on the most remunerative boards of directors
in Rumania. Rumor had it that the great European
powers, including Germany and England, paid large sums

to the King's favorite. All this, if true, would be in the best tradition of the Balkans.

But even Urdareanu's bitterest enemies admitted that Urdareanu adored the King and was completely loyal. They even admitted that Urdareanu advised Carol according to the best of his knowledge as to what was best for his King. What his enemies resented was that this "best knowledge" was a primitive kind of unscrupulous shrewdness, and that what Urdareanu thought was the best interest of Carol was rarely the best interest of Rumania.

On the eve of the fall of France, Carol of Rumania was faced with momentous decisions. The Great Rumania was at stake and so was his throne. Until now Carol had succeeded in being all things to all men. On one side he kept to the letter of the German-Rumanian trade agreement, closed shortly before the war, which guaranteed the Germans grain, wood, and 1,500,000 tons of oil per year. He also showered good old Dr. Fabrizius, who was very responsive to signs of royal favor and happened to be a relative of Ribbentrop, with his loveliest decorations. On the other hand he looked the other way when the English and the French planted hundreds of their agents around Ploesti and on the Danube and let them sabotage oil wells and German shipping whenever they could. Also there still existed the British guarantee for Rumania. As far as it went, Carol's had been a clever enough political game. Vainly foreign diplomats tried to figure out whether this great-grandson of Queen Victoria believed in the final British victory and just played the Nazis along in order to avoid trouble, or whether this heir to the blood of Germany's great dynasty was really pro-German at heart and waited for the right moment to jump on the Hitler bandwagon. Carol loved to leave people guessing, finding it highly practical. He loved, too, to play one against the other, which he did also with political parties, friends, advisers, and envoys of great powers. But anti-liberal, pro-fascist Carol was really neither pro- or anti-German, nor pro- or anti-British. He was only pro-Carol.

What worried Carol most about the swift German victory in France was that it put a stop to his beautifully ambiguous game. The South of Europe was from now on at the mercy of the Führer and so was he. Hitler alone could stop the Russians, Bulgarians, Hungarians from falling on Rumania. *If* Hitler wanted to stop them. The smart thing for Carol to do seemed to be to adopt an out-and-out Axis-policy, to forget England for the time being. Carol would not have minded this except for two reasons: one was the possibility that the British might win in the end, as they always did. In this case it would be awkward, to say the least, to have put all the Rumanian eggs in the German basket. There seemed to be no solution for this problem, for, if he wished to make a success of his out-and-out Axis policy, Carol had to submit gracefully, in which case he could not go on the record for future British reference as doing it under duress.

The other more immediate reason why Carol was apprehensive about taking the plunge into the Axis orbit was that he was afraid it was already too late—five minutes after twelve.

Carol knew that Hitler had resented his acceptance of the British guarantee, but this was not the worst. The worst was that the Führer could be expected to present a bill for the death of Corneliu Zelea Codreanu. Tall, dark, vital, Codreanu had been the leader of Rumania's green-shirted fascist movement, called the Iron Guard or the Legion of the Archangel Michael. And according to reliable German and Rumanian sources, his gruesome end was directly connected with the only visit Carol paid to the Führer in the autumn of 1938, in Berchtesgaden. This meeting between Carol and the Führer seemed to have been quite cozy up to a point. Then suddenly, with the abruptness peculiar to him, Hitler is said to have fixed his blue eyes severely on his royal visitor and said, "You know, sir, to me there exists only one dictator of Rumania and that is Codreanu."

The Führer's remark must have been a shock to Carol. He had hoped that at last Codreanu, recently condemned to ten years of hard labor for high treason, and behind prison bars, was the forgotten man of Rumanian politics. Now the Führer's remark made it clear that Codreanu was to be feared even behind the highest prison walls, and a few weeks later Codreanu was shot "in flight."

So far Hitler had made little of the murder of Rumania's fascist number one, but Carol expected him to take the matter up at the proper moment: the moment when Carol was most in need of his good will. So to the last Carol's throne depended on the outcome of his duel with Codreanu. It was even more difficult, though, to fight the dead Codreanu than it had been to fight the living.

Carol's relation to Codreanu, son of a Rumanian high school professor, was stranger than fiction. It made even his relations with Lupescu, tested and approved as the great royal romance, seem somewhat pale, for while Carol's love of Lupescu was the cause of, or at least the pretext for, his first exile and the subsequent alienation of his people, Carol's jealousy of Codreanu caused the vicious circle of revenge and violence which stained his reign. Finally, as I witnessed, the collapse of Carol's reign could be traced directly through a haze of blood and hate back to the King's jealousy of Corneliu Codreanu, called by his followers the Capitano.

Carol's savage jealousy sprang from the fact that Codreanu was and did everything that Carol wished to be and do. As far back as 1920, when he first heard of Mussolini, Carol wished to found a fascist movement in Rumania. And Codreanu founded this fascist movement. Carol wished to be loved by his people, especially by the young. And Codreanu was a Pied Piper who stole the hearts of his people, especially the young ones. Carol wished to be a tribune in the imagination of Rumanians, instead of king. And Codreanu was a tribune who stood in the imagination of the Rumanians as both martyr and prophet.

Though strangled on a cold November night in the forest of Ploesti, Codreanu still dominated the Rumanian political scene as counterpoint to Carol. He was still very much alive: people told you about him, all emphasizing an elfin quality about his tall, dark handsomeness, something which set him mysteriously apart among men and made him seem to belong to the forests, seas, and mountains. Of all would-be dictators he was the only one who did not rely on speeches but on silence. On a white horse, in the white costume of the Rumanian peasant, the Capitano, people told you, used to ride through the villages of Moldavia and Walachia, acclaimed by the peasants as the envoy of the Archangel Michael. He did not have to speak, and more often than not the authorities forbade this, but he was there, smiling his childlike radiant smile, and people loved him and believed in him.

So great was Codreanu's effect on the Rumanian masses that when he was tried for the assassination of the Police Prefect Manciu at Turnu Severin, tens of thousands waited before the courthouse. After his acquittal—he acted, said the verdict, in legal self-defense—he married, and ninety thousand Rumanians from all over the country in thousands of vehicles formed a bridal procession more than four miles long. The newsreel of this bridal procession was confiscated and burnt by the Government as a document endangering public order and security. This was in 1925!

Codreanu was a lawyer in private life, having studied law in Rumanian and German universities. But he did not spend much time on his profession, as he was in jail a good deal or, to recover from imprisonment, lived in the mountains with shepherds building his own huts. Or he went to live in France with his wife and did humble menial work there. The Capitano was more a mystic nationalist than a nationalist politician. The Rumanian people to him were the oneness of all Rumanians, the ones alive and the ones still unborn and the souls of the dead. To him the state was only a garment, wrapped around the body of the nation. To strengthen this body was the only task of government. Codreanu wanted to create the new Rumanian man, because Rumania suffered no lack of good programs but a lack of men to carry them out. The Capitano wanted Rumania to belong to the Rumanians, to all Rumanians, that is. From this basic formula he developed, as a young anti-communist student in Yassy in the early 1920's, his battle slogans: slogans against the

Jews, who under the pressure first of Germany and then of the Allies were just achieving equal rights in Rumania; slogans against the party system and parliamentarianism which, he felt, was an empty copy of western liberalism, foreign to the real interests of Rumania; slogans for the liberation of the suppressed peasant.

In 1927, following an inspiration received before the ikon of the Archangel Michael in the chapel of the Vacaresti prison, Codreanu founded the Legion of the Archangel Michael. He had then almost ten years of fanatical national struggle, persecution, violence, and prison behind him; and also remarkable successes. But neither he nor the five comrades with whom he founded the Legion had a political program. Never proclaiming his own political power as essential, Codreanu visualized the Legion of St. Michael as a religious order and a school of character education, rather than as a political party.

The basis of this religious order was the "cuib," the nest, or, as the vernacular of western fascism put it, the cell. The cuib had a maximum of thirteen members. As soon as it had more it split automatically in two cuibs and so on. Codreanu did not nominate the cuib-leaders, but gave every man a chance to gather around him as many congenial souls as his moral capacity allowed him to hold together. Only when the individual proved that he was a magnetic, convincing leader of men was he confirmed head of a cuib.

At the gatherings of the cuib the member had to forget all his petty worries and dedicate his thoughts to Rumania and to Codreanu's six laws of discipline, work, silence, education to a heroic existence, mutual love, and honor. To the existence of these firmly knit small cells the movement owed its survival throughout the years of inexorable persecution. The Legion made a very strict selection among candidates for membership. Codreanu ordered that of twenty would-be members, nineteen should be refused; the ones accepted had to serve for three years before they were solemnly received in the Legion. Thus the Legion really contained the élite when, in 1930, it became the backbone of the newly created organization of the Iron Guard.

During the Rumanian political campaign of 1933, eighteen thousand legionnaires or, as they were now called, Guardists, were put into prison and mistreated. Finally the Duca Government outlawed the Iron Guard and, as an answer, a Guardist bullet ended the life of Duca himself. For a fascist movement which allegedly was more a religious than a political movement, Codreanu's Guardists were amazingly quick on the trigger, but then this was the reaction of passionate and desperate nationalists to persistent cruel persecution by a corrupt ruling class.

Codreanu and forty-odd leaders of the Guard were accused of the moral and intellectual authorship of Duca's murder, but Codreanu could not be found. He had done an extraordinary disappearing act, disappearing right into the lions' den. He went to Max Ausschnitt, the big Jewish industrialist, and friend of the King and Lupescu, and said: "If you don't find a way to save me, you'll be bumped off next."

Ausschnitt knew that Codreanu meant what he said and went into a huddle with Lupescu. They decided to hide the fugitive in the house of one of Lupescu's cousins. Here Codreanu stayed until he decided to surrender to the court. Later he was acquitted of complicity.

At this time Hitler was in power in Germany and the powers-that-be in all European countries were making peace with their respective fascist movements or trying to liquidate them. Prompted by Lupescu, Carol tried first to make peace with Codreanu. The two met at the house of Malaxa, the other big Rumanian industrialist. Nothing about their talks has ever been published, but rumor has it that Carol suggested a sort of partnership to Codreanu. Not that he wanted to share the throne; he wanted Codreanu to share the Guardist leadership. But while Codreanu was emphatically royalist, he could not possibly share the leadership of the Guard with Carol—not as long as the Guard opposed the corruption and abuses of Carol's regime.

Codreanu used the temporary truce and the funds which were said to have come to him from Ausschnitt and Malaxa in this period of appeasement to hold mass meetings and strengthen his movement. His success was overwhelming. At the elections of 1937 he and his party got sixty-six seats in parliament and thus became the second strongest party in Rumania. It was then Carol realized that Codreanu could be neither appeased nor kept from coming to power by legal means. Carol's jealousy won the better of him. He wanted to show Codreanu that the King was still stronger than the Capitano and decided to pit himself in person against Codreanu and meet the revolution from below with revolution from above.

In February 1938 he dissolved all political parties and set up a royal dictatorship, thus preventing the meeting of a parliament in which Codreanu's men had their sixty-six seats. But the main idea was to steal Codreanu's thunder by establishing a dictatorship of his own before Cod-

reanu got around to it. From now on it was war to the
knife between Carol and Codreanu, at least on the King's
side.

Then something happened which sharpened Carol's
jealousy. Some of the Guardists who had fought with
Franco in Spain brought their dead comrades home, and
the Rumanian people gave them a truly triumphal reception. Wherever their train stopped they were greeted by
thousands. The clergy turned out to give them the blessing of the orthodox church. Mothers brought their children to have a look at the heroes. In Bucharest people got
really wild and marched the returned Guardists up the
Calea Victoriei like conquering heroes. Carol watched the
procession from his palace window, listening to the enthusiastic shouts and Guardists songs. As a result of it he
decided to liquidate the entire Guardist leadership.

So, though Codreanu had never resorted to violence or
to rebellion against the King, possibly because he never
thought of achieving power by force, he was arrested and
brought before a military court. To start with he was only
condemned to six months in prison for libeling former
Prime Minister Nicholas Jorga, but after an enormous
press campaign had set the stage for it, the last and biggest
Codreanu trial was held before the military court—a trial
for high treason. This time, though the highest officers,
scholars, priests and even political opponents termed the
accusation of treason as absurd, Codreanu was condemned
to ten years at hard labor, the principal proofs offered by
the prosecution being a letter found at a tailor's, said to
be written by Codreanu to friends in Berlin and to prove
a forbidden connection with the Wilhelmstrasse, and Codreanu's own statement to the effect that, should he ever

come to power, Rumania would join the Axis forty-eight hours later.

With the verdict of this court martial the Capitano and the Iron Guard seemed to be liquidated for good. By the thousands, Guardists were put in prison. It seemed as if the backbone of the Guardist movement was broken. Then came the bloody finale in the forest of Ploesti, which may have been caused by Hitler's nasty remark that for him there was only one dictator—and that this was Codreanu.

On November 30, 1938, Carol's Government announced that on a transfer of prisoners from one jail to another fourteen Guardists, among them Codreanu, had been shot "in flight." Official announcements could not for long silence the rumors or cloud the truth. The prisoners had not tried to flee; they were helplessly bound and gagged in two motor trucks allegedly bringing them to the military prison of Fort Jilava. Nor had they been shot; they had been strangled from behind. A corporal who sat behind Codreanu threw a leather strap around the Capitano's neck and pulled the noose tight. Acid was poured over the corpses and they were buried in Fort Jilava. A heavy slab of concrete was put over the grave to keep it shut.

Strangely enough, the violent deeds with which the Capitano had been connected through the years never hurt his prestige with the Rumanian people. Somehow people don't mind murder when they feel that the assassins don't do it for personal gain or revenge but for what they believe to be the good of the country. So the Rumanian people never lost faith in the Capitano. Carol's propaganda ground out the vilest stories about Codreanu being paid by the Wilhelmstrasse or that he had sold out

to the Jews and Freemasons. But such stories never caught
on with the Rumanian people. To them the Capitano remained a saint and a martyr and the apostle of a better
Rumania. Even skeptical ones who did not agree with him
in political matters still grew dreamy-eyed remembering
Codreanu.

As Carol on the day of the fall of Paris faced his problems, he must have put "reconciliation with the Iron
Guard" at the top of the agenda. There was not much of
the Guardist leadership left; they had been liquidated by
the thousands in these last two years, and there was only
the third- and fourth-grade leadership left alive, most of
whom had fled to Germany and Italy. But the rank and
file were still very much there. Though the party itself
was outlawed, the Capitano's cleverly devised cuibs of thirteen were indestructible and ready to spring into action
at any moment to take revenge for their Capitano. These
had to be reconciled, in the first place to placate Hitler
but also to keep them from becoming a terrific menace at
Carol's back.

Carol that night was in as bad a spot as a king and dictator can be. He was surrounded by three enemies, of
whom every single one wanted a slab of Rumanian territory. He had not a single ally to his name, only a British
guarantee which was more of a handicap than a help. His
armed forces were such that they could only fight the Hungarians (alone) or the Bulgarians (alone). They could certainly not fight the Russians, or the Hungarians, Bulgarians, and Russians together. Being a personal dictator,
Carol ruled without the support of a party. Being head-
strong and arbitrary, he had in the ten years of his rule

alienated all the leaders of the former parties, men like Juliu Maniu, the leader of the peasant party, or like Georges Bratianu, Jon Bratianu's son, leader of the liberals. He had alienated the army because its best chiefs, like General Jon Antonescu who had dared to say what was wrong with the army, had been disgracefully treated by him. Carol ruled in a vacuum, thinly populated by Lupescu, Urdareanu, and the "camarilla," mostly a corrupt crowd of racketeers, big industrialists, and police chiefs, every single one of whom could be voted the most likely to be killed by a Guardist bullet. Carol's only hope this night was the Führer—if the Führer wanted to save him.

2—ATHENE PALACE

In this summer of 1940 the Athene Palace was the last cosmopolitan stage on which post-world-war Europe and the new-order Europe made a joint appearance. There was, of course, the Hotel Aviso in Lisbon, Portugal, but there the old society, harried and terrified, just waited around for boats to America. There still was the Serbsky Kral in Belgrade, Jugoslavia, where the two orders mingled, but here the setting as well as the cast lacked glamour. In the Bergues in Geneva or the Dŭnapalato in Budapest, there was no play on at all. Only at the Athene Palace, a glamorous setting in the traditional style of European Grand Hotels, the cast of post-world-war Europe and the cast of the new order, all-star casts both, still had equal billing and the play itself was full of suspense.

This was the plot: Neutral Rumania, a small country, but rich in wheat, and the fifth oil producing country in the world, was striving to keep her independence. To the Allies and to the Nazis this small Rumania was the most important Balkan country, and both did their utmost to

38

draw her into their respective orbits. The Nazis had a positive interest in Rumania: they were after the oil and wheat; they needed the friendly neutrality of Rumania because the Danube runs through the country and they needed the Danube to ship their goods from Russia and the other Balkan countries. And last but not least Rumania was of the utmost strategical importance for any move against the Balkans or against Russia.

The Allies' interest in Rumania was equally strong, though negative: importing their oil from America and Iraq, and their wheat from the Dominions, they had no need for Rumanian oil and wheat, nor was the Danube of much use to them or had they much chance of getting troops to Rumania themselves. If the Allies tried hard to draw Rumania into their orbit, it was solely in order to prevent the Nazis from getting Rumanian oil and wheat and from shipping their goods on the Danube and especially from deploying their troops in Rumania.

In the lobby of the Athene Palace, old post-world-war Europe and new-order Europe were acting out their parts in this drama. It was an epic setting, for in the last twenty-five years this lobby had been the forum of the Balkans. Here secrets of the alcove, secrets of court, secrets of diplomatic pouches were whispered into ears that miraculously turned into microphones. Here opportunities were made and destroyed; here stories were invented and from here spread like epidemics; here the skeletons of all the Balkan closets were promenaded and laughed at, and gossip sold short the honor of every politician and the virtue of every woman. Nobody minded it, not even the victims.

This summer there were in the Athene Palace spies of every Intelligence Service in the world; the diplomats and

military attachés of great and little powers; British and
French oil men on their way out, and German and Italian
oil men on their way in; Gestapo agents and Ovra agents
and OGPU agents, or men who were at least said to be
agents; amiable Gauleiters and hard-headed economic experts; distinguished Rumanian appeasers and the mink-
clad German and Austrian beauties who were paid to keep
them happy; the mink-clad Rumanian beauties who were
paid by Udurianu to make the Italian and German ministers talk and who were also paid by the German and
Italian ministers to make Udurianu talk.

As the drama of bloodless German conquest later on
drew to its bitter end, the old order dropped out of the
play. Then wild-eyed greenshirt dignitaries, catapulted
into power from a concentration camp, would make their
debut in the lobby. Hopeful Axis businessmen would
swarm here to buy themselves a Jewish department store
or a mine for practically nothing. German Generals, quiet
and scholarly, would talk here of their old campaigns and
think up new ones.

At one time or another Franz von Papen, Hitler's am-
bassador to Ankara, smiling and optimistic, would rest in
the lobby of the Athene Palace on his way from or to
Berchtesgaden. Suave Dr. Clodius, Hitler's economic wiz-
ard, would recover his breath here after endless discussions
with General Antonescu. Baldur von Schirach, Gauleiter
of Vienna, would revive here after the endless re-burial
of Codreanu. Even Frau Himmler, wife of the Gestapo
chief, looking like Elsa Maxwell, came and ate big por-
tions of whipped cream.

To the Nazis the lobby of the Athene Palace became
a kind of reservation of pre-Nazi life in Europe, and while

they conscientiously tried to destroy this life everywhere else, they did their best to hold onto it here. They enjoyed the flavor of respectable sin which surrounded the demi-mondaines. They marveled at the dignity which a long life of corruption had given to Rumanian older statesmen. They were deliciously disquieted by the liquid-eyed daughters of princely houses who made them go to bed with them before they had a chance to check up on their Aryan grandmothers. Here in the lobby of the Athene Palace, where the past of Europe was breathing its last, the Nazis, like Landru weeping over the corpses of the lady loves he killed, indulged in man's most exquisite enjoyment—sweet sorrow for what he has destroyed.

As I came downstairs, on my first evening at the Athene Palace, the long wide lobby took on perspective through the open folding door. Pairs of heavy yellow marble pillars made three aisles in the lobby and people sat in large clusters along the walls of darker, rust-colored marble inlaid with narrow, gold-framed mirrors. People sat in small clusters, too, in the middle aisles against the pillars in chairs and settees covered with raspberry-colored plush. The carpets were Bordeaux red and the general effect was wintry. There was no sunlight in the lobby of the Athene Palace or any light of day, for there were no windows, only artificial light. Connected with the lobby by two arches was a light green salon, a charming room with long low sofas and long low tables before mirrored walls. A large gold-framed photo of Carol in uniform on an easel stood as a kind of door stopper in the open glass door, opening on a small courtyard which served as a summer restaurant. The tables there, laid for dinner, looked empty but expectant, and white-clad waiters stood about cleaning their nails.

I sat down at a large table in the corner of the lobby, where the foreign newspapers were laid out—French and English and German newspapers, as behooves an international hotel. But the single number of the London *Times* was four weeks old, while the *Voelkische Beobachter* and the *Boersenzeitung* were yesterday's. This was, incidentally, the last number of the *Times* I was to see during all my seven months in Bucharest, while the *Matin* came through belatedly from Nazi-dominated Paris, carrying the same news one had already read in the *Voelkische Beobachter*.

Usually European Grand Hotels have a band playing in the lobby which submerges all noises, but there was no music in the lobby of the Athene Palace. Here one heard peoples' shoes creaking on the parquet between the Bordeaux-red runners, and the ring of glasses on the marble-topped tables and the rustle of newspapers and the hum of voices.

It was a strangely subdued hum of voices, coming from people who sat in clusters, put their heads close together, and whispered. The backs of the people in each cluster were turned to the backs of the people in every other cluster, and there seemed to be missing from the Athene Palace that evening the discreet current of friendly curiosity that makes for the much-touted "atmosphere" of European Grand Hotels. For today the Germans had won the decisive round in the battle of the Balkans. France, their chief opponent, was now out of the picture. Tonight the Allied clusters tried to conceal their shock, while the Rumanian clusters tried to conceal their apprehension and the Nazi clusters tried to conceal their satisfaction. And from a charitable instinct each cluster acted as if the other was not here at all.

Only one cluster was different. Here were two elegant old men who evidently enjoyed the Athene Palace scene, looking around and talking with spirit. Theirs was a carefully chosen table against the wall. No one could escape them on the way to the green salon and the summer restaurant or to the bar off the far end of the lobby. These two old men, I was to learn, were known as Old Excellencies. Everyone in Bucharest knew the Old Excellencies. The two I saw tonight in the lobby of the Athene Palace were only a kind of token force of a large army of some seven hundred living Rumanian former cabinet ministers, and of innumerable diplomats, and generals.

The Old Rumanian Excellencies of the Athene Palace appeared at their favorite table in the lobby every day before noon. With an interruption only for luncheon and dinner, they stayed till after midnight, drinking Turkish coffee and commenting on everything in sight. I could never quite believe that the Old Excellencies had houses and beds like other people; it seemed more likely that they dissolved into the air when the lights were put out after midnight, only to materialize at noon next day, complete with white linen spats and the black-rimmed monocle through which the experienced eye looked over women's points. For no matter what had been their political position, the Rumanian Excellencies' real life work had always been to be charming to women with but one purpose in mind, and their successes were legendary and to many enviable. A French traveler, coming to Bucharest in 1860, wrote, "In Bucharest one makes love or one talks about it." The Old Excellencies bore him out. They were wicked old men; their thoughts and talk ran strictly along pornographic lines. They were curious and gossipy and unprincipled, saying and thinking the worst about everybody, with the distinction that they never thought the worst of the worst.

The Old Excellencies rescued me from my solitary *Voelkische Beobachter*. A tall one with the face of a sick greyhound bent over my hand with a deep bow that came from another era. I noted the red ribbon of the Legion of Honor in the lapel of his black coat and the slight smell of arabi which came from his white mustache and emphasized the mauve-decade look about his fragile appearance. I thought that he must have been superbly aristocratic before age yellowed him, and somehow he conveyed to me the conviction that we had been friends at some time or other and that it was entirely my fault if I could not remember when and where. Much later I learned that I had never before met the old gentleman, but that to accost ladies smoothly and convincingly was one of the arts which each of the Old Rumanian Excellencies had at the tip of his fingers. Looking over the back of the sick greyhound who bowed before me, I could see that the other Excellency, gray-haired and heavy-eyed, under very black eyebrows, had the pointed beard of the late Jon Bratianu.

A complex odor floated about the table of the Old Excellencies, as the greyhound maneuvered me to the settee behind their strategic table. There was the vivid scent of Turkish coffee coming from the small, handleless cups and of the Turkish cigarets which the Old Excellencies smoked endlessly. Mingled with this was the sharp scent of toilet water and the sweet smell of arabi. But uppermost was the smell of the copper-colored liquid which came in their cocktail glasses—"amalfi," the Excellencies hastened to explain, a combination of vermouth and tzuyka, the national plum schnapps.

"Have an amalfi, Madame," Bratianu-beard broke the silence, and without waiting for my answer he smacked little kisses into the air, which was, I learned, the Rumanian way of calling the waiter. A swarthy little barman came up to the table from across the room, and Bratianu-beard said, *"Un amalfi pour madame,* Henri." And then he said to me, "Henri knows everything. For 2000 leis he tells a true story and for 1000 leis he tells a very plausible story."

Henri's smile made glittering slits of his black eyes and he said, "If madame wishes to change dollars, I have always use for dollars."

The Excellencies explained the miracle of the Rumanian Black Bourse. Officially, they said, the dollar was 210 leis, but the Black Bourse would pay at least 500 leis for the dollar. I asked wasn't there a law against changing at the Black Bourse, which the cynical Old Excellencies thought the funniest thing anybody could say. Of course, they said, there were plenty of laws against the Black Bourse, but who cared about laws, and if the police should get fresh with me, they themselves would fix me up. I figured that at the Black Bourse exchange my luxurious quarters on the first floor cost less than a dollar per day. Corruption really made life pleasant all around. . . . The piccolo brought the amalfi and I compressed my nose from inside and drank it down, to please the old gentlemen. It made me feel extraordinarily good and strong.

Under the tutelage of the Old Excellencies I began to see the Bucharest scene. I learned which cabinet minister was having an affair with what lady, what was the *specialité* of which cabinet minister, and what was the price of what lady. That every lady had a price was a foregone conclusion with the wicked old men, but only from 20,000 leis up did they consider her a lady. It was the same with the politicians; they also had a price, and if they were expensive enough they could be considered statesmen. However, there were exceptions among the statesmen. The Old Excellencies talked about two who did not take money. One was Juliu Maniu, leader of the former Peasant Party, who had been in the opposition for over ten years. The other was General Jon Antonescu, who once had been Minister of War and who, though no Guardist himself, had been a friend of Codreanu. It was obvious that the Excellencies found both these incorruptibles rather irritating.

The Excellencies were full of good advice, forthcoming after a tall, heavy man in his forties came up to our table and made a slow, deep bow. He held the bow as he murmured in deferential tone, "Your Excellencies . . ." I noted that he had the face of a seal and breathed very loudly through his short nose. The old men were extremely cordial to him, presented him to me, and he kissed my hand with very moist lips. But hardly had he moved on when Bratianu-beard said, *"Voilà le gigolo le plus dangereux de Bucharest."* I could not imagine that any woman would pay for this rather unappetizing animal, but the wicked old men smiled and assured me that he was "formidable."

Though everybody knew that he lived on women and blackmail this man was received in Bucharest society. For everybody was deadly afraid of him, as he worked for Moruzov's Secret Police. The Old Excellencies were most voluble about Moruzov's police. A long unbroken line went from it back to the era of Turkish domination, giving it an oriental flavor. Contrary to the Gestapo and the OGPU, it was not the police of a regime or a party. It was a more personal sort of police, the police of a suspicious king out for minute, inside information about the lives and the loves of his courtiers and gentry—information he manipulated for his personal aims in the byzantine manner. According to the Old Excellencies practically everybody at the Athene Palace was on Moruzov's payroll: waiters, valets, porters, chambermaids, the fatherly spectacled porter and the swarthy little barman with his glittering eyes, the doorman, the woman in black with a white apron in the lavatory off the lobby, the apple-cheeked page boys in their turquoise uniforms with their little monkey caps strapped around their chins and, of course, the demimondaines who sat professionally in the lobby. Most of these were working too for the Gestapo or the British Intelligence as a sideline.

All these spies told the police what people ate and for how much and with whom, who came to see them and how long they stayed, what they said, and when they came home at night and with whom. If there was nothing to tell, they made it up. The Excellencies explained that this was the really dangerous part of it, the made-up part. If somebody did not like you, he just went to the police and reported that you said that the King was a racketeer or, even worse, that you slept with the Russian Minister and had communist sympathies. This was why nobody could afford to offend people like the unappetizing gigolo.

The beard à la Bratianu spoke. "Watch your step, Madame, and confide in nobody except in us," and the Greyhound chimed in and said, *"Nous sommes les seules personnes discrètes à Bucharest."* I wondered what the indiscreet persons in Bucharest were like if the discreet persons were like these wicked old men, who at that point bowed respectfully to a woman of extraordinary dark beauty seating herself at the next table with her escorts, all in evening clothes. Taking off her sables, the lady showed beautiful, very white shoulders and arms over her brilliantly black tight-fitting dress. The Greyhound whispered, "That is the friend of the German and the Hungarian and Italian ministers. They all pay her for telling what Urdareanu does. And Urdareanu pays her to tell him what the ministers are up to. The perfect arrangement." He indicated an old-looking young man as the husband of the versatile beauty and said that she was wonderful to him and had made his career. Bratianu-beard contributed that her breasts were the best thing about her and that she had *"Une specialité, mais une specialité! . . ."* He lowered his voice as he told me the secret of the lady's diplomatic success.

There was more movement in the lobby now. People from the bar, on their way out, passed people coming from the vestibule on their way into the bar and the restaurant. From the little courtyard beyond the green salon the ring of silver on china and the scraping of iron chairs on flag-

stone told the appearance of the first dinner guests. Little
gusts of cool wind entered through the open door past
Carol's large photo. Bratianu-beard nudged me and said,
"Have a good look at the man who is coming in now."

My eyes followed and fell on a little rotund man in a
white shantung coat over dark trousers who fairly shot
into the lobby. From the distance his face was a bald expanse of baby pink flesh, but as he came nearer he showed
cold eyes and a secretive, intelligent mouth. He made the
most of a few blond hairs by combing them with great
care. He was Colonel Gerstenberg, the German air attaché.
In the world war the Colonel had belonged to the famous
Richthofen Squadron, to which Field Marshal Goering
had also belonged, and the two were still friends. The air
attaché, the Excellencies said, was really the head of the
German Military Intelligence in Bucharest. He had held
the same job in Warsaw before, and the parallels suggested
by this fact were so disagreeable that no one cared to mention it. Before this the Colonel had been in Moscow. His
knowledge of Eastern Europe was certainly complete.

The Colonel crossed over to a group of men, sputtered
in short, rapid, chopped-up phrases and shot out to the
courtyard. As he joined and left them, the men flicked
their hands shoulder high in the casual version of the Nazi
salute, which was the only way I knew they were Germans.
At that time the Germans abroad had orders not to wear
their party buttons, and only officials wore a modest sign
in the form of a metal eagle with a microscopic swastika
under his wing. The idea of the order was probably not
to frighten the Europeans more than strictly necessary.

In other ways, too, these Germans—representatives of
German industrial firms, directors of banks and of Ger-

man oil companies—looked more European than German. They seemed a hand-picked lot: no rolls of flesh on the backs of necks; none of the closely cropped skulls which have marked George Grosz' caricatures of Germans. These Germans in the Athene Palace, I thought, were living testimony to Hitler's subtle way of dealing with bourgeois capitalism. They could not look more prosperous and elegant. Their appearance seemed to say, plenty of people are making plenty of money in Germany. And while money in itself did not give them power in Hitler's state, they were at least allowed to enjoy the pleasant paraphernalia of money. Here lay the chief difference between the way Stalin dealt with private capitalists and the way Hitler did.

There was another table of Germans, looking slightly less worldly but even more prosperous. These were Nazi party officials and Gestapo agents, stationed in Bucharest for a temporary survey. They had brought their women, some of them expensive-looking beauties in silver foxes. Outside on the Square they had long shining Mercedes parked, ready to take them to the most expensive restaurants where they would eat the most expensive food and drink the most expensive wines. The Nazis themselves had a wide range of jokes about these prosperous bosses. The best went like this: "Daddy," asked the son of a boss, "what is a plutocrat?" Daddy: "A plutocrat is a man who comes to power through money." The boy considers this for a moment, then says: "Then you are a crato-plut, daddy, for you came to money through power."

This new "cratoplutic aristocracy" which came into being in Hitler's Germany was not to be ignored. The Führer, intelligent Nazis said, with his never-failing insight into human nature knew that one could not make revolution with saints. Frugal though he was himself, he did not mind his big and little paladins getting their compensations in terms of worldly pleasures and possessions, or at least in every conceivable comfort. Country estates, fast motor cars, private planes, and the most expensive streamlined cuties—nothing was too good for his boys. Hitler probably regretted that he could not make princes and dukes of them as Napoleon had done. But then Napoleon's boys ended up by becoming so soft that they wanted just to hold on to their loot.

The night of the fall of Paris, the Germans in the lobby of the Athene Palace disappointed their audience, who had expected them to celebrate in a big way. No victor could behave with more reticence and dignity. The Hitler Germans were really getting very smooth, but it was not much use. Their impeccable behavior, I discovered, rather irritated the Rumanians, who sneered: "The German minister has told them to be extra-careful not to offend our pro-French feelings. They expect to win us over by *politeness!*"

The Old Excellencies did not like the Germans, but they were even more critical of the Allies. The Allies, they explained, had a considerable head start on the Nazis because the Great Rumania owed her existence to the Allied victory in the last war and because the sympathies of the Rumanian ruling class had been all with them. In view of these initial advantages the Allied performance had been lamentable. What the Old Excellencies found especially aggravating was that Allied attempts at sabotage in the oil region, as well as their clumsy efforts at blocking the Danube, had failed deplorably. *"Des dilettantes! Des idiots!"* said the Old Excellencies of Allied diplomats and intelligence agents. "They could not even buy a statesman so that he would stay bought." In the eyes of a Rumanian worse could be said of no man.

As if to illustrate his point, a dark thin gentleman with a little thin mustache moved towards our table. A big gray pearl in his black necktie matched his gray flannels. Here was the French envoy, M. Thierry, who fell back into the cushions exhaustedly, staring bleakly around him with small myopic eyes while he took a handkerchief from his breast pocket and began to wipe his glasses. The Old Excellencies informed me that this man had a Jewish wife, a Rothschild daughter, a fact to which they ascribed the minister's mournful appearance rather than to the fall of France. The Excellencies were pessimistic about the fate of the Jews in France, which they still discussed in the terms of the Dreyfus affair.

M. Thierry, that night, was only in the first phase of his difficulties. A few weeks later the Germans published documents, found by them on their campaign in France and never denied by the French, from which it appeared that Thierry was up to his ears in the unsuccessful Rumanian sabotage. The Germans were surprisingly sporting about the matter and hardly bothered Thierry personally, for to them sabotage was clearly just part of a diplomat's job and it was unfortunate if he failed as Thierry did. Recalled from Bucharest shortly after, M. Thierry quietly faded out after spending a few more thoroughly uncomfortable weeks—a very insignificant man in a very significant post.

Thierry was the diplomat of a system which had become unsure of itself and had made the most contradictory policies. While French statesmen in the last twenty years had considered Rumania solely from the point of view of what support they could get from her, instead what support France, the *grande nation*, could give, they allowed fraudulent French industrialists to dump worthless war materials on Rumania. That Rumania had no air force to speak of, though the Rumanian people sacrificed billions of leis on "air force stamps," was the sole fault of the French. The French industrialist, Paul Louis Weiller, builder of what some called flying hearses, had with the help of high Rumanian officials secured a monopoly. The quarrel between Weiller and his corrupt Rumanians on one hand and the honest and patriotic Rumanian engineers on the other hand not only ended in jail for the engineers but virtually stopped Rumanian airplane production during the crucial 1930's. Rumania could not have helped the democracies in 1940, even if she had wanted to.

Though this was only one case in point—there were many others—the prestige of France was still very high with the Rumanians, so much so that when Rumanians said "Allies," they really meant "France" and when they said "Allied diplomacy," they really meant "French diplomacy." To the Rumanians England, the Empire, the Anglo-Saxon way of life, were admirable but something as exotic and faraway as the Chinese civilization of the sixteenth century. In spite of her failings of the last twenty years France had been the dominating force in Rumania and the liberal order ruled only through the medium of France. This was a basic fact not only about the past but also the future. It showed that here no Anglo-Saxon order could impose itself without the agency of a great continental power. Any Anglo-Saxon order—any order at all— had to be represented, translated, interpreted by France,

Germany, or Russia. And this went not only for Rumania but for the whole Southeast of Europe. Nowhere in these parts of the world was England real enough to be accepted as a dominating force.

This was why, tonight, after the fall of Paris, the English were already licked in Rumania, though they did not acknowledge it. It was not so much that the defeat of France confirmed the notion of the supposed invincibility of the German army but more that the fall of France robbed the English of their viceroy in Rumania. This viceroy was France.

I asked the Rumanian Excellencies where the Englishmen sat, and they pointed out some tall young men sitting with their loosely jointed frames slouching in low armchairs who moved not at all or in a slow-motion fashion, about them the same aura of elegant boredom that distinguishes the heroes of Michael Arden. If the tragic events of the day had moved these Englishmen, they certainly did not show it, but gave the impression of being superbly sure that England would win the last battle. I did not know whether to admire them or worry about them.

These unconvincing, relaxed young men were, the Excellencies said, British diplomats, oil men, journalists, and Intelligence Service agents. Their minister, Sir Reginald Hoare, rarely appeared at the Athene Palace and was not very convincing either. The English here had always relied on the French to communicate the belief of ultimate Allied victory to the Rumanians.

Americans, and even Englishmen in Rumania, were harsh on Sir Reginald and his crew of relaxed young men, blaming them for being no match for Hitler's alert hardworking boys. But even if the English had been diplomatic geniuses, it would have made little difference. They could not have counteracted the growing realization in Rumania that her economic destinies were naturally bound up with Germany—a realization which had even begun to dawn on anti-German circles in Rumania and convinced them that, no matter whether Germany won or lost the war, Rumania would have to lean on her in the future. Above all, the English could not have counteracted the loss of France as the acknowledged representative of the liberal order on the continent.

Now the Excellencies turned their attention to a lady who crossed the lobby and sat down with the young Englishmen. She walked on narrow feet with toes turned out exaggeratedly, and there was, too, something exaggerated in the deep bow that she gave to the Excellencies and the enraptured smile that accompanied the bow. I noted that she was thin, indifferently dressed in black, and that her haggard face was painted into a chalk-white mask. The lady was the Princess Antoine Bibescu, née Elisabeth Asquith. I said "Oh," respectfully. Elisabeth Bibescu had been, in the twenties, the answer to every intellectual's prayer. Many of my friends still called this brilliant daughter of brilliant Margot Asquith unique. Her voice rose shrilly above the subdued hum in the lobby with the loud self-assurance of a woman who is used to sounding off every remark like a bon mot.

The Antoine Bibescus—he was Rumania's minister to Washington in the twenties—were pro-Ally by inclination and tradition. The fall of France was a terrible blow to the Princess and she had no illusions about Rumania's surrender to the Nazis. In months to come she organized a salon for the English and Americans, French de Gaullist sympathizers, and leftist or Jewish Rumanian intellectuals. Rumor had it that General Antonescu himself advised Antoine against carrying on this salon. However that may be, Elisabeth Bibescu's salon died down for lack of support, because the members left or did not dare be seen with the Princess. This left Elisabeth Bibescu much time for loathing the Huns, which she did with abandon.

At 9:30 the clusters in the lobby had begun to break up: now it was the wonderfully late Rumanian dinner time. The big lobby had become so still that the ring of silver on china and the scraping of iron chairs on flagstone from the courtyard seemed very noisy. Maids in black dresses with little white aprons began to empty ash trays and shake cushions back into shape. Clusters of people who up to now had been content with the small tables in the middle aisle moved over to the larger tables by the wall. Where the French envoy had been, there was now a group of olive-skinned young men with smooth black hair and dark luminous eyes, who reminded me of South Americans. They were the young Brancovans, Katargis, Ghykas, Soutzos, and other descendants of phanariotes and hospodars, the noblest blood of Rumania. They were poor because the land reform of 1925 had done away with their big estates. Yet most of them had never done an honest day's work.

Most of these young upper-class Rumanians were pro-French and anti-German, and at the same time most of them were pro-totalitarian and anti-liberal. Their brothers and cousins had followed Codreanu, fought for Franco, were put in jail by Carol's police, and some even killed. One of these was Prince Cantacuzino, of whom they were all very proud. Cantacuzino was once accused of plotting against the life of Lupescu. Before the court which tried to prove that he had acted on behalf of the Iron Guard, the Prince denied that the Guard had anything to do with the plot and shouted, "I wanted to kill Lupescu because she was my mistress and has betrayed me." Nobody believed this was true, but everybody was pleased that he said it. The Prince was acquitted, to be killed a few years later by order of Carol's police.

But that was not all. Ten minutes after the Prince's death, Carol had his mother, the old Princess Alexandrine Cantacuzino, locked up in one room of her palace for fear she would make trouble. The Princess had been one of Queen Marie's closest friends, one of the great ladies of Rumania, founder of orthodox Catholic schools from kindergartens to business colleges—schools so perfectly organized that they stick out like sore thumbs from anything else of the kind in the country. Yet the old princess had been held incommunicado for almost a year now, her windows leaded, water and light cut off, and no doctor, lawyer, or servant allowed to see her. The princess was worse off than in a Rumanian prison, and Rumanian prisons were no picnic.

So the young princes, though they did not all approve of the Iron Guard, certainly were against the status quo and considered Carol a heel. Even the Old Excellencies themselves took a grim view of the future of a country where such things could go on, but they were happily unable to concentrate for long on the future. People as they appeared on their immediate horizon distracted them. "There, Madame," the Greyhound breathed into my ear, "is a man who is a great friend of His Majesty. He sleeps with his daughter. A lovely girl." He said it as casually as if there was nothing more natural than for His Majesty's friend to commit incest, and Bratianu-beard offered details of the sort in which the Old Excellencies excelled. Then, without any transition, they again began to talk of the Iron Guard.

The Guard seemed to them no immediate threat to Rumania because the intellectual leaders of the Party, some twelve hundred of them, had all been killed. They rather disapproved of the killing of the Guardists on the ground that it was "unsound." They especially disapproved of leaving the corpses lying around on the Square, as Carol had done with the Guardists who killed Calinescu. Carol's police had spat on the bodies and trampled them before the eyes of the populace. "Leaving them," the Greyhound said, *"je vous assure,* Madame, with their brains hanging around like calves' brains at the butcher's." The Old Excellencies felt that Hitler—they pronounced it Hitlér—would soon see to it that these murdered Guardists were revenged. And that he would make Rumania suffer for Carol's sins.

I left the two Old Excellencies sitting in the now empty lobby and walked to the bare white vestibule, where a group of midget-like page boys in turquoise-blue uniforms, apple-cheeked, and with knowing eyes, sat on a stone bench and dangled their legs. Theirs was a strategic position. They had only to turn their heads with the little monkey caps to the right and they could watch the revolving door, the entrance hall, and the desk. Turning the monkey caps to the left they could see the lobby, part of the bar, and most of the green salon beyond it. Before their noses were the stairs, the two elevators, and the telephone booths. Booth number two was half open now and the page boys listened with fascination to an American voice yelling at somebody in Berne, Switzerland, as if it were not the phone wires but vocal power alone which had to cover the distance. The American voice was trying to tell Berne that things looked black all around in Rumania. For a second the disheveled figure of a man in shirt sleeves, with necktie torn loose and collar open, popped out of the booth and wiped a perspiring brow. Then he dived back in and his shouts became more frantic.

They followed me as I mounted the yellow marble stairs.

3—THE GERMANS

With the fall of France the Germans became the whole show in Rumania. The French in Bucharest split overnight into the Frenchmen of Vichy and the Free French, and as such suspected and spied on each other. As far back as Dunkirk the French and English in Bucharest had not been on speaking terms and after the French armistice and the Oran incident, the schism was complete. So while the Free French left as quickly as they could for territories outside the German orbit, the French of Vichy led an isolated existence, even after cooperation with Berlin had become the order of Vichy. In Bucharest there was no pretext of Vichy and Berlin cooperating.

The English were, of course, still around, but this was all you could say of them. Nobody asked any more what the English expected to do. They could not do a thing.

Politically the English in Bucharest became the forgotten men.

Even the American journalists, who drifted to the Athene Palace before luncheon and dinner every day to sample the latest rumors, reluctantly agreed that in Rumania now everything hinged on Hitler. At this time only the American news agencies had their representatives in Bucharest, and a few newspaper correspondents had floated to Rumania from Finland, Norway, and Holland on the chance that the war would come to the Balkans. For the AP there was Robert St. John, a thin, pale young man with a brown beard who looked like the Christ of the Oberammergau Passion play, except for his Dunhill pipe, and who was later wounded in Greece. There were two Stevenses. The older, Stevens of the United Press, a thickset, red-faced man, had spent a lifetime in Bucharest. Gossip at the Athene Palace said he was originally a boxer. Young Edmund Stevens of the *Christian Science Monitor* was coolly sophisticated in a slow-moving, slow-speaking way. Having lived in Italy and Russia for many years he took European wickedness in his stride. Spencer Williams had come fresh from ten years of Soviet Russia which had made him allergic to all sorts of dictatorship. And Betty Wason, a diminutive ingénue from Indiana, had been in Norway when the Germans came and had told it to the folks back home over the Columbia Broadcasting System. Engagingly unaware of the fact that there had been disagreeableness in the world before Hitler, she was on the way to becoming an expert on European affairs. The American journalists expected the establishment of a German protectorate over Rumania or something of the kind any moment now. To them the people to watch here were the Germans.

The most sinister German around, and about the most powerful, they told me, was Gauleiter Conradi, the head of the Nazi Party in Rumania. Gauleiter Conradi never appeared at the Athene Palace or elsewhere in Bucharest. In fact Gauleiter Conradi rarely moved from the high pillows in his bed, for he was paralyzed from the waist down, a fact which only enhanced his uncanny prestige. But even though the Gauleiter rarely went out, he managed to know everything. To the Germans in Rumania the thought of their Gauleiter was as uncomfortable as the thought of the Last Judgment is to the faithful, and all were terrified of him: princesses and Volksdeusche chambermaids; German schoolteachers in Transylvania and German businessmen; the German minister and the charwoman of the German legation—the only difference being that the minister was more afraid than the charwoman.

Gauleiter Conradi was about sixty, and on his heavy torso—I was told—sat the head of a Roman emperor. All day long agents passed in and out of his shabby bedroom and reported to the severe figure against the pillows. Each came alone, made his report, and left immediately— waiters and pageboys from the Athene Palace, officials of the German legation, maids to the high-priced ladies, secretaries to businessmen, all stood stiffly for a few moments by the side of the Gauleiter's ugly bed.

The Gauleiter heard everything. When Frau Dr. Fabrizius, the German Minister's wife, bought clothes at Neumann's in Brasov, the Gauleiter took the case up and brought it before the Brown House back home. Neumann's, which sold the finest and most expensive clothes in Rumania, was a Jewish shop, and though the lady was a relative of Herr von Ribbentrop, she never again shopped at Neumann's. When the pretty wife of one of the secretaries of the German legation began an affair with the gigolo I had seen in the Athene Palace lobby, the Gauleiter cracked down on the lady and her husband with a speed and a violence that left them terrified, though the more moderate legation decided to hush the matter up.

Relations between Gauleiter Conradi and the official German legation in Bucharest were a reflection of the relationship between Nazi Party and Nazi State in Germany and of the struggle for power which has gone on between State and Party from the beginning of the Third Reich. The Party, mainly interested in the devotion to national socialist principles, was out to punish anybody who would not conform. The State, mainly interested in the efficiency of its personnel, was ready to overlook sins against the party line, provided a man was good at his job. Since the war the Nazi State, with the armed forces at its disposal, had won the ascendancy over the Nazi party. Which is why Gauleiter Conradi, the boss of the Nazi party in Bucharest, now won increasingly few battles with the German minister, who represented the Nazi State.

Journalists at the Athene Palace said that the German government accounted for thousands of people in Bucharest and that these people occupied at least a hundred houses, which may have been an exaggeration. However, the Third Reich in Bucharest functioned in several hierarchies, all more or less independent of each other. Aside from the Nazi State and the Nazi Party hierarchies, there was a separate hierarchy which represented the Gestapo, and another which represented the Propaganda Ministry. There might be others, of which no outsider like myself could know. In this exceedingly opaque organization it was almost impossible to ascertain which official Germans belonged to which hierarchy, since all of them had "German Legation" on their visiting cards and all carried diplomatic passports. It was difficult, too, to get Germans to talk; they did not like it to be known that several hierarchies ruled the Third Reich and always insisted that there was only one with several functions. But every once in a while something happened which showed that this could not possibly be so.

The German set-up in Bucharest was further complicated by the fact that there were two actual German legations. The regular German legation occupied five houses in the Strada Victor Emmanuel III. Its head for several years had been Dr. Fabrizius, a tall, pot-bellied, stuffed-shirtish career diplomat in his fifties, called "Pappi" behind his back by the young attachés of the legation who loved to point out his likeness to Weiss Ferdl, a Munich cabarettist famous for his frank jokes about the Nazis and his ability to retain the friendship of Hitler in spite of them. Ardent Nazis criticized Dr. Fabrizius for playing around with the "wrong people," meaning Carol, Lupescu, and Udurianu, and for treating the Iron Guardists as unimportant. Pappi, they said, had not moved a finger to help Codreanu and his followers or they would surely not have been killed—which was probably unfair, for Pappi only did what Berlin told him to. Pappi, the ardent Nazis said, was a diplomat's diplomat, and not quite in tune with the new order.

The other German legation was decidedly new order.

Housed in the Strada Wilson opposite the Rumanian Ministry of Propaganda, with cars parked before it and along the street from morning to night, there was no elegant diplomatic nonsense about this legation, which was more like a permanent economic commission, and was headed by Dr. Neubacher, Germany's minister plenipotentiary for economic questions in the Balkans. Neubacher worked with a staff of economists from the Section "W" (Wirtschaft, or economics) of the Foreign Office, from the Ministry of Economics, and from the Ministry of Agriculture. He also employed experts who had never before been in Government service but were businessmen with wide experience in the Balkans.

Unlike Dr. Fabrizius, the diplomat's diplomat, Dr. Neubacher was a newcomer to diplomacy. Until a few months ago he had been Mayor of Vienna; nominally he still was. He was as unstuffed-shirtish as he possibly could be, calling himself an old revolutionary and bragging a little of having been in Schuschnigg's concentration camp for thirteen months. Belonging to the old Guard of Austrian Nazis who had paved the way for the Anschluss, Dr. Neubacher was well into his forties, a slight blond man with the profile of a tired eagle. When he smiled, as he did easily, his face crumpled into innumerable wrinkles and his eyes danced. One assumed that women must be greatly tempted to make Dr. Neubacher smile.

Men with portfolios dashed to and fro in the entrance hall at the German legation in the Strada Wilson, and the telephone rang constantly. Invariably the clerk at the desk would say into the telephone, "Heil Hitler, His Excellency is in conference. Can I connect you with one of the

other gentlemen?" This augured badly for an interview
I hoped to have with Dr. Neubacher. It was almost noon,
quite a while since I had sent up my card, on which I had
scrawled "American journalist."

Because of his militant Nazi antecedents, a recognized
genius for economics, and a long friendship with Goering,
Dr. Neubacher, the American journalists in Bucharest
were convinced, was the real Nazi works in Rumania,
while polite Dr. Fabrizius was just window dressing. But
the American journalists in Bucharest, though they considered the Nazis the whole show in Rumania, almost
never interviewed them—probably because they had more
hatred of Nazis than curiosity about them. I had the curiosity, too.

In half an hour a pretty blonde secretary told me that
Dr. Neubacher would receive me: apparently he was curious to see an American journalist who was curious to see
him. It was a novelty. As he made me sit down in a comfortable armchair and took one himself, he gave the impression that he had oceans of time and was delighted to
spend it all on me. This was part of his charm. I thought,
as we talked, that there should be a law against Nazis hav.
ing charm, and thought how smart it was of Hitler to use
so many Austrians in his conquest of the Balkans, which
he did chiefly because of this charm.

In Bucharest Austrian diplomats and consular officials
whose loyalty to the Third Reich seemed to be satisfactory had been recruited after the Anschluss and the Nazis
imported many more later. It was a smart political move.
The Austrians had a centuries-old tradition of ruling a
motley crowd of nations under their flag—at one time there
had been fourteen—a tradition which the Prussians lacked.

While the Austro-Hungarian Empire broke down in the end, it is nevertheless true that for a long time it had succeeded in making Austrians of Czechs, Ruthenes, Hungarians, Croats. You have only to look at their cities: Zagreb, Prague, Budapest, even Cracow are Austrian cities to this day. The ingratiating manners of Austrians spring from imperialistic experience and from an almost oriental *laisser-aller*, which made Hitler's new order more easily digestible than the Prussian ways of iron discipline. That's what made the Austrians an integral part of Hitler's imperialistic scheme, and the Austrian Nazis knew it. In fact they felt very cocky about it. They would tell you that it was really Austria who had conquered Germany, not vice versa, only that the Germans did not know it yet.

Dr. Neubacher sat hunched forward, elbows on knees. His was a most unbusiness-like office, full of gilt chairs and tables that must have come with the house when the Germans bought it. Only one personal touch stood out: the antlers of a stag which the Doctor, he told me, had shot in the Carpathians. The shutters were closed against the hot midday sun and no noise of autos dashing up to the entrance penetrated. A large map of the Balkans hung behind us on the wall.

Dr. Neubacher spoke with vivacity, warmth, and enthusiasm, punctuating his sentences with little round gestures of the hand that did not hold his cigaret and appearing rather to like questions, smiling just a little if they became too insidious. When he got enthusiastic he rose and walked slowly up and down the room with his hands buried in the pockets of his gray flannel trousers. Once we both walked up and down the room, side by side, stopping at intervals like two old men taking a constitutional.

As he talked with enthusiasm about the plans and ideas
of the Third Reich, I thought of the times when Nazi
diplomats at the slightest provocation would confess that
they were really liberals at heart and served Hitler only
"to avoid the worst." The time of apologetic Nazi diplomats now seemed past. If they had not been old Nazis to
begin with, victorious Hitler had won them over to the
Third Reich.

"I have much to tell that is new and interesting," Dr.
Neubacher said, "but journalists want only to hear about
the actuality of the war. Yet for Germany the war is merely
a sideshow. Our main activities are concerned with the
organization of Europe after the war."

This economic organization of the Balkans, Dr. Neubacher's special sphere, was not so much intended to
service Germany's war needs as it was really the first step
toward the peacetime development of Europe, the rosy-
fingered dawn of Hitler's New Era. Whether Germany got
foodstuffs and oil from the Balkans or not, Dr. Neubacher
emphasized, did not in the least influence the outcome of
the war, as Germany had enough supplies stored, no matter how long the conflict.

Like all German economic experts, Dr. Neubacher
denied that oil could make or break their war efforts, or
that the Rumanian oil was of decisive importance. Germany, he said, had found so much oil in the newly conquered areas that it more than made up for the oil so far
used in the war. Moreover the oil reserves Germany had
stored before the war would be enough to carry on a full-
dress war for several years. Besides, considerable oil was
produced in Germany and the German-dominated neigh-

borhood. It added up to 2,000,000 tons of natural oil a year in or near Germany's frontiers.

But most important was the production of synthetic oil, which had been immensely increased in the last two years. This production was, at the end of 1939, 2,008,000 tons, and this year the output would at least be doubled. Moreover, "Treibgas," a mixture of propane and butane, the production of which had automatically increased with the production of synthetic oil, would be used for all trucks, auto-buses, traction-engines, and would make for a further decrease of consumption in liquid oil.

The above-mentioned oil sources were always accessible to Germany because they could not be disturbed by political changes or difficulties of transportation. The same was not true of German oil supplies from Russia and Rumania, which depended on transportation and were therefore limited. Of Rumania's yearly oil production, which decreased from 8,004,000 tons in 1936 to an average production of 6,000,000 tons in the last four years, 1,500,000 tons per year went to Germany according to the German-Rumanian treaty. But even the transportation of this small amount was difficult and Rumanian oil could not be counted on for war use proper. The war was not everything, however. Germany used in peacetime four to five million tons of oil per year. Wartime restrictions had reduced this peacetime consumption by 30 per cent. If Germany could get the whole output of Rumanian oil, she could abolish the present restrictions on private auto driving. The Führer would like his Germans to drive their cars in spite of the war.

These were the rather sanguine terms in which the Germans viewed the oil question at the time. Evidently in doing so they excluded the possibility of a Russian campaign, when the 6,000,000 tons of Rumanian oil would come in handy. Also while they always talked of a "long conflict," it appeared to me that they never seriously believed in a long conflict. For instance, Dr. Neubacher pooh-poohed the importance of Rumanian grain for the German war economy. Germany, he said, had stocked enormous amounts of grain. Also the harvest all over the Balkans was so bad this year that very possibly they would have to import grain there to keep the Balkan people from starving. It did not seem to occur to him then that next year might be a war year, too. All the Germans were at this juncture convinced that the war would be over before winter. Later, when it became evident that this would not be the case, they admitted that the Balkan produce would be important for keeping "friendly countries" in food, meaning especially Italy. But they never admitted that it would make a difference to themselves one way or the other.

Germany's economic organization of the Balkans, Dr. Neubacher went on, was the first part of a plan by which German economists would later set up the European continent as a single Grossraum, which instead of the individual countries would form the economic unit of the future. A common plan would regulate production in every section of the European Grossraum and the exchange of goods and collaboration between these sections. Already the Germans knew what they wanted to do in Rumania and already they had begun.

The aims of the new economic order of Europe were to abolish unemployment everywhere through full utilization of the productive forces of every country; regulation of international exchange on the basis of barter; breaking of the British monopoly on raw materials, and therefore of the arbitrary power of capitalistic speculators; and—to get down to cases—to increase the buying power of agricultural peoples such as Rumania through improved methods and crops.

Barter, Dr. Neubacher said, was wrongly decried in the democracies as a German means to enslave the small nations. Actually barter had done wonders to develop the small nations: Rumania was an example. In late years the so-called gold countries had been so stingy about their imports from Rumania that the Rumanian funds in these countries did not allow them to buy sufficient machinery to develop Rumanian plants. Instead German-Rumanian barter worked on a basis of machinery in return for produce and functioned without a hitch, war or no war. By way of exchanging their agricultural products and oil Rumanians got all the German machinery they needed. Right now—in the middle of the war—Rumania was building a pipeline from Mannesmann in Düsseldorf and had increased her output of ores through German machinery.

The Germans, Dr. Neubacher explained with smiling satisfaction, were not doing this as benefactors of the Balkan countries, but because their economy and the economies of the Balkan countries complemented each other. The Allied countries were interested in just one Rumanian product—oil—and if they bought anything else from Rumania it was sheer charity. But what Rumania and the other Balkan countries needed was equal export of all products, especially agricultural, for this would make them independent of the hazards of the world market. And it just so happened that Germany needed Rumania's agricultural products as well as her oil.

At the moment German specialists and organizations were working hard with Rumanian farmers to make fatter pigs and chickens and better breeds of sheep and cattle. The Germans, Dr. Neubacher took pains to make clear, did not let themselves in for such a face-lifting process in order to make Rumania beautiful but in order to procure fatter hams and bigger eggs for Germany.

It sounded, as Dr. Neubacher described it, superbly practical. Under the easy flow of his rational words, however, I detected a fanaticism peculiar to the Germans which connected with something I had read long ago. The English, I remembered reading, conceive of the world as always bridally adorned and beautiful, needing to care for it only a loving, guiding hand; whereas the Germans conceive of the world as constantly in a state of disorder, a chaos which must be cleaned up and ordered anew by the right kind of hard work. This conception, it seemed to me, was really at the bottom of the plans for the new order. After centuries of frustration the Germans at last saw themselves in a position to run Europe as they thought it should be run, and they were going at it with a vengeance. All the protestations about the organization of the economics of the Balkans being the practical and logical thing to do were just the Nazis cloaking the deeper motive of bringing German order into a world which the Germans considered disgustingly chaotic.

Dr. Neubacher thought the greatest future of Rumania lay in oleiferous plants, especially the soya plant. Until a few years ago the Germans had imported the soya from Manchukuo, but Nazi economists had decided that such an important plant should be grown nearer home, where it would be accessible regardless of political disturbances and transportation difficulties. Experiments showed that Balkan soil was favorable for soya, and in 1934 the I.G. Farbentrust, on behalf of the German Government, started working with the Rumanians on soya. They gave the seeds to the peasants for nothing and guaranteed a fixed price for the harvest—which, of course, was the most wonderful thing that ever happened to these most downtrodden of farmers, who never before had got a fixed price for anything and had always been cheated by the middlemen into the bargain. (In fact, one of the great surprises brought by soya to the Rumanian peasant was the discovery that his scales were right, after all.) When the Rumanian peasant had cultivated his beans, he was even more pleasantly surprised. One wheat-planted hectare (2.47 acres) had brought only 3500-4000 leis, while a soya-planted hectare brought 5460 leis: an enormous difference for the small Rumanian farmer, who had only five or six hectares to his name. The 1400 hectares which had been planted with soya in 1934 had by 1940 increased to 140,000 and would be increasing every year.

Dr. Neubacher's justified pride in German soya diplomacy came, however, to a premature end. For the bulk of Rumanian soya, 100,000 out of the 140,000 hectares, was situated in Bessarabia which a fortnight later, in the end of June 1940, was annexed by the Russians. This lost the Germans much hard work and financial investment, together with the year's Bessarabian soya harvest. Some 10,000 soya-planted hectares in the southern Dobrudscha went to Bulgaria a few weeks later when this district was ceded and another 14,000 soya-planted hectares in northern Transylvania went at the same time to the Hungarians. As the Germans had made a similar soya diplomacy in Hungaria and Bulgaria as in Rumania, though not on such a big scale, they at least got the harvest of these 24,000 hectares. Still, the bulk of Rumanian soya cultivation was lost, at least temporarily. By autumn 1940, only 16,000 soya-planted hectares were left in Rumanian territory, and the exportable soya harvest for the year amounted to not more than 12,000 tons. All this has been changed again by the course of the Russian campaign. As this is being written, Bessarabia is back with Rumania, and the Germans may plant soya there again. Still, while I stayed in Rumania the fate of German soya diplomacy gave me the first inkling of the great gap that existed between planning and reality, even if the planning was done by Germans. The most thoroughgoing and efficient plans were apt to come to naught simply because fate decided otherwise, and the Germans were no supermen—which is a good thing to remember.

The intensification of agriculture alone, Dr. Neubacher said, was not enough to prepare Rumania for the Grossraum. To raise the living standards of the agricultural Southeast, the surplus agricultural population had to be absorbed. Too many people worked the piteously small Rumanian farms and most of the time just sat around and did nothing. Only increased industrialization of the Balkan countries would solve the problem of the agricultural surplus population, and it was one of the democratic misconceptions, Dr. Neubacher said, that the Germans would make the agricultural countries abandon their industries and limit them to agriculture. On the contrary, Germans encouraged the industrialization of the Balkans. Industrialized countries, German economists had found out in their dealings with South America, are richer than non-industrial countries and can, therefore, buy more goods. An industrialized Rumania, while absorbing her agricultural unemployment, would become a better client for Germany.

Of course industrialization of the Balkans would have to be reasonable. Rumania would have to concentrate on the industries for which she had the raw materials right in the country. Products for which she would have to import the raw materials would be better imported ready made. The industries which Germany was eager to cultivate in the Balkans were those connected with the preservation of foodstuffs. Even now German firms were establishing plants for canning and freezing foods. In a short time, Dr. Neubacher said delightedly, the Balkans would be the California of Europe.

Thus the Nazis plan for the colonization of the Balkans. . . . It was an exceedingly rational, intelligent, imaginative plan. Nobody could possibly have conceived of it but the Germans, with their immense belief in the necessity of an ordered universe. The Germans alone had the skill and thoroughness to achieve it, and were the only people in the world who were not a bit afraid that a planned and efficient world would be an awful bore.

There was only one question more to ask in connection with the economic organization of Rumania, a question which at the time was in anybody's mind: did the Germans intend to make Rumania a protectorate or a fascist state in order to carry through their economic plans?

Dr. Neubacher was very definite in his "No" to this question. "We haven't got any political interest in Rumania," he said. "We have only one aim, and that is to keep quiet in the raw-material sphere. We don't wish to Germanize Rumania or to make her fascist. Any strong government which has the authority to keep quiet in the raw-material sphere will do."

The worst about this was that Dr. Neubacher was sincere. For seven months I was to hear the Nazis protest wistfully that the Balkans were their economic, not their political, sphere of interest and that they really did not want to establish a protectorate in Rumania. They still protested when the chances for "any strong government which had the authority to assure quiet in the raw-material sphere" were about as remote as the millennium and they had a full-sized, noisy revolution in the sphere instead. This reluctance to take political responsibility all but wrecked their wonderful economic planning in Rumania, at least temporarily. It showed that the Nazis are not above making great tactical blunders.

Now Dr. Neubacher's secretary put her head through a crack in the door and beckoned. It was, I discovered, after one o'clock, but Dr. Neubacher assured me that he had nothing to do until his wife picked him up for luncheon. The secretary slipped out again and Dr. Neubacher went on, skipping now from one topic to another. He ascribed the German successes in the war first to the person of Hitler. "What a genius!" he said and I could see he meant it. "Even if we had been beaten in France, and the French had invaded Germany, we would have followed him back to East Prussia and further back to Poland, knowing that he must win in the end." The German army, he said, was a revolutionary army and therefore bound to win. "Revolutionary armies always win," he said, "though they are usually ill-equipped. This time the revolutionary army has the dynamism, *and* the bombers and tanks."

Next in importance he considered the unity of the German people and after that the blindness of the democracies. The British and French and American journalists who wrote that German tanks were of papier-mâché, and that German generals were revolting against the Führer, had been a great help to Germany. Most of the people who spread these tales, he said, were refugees, and Berlin jested that after this war they would erect a monument not to the "Unknown Soldier" but to the "Unknown Refugees."

As Dr. Neubacher paced up and down the quiet room with the gilt chairs, talking easily and with intelligent frankness, I could not help thinking: Here is a man who was Mayor of Vienna when the SA made the Jews clean streets and worse. How, then, could this apparently civilized and decent human being permit other human beings to be humiliated and tortured? Why, in short, had he permitted the Viennese atrocities to happen? Dr. Neubacher shrugged his shoulders. "One must give every revolution a short holiday. It's a necessity of revolutionary dynamism. Of course, if the atrocities had gone on a day longer, we would have shot into the boys. I know Americans are outraged about this kind of thing. To them the ugly byplay of revolution overshadows the achievements. They are too puritan to appreciate revolutionary dynamism."

A long Horch limousine waited for Dr. Neubacher in the doorway of the legation as we went out. Two stiff little flags framed the radiator, one with the swastika and the other with the crest of the city of Vienna. Frau Dr. Neubacher, as pretty a Viennese as they come, looked not more than thirty—but she was, for there beside her in the car were Fraulein Neubacher and her fiancé. Peach-like skin, radiant eyes and lovely blonde hair, looking from the neck up like a young Marie Antoinette and from the shoulders down like a sporty young lady, with wide shoulders and narrow hips and a blue sleeveless linen dress without hat or stockings: this was Fraulein Neubacher. Her fiancé was a young diplomat of excellent German family. They would found a nice Nazi dynasty.

I left the legation and walked back to the Athene Palace across the Royal Square, calm and still in the blazing mid-day sun. The crane before the red brickwork of Carol's unfinished annex was locked for the siesta hours, shops were closed with the shutters down. A solemn Rolls Royce swung into the drive of the Palace and discharged a dig-nitary before a door opened by a white escarpined foot-man. A white-clad peasant tended the gigantic gladiolas which bordered the patch of lawn. I thought of Hitler's new order as Dr. Neubacher had explained it. Rumania in the Era Germanica sounded like a good place for peas-ants—that is, for eighty-five percent of the Rumanian people. But for the remaining fifteen percent it would be a hell of a bore or a hell of a hell.

4—FIFTH COLUMN

Frau Edit von Coler rarely
gave people in the Athene Palace an opportunity for a
good look at her, though she lived in the hotel and had
been there for two years. She seldom sat in the bar or in
the lobby, allowing the curious their most satisfying
glimpses of her when she passed quickly through the entrance hall or when she drove down the Calea Victoriei
in her long gray Mercedes. In the two years she had been
at the hotel, Frau von Coler had been talked about nearly
as much as Lupescu. People in the lobby called her "la de
Coler" and said she was a sister of Heinrich Himmler.
Numerous unflattering stories were passed around about
her, describing her alternately as an overblown frau or
blonde vamp and linking her name with that of the rich
and powerful Malaxa, Carol's friend, or the handsome
Nazi commissar for oils.

Everyone at the Athene Palace considered Frau von

Coler as a Mata Hari, 1940 fashion, a simplification which
made everybody happy. But actually Frau von Coler was
as remote from Mata Hari as a panzer division of 1942
is from the cavalry of 1914. Mata Hari and her sisters were
dumbbells in an era when bare skin was supposed to make
generals lose their heads to the point of leaving secret
plans on a lady's bed table. Glamour was their only stock
in trade. In the high game of war and peace they ranked
with the charwomen designated to empty the wastebaskets
in foreign legations and the offices of military attachés.
The real drama of the Mata Haris, which never was sufficiently exploited by Hollywood, was the enormous gap
between the risks the poor creatures ran and the exasperat-
ingly modest results of their most successful endeavors.

Frau von Coler was an entirely different proposition. To
begin with, contrary to what the Athene Palace wished
to believe, she was not Hitler's spy, but a Hitler propagandist. Her task was infinitely more complex than the
task of a spy, and conceived in a much more realistic vein.
Seduction was no longer enough. The propagandist had
to combine the diplomatic genius of a Jules Cambon
with the salonist talents of a Récamier.

Yet her superiors, aware of the sad fact that the number
of generals and statesmen who leave their secret papers
was very small, still believed that an alluring woman's
boudoir was a good place to make friends and influence
people. And to make friends and influence people was a
propagandist's business. Instead of waiting for the moment
that actual secrets would fall into her lap, she was expected
to find out trends and moods in influential circles, and
the character, beliefs, and weak spots of decisive figures
in politics. Aside from being a good psychologist, the

propagandist must influence the right people by argument, using her skill and charm to plant suitable information rather than to extract it.

Frau von Coler, as would be expected, never admitted that she was a German propagandist. The woman who for two years had done more than the German legation and the Gestapo combined to wean Rumanian statesmen and society away from the French, and to make Nazi Germany palatable to them, was registered as one of two Bucharest correspondents for the *Deutsche Allegemeine Zeitung* in Berlin. This accent on a comparatively unglamourous, intellectual metier was very 1940; in 1914 mystery women were never journalists. Incidentally Frau von Coler was quite a good journalist, writing very creditable articles on Rumania for her paper, chiefly on agricultural questions. For strangely enough, Hitler's propagandist in Rumania had been secretary to Herr Darre, Nazi Minister of Agriculture and a genius in his field, and had a great knowledge of agriculture, even going so far as to establish a model chicken farm on the outskirts of Bucharest, which was one of von Coler's efficient ways of making friends with the Rumanians by doing something about their problems. This Hitlerian touch of "blood and soil," in combination with the legends of glamour and mystery which surrounded the lady, was more irresistible than all the stories I had read about Frau von Coler in American magazines and heard at the Athene Palace. It was what made me more curious to meet her.

So one day I sent Frau von Coler a note of introduction from an American journalist who knew her in Berlin. The response was impersonal but prompt. Frau von Coler, a secretary informed me over the phone, was taking friends to see a picture at the Rumanian Ministry of Propaganda that night and would be pleased to take me along. She was meeting her guests at the Ministry, but as I too lived at the hotel, would I not meet the *gnädige* Frau in her apartment?

At 8:30 that evening I knocked at the door of von Coler's apartment on the fourth floor of the Athene Palace and was led by a secretary into the salon. The salon was rather banal, with gilt Louis Seize chairs covered with rose brocade, but there was something pleasantly lived-in about the room. Chairs and sofas stood at sociable angles, and beside the most comfortable chair was one of the best German-made radios. The door to a balcony stood open and the fragrance of the warm summer night mingled with the fragrance of the roses and carnations in the room. On the tables was a wide assortment of books and magazines in German, French, and English and as I looked over the titles a medium-sized slender blonde entered the room quickly, greeting me with a cordial handshake.

Here was a roundish face with a firm mouth and a little nose, a lovely skin and gentian blue eyes which went straight at you in a searching but friendly way. Over the smooth rounded forehead, that of an intelligent child, bamboo-colored hair was brushed tightly back and plaited into braids which were pinned flat on the back of her head. Peasant girls of the Black Forest wore their hair that way, and on Frau von Coler it looked exceedingly chic and soigné. She was, I thought, blood and soil all right, but streamlined by Elizabeth Arden and dressed by Molyneux. The silver foxes of her coat were the best to be had, and underneath the coat I noted a casual little print which looked rare and expensive. As jewels she wore heavy golden chains around her arms and lovely golden earrings with moonstones. Moonstones went very well with her blondeness.

Frau von Coler talked quickly with a simple and direct friendliness about a number of things. She mentioned the fall of France, and said, "I am so happy that the French declared my beloved Paris an open city. It would have been too terrible if we had had to bomb the Louvre or the Place Vendôme." She really sounded as if this aspect of the great German victory pleased her more than anything.

I felt perfectly at ease with Frau von Coler and so asked her point blank whether she was really Herr Himmler's sister. We were waiting for the elevator and she was stripping her gloves down over her fingers. She laughed and shook her head and said, "It's the best story about me, but unfortunately, not a true one." And she told me that she did not mind the stories that went around the Athene Palace about her, except that one which said she was fifty. That story, she said, was as unfair as it was untrue.

We ran to the Ministry, for it was late and the distance was too short to use Frau von Coler's sleek car. The Square, as we dashed through it, was empty and the windows of the Palace were dark. Running along, Frau von Coler told me breathlessly that we were to see the private showing of a French picture which was banned in Bucharest. She squeezed my arm a little and said, "I think it's fun to invite my friends to a forbidden French picture. You would not expect a German in Bucharest to invite them to a French picture in the middle of the war." She chuckled contentedly, evidently pleased with her own unexpectedness.

Frau von Coler's guests waited for her in the projection room of the Ministry in the Strada Wilson, a big new building which had sounded hollow as we ran through its empty corridors. For me there was a confusing moment of presentation before the picture began. A dozen or more black or blond or gray heads bending over my hand, as whiffs of brilliantine entered my nostrils and mustaches tickled my fingers. Frau von Coler pronounced the names hastily. All the Rumanian names sounded like Jonescu and the other names—German ones—swarmed with titles: counts, barons, a prince or two. The three ladies in the party, besides the hostess and myself, were young and good looking.

The forbidden movie was called *From Mayerling to Serajevo,* and nobody knew why it was forbidden, not even the gentleman from the Propaganda Ministry who had arranged the showing of the film for Frau von Coler. Someone suggested that the picture was forbidden because the assassination at Serajevo might put ideas into the heads of the Rumanians about their King. Others guessed that the picture was forbidden because the morganatic marriage of the Archduke would remind the Rumanians of their King and Lupescu. The gentleman of the Propaganda Ministry shrugged his shoulders discreetly and smiled.

After the film Frau von Coler's party repaired to her apartment at the Athene Palace. Sandwiches and raspberries with cream were passed around, and glasses of Maibowle. There were several men to every woman, not more than twenty people altogether. Groups formed easily, in a fluid way; talk was lively, free, good-tempered, and, at moments, brilliant. On the surface it was a simple,

unpretentious gathering of well-bred, intelligent people.
Yet it was exactly this kind of gathering which had made
Frau von Coler a spectacular success as a propagandist and
which was significant in the scheme of the Nazi fifth column in Rumania.

All revolutionary propaganda, inasmuch as it works
on the decisive groups of the status quo abroad, has the
aim of breaking the resistance of these groups by putting
up a show of normalcy: a show meant to convince these
groups abroad that the corresponding groups back home
have retained their privileges under the revolution; a
show which makes the propagandized groups end up by
saying, "All these atrocity stories are untrue. *My* kind of
people are very well off under that revolution."

In the case of Rumania the task of Nazi propaganda,
practically achieved at that time, had been to sell Rumanians of wealth and influence—key men of industry,
banking, and assorted intellectual and artistic professions
—on the idea of collaboration with Nazi Germany. It had
not been an easy task. Aside from being pro-French, these
Rumanians had been frankly frightened: the wealthy had
been unfavorably impressed with stories of the Nazis doing
away with wealth; the women had been unfavorably impressed with stories of the Nazis doing away with lipsticks
and rouge; and the intellectuals had been unfavorably
impressed with stories of anyone who opened his mouth
going straight into a concentration camp.

Frau von Coler's unpretentious little parties came in
nicely to retouch this unattractive picture of the Third
Reich. The idea of these parties was to reassure Rumanians that the "right" people, which meant the equivalent
of their own kind, led a normal and pleasant life under

Hitler's dictatorship. The idea was to convince the rich in Bucharest that the rich in Berlin made money and enjoyed it; to convince Rumanian intellectuals that German intellectuals could talk as freely as they could themselves; to convince Rumanian women that German women were beautifully dressed and made up.

Not that Frau von Coler rationalized about her aims and methods the way I do it here. A born hostess and a kind woman, it was natural for her to create an atmosphere of ease and friendliness. Also it would be a mistake to say that the normalcy which she built up in her salon was a fake put up for the occasion. This was not the case at all. The strange thing about revolution, any revolution, is that it retains a fund of normalcy, in addition to and underneath the noise and the terror. No writer or journalist makes much of this normalcy in revolution because it is not news, which is one of the reasons why all descriptions of revolution are one-sided, with all the light thrown on the atrocities.

Frau von Coler, on her part, falsified the picture of revolution in the opposite direction, in that she concentrated all light on "normal life under the Nazis," isolating it from the atrocities and thus showing it in a purity which was too idyllic to be true.

The main actors in Frau von Coler's idyll of Nazi life were German aristocrats who were charming and politically innocuous, and German aristocrats who had gone Nazi. They were German bankers, industrialists, and diplomats who had made their peace with the regime as they had with the Weimar Republic. They were German intellectuals and artists who were washed to the surface by the Nazi revolution or confirmed by it.

On this particular evening—which was more in the nature of an epilogue, because by then the Rumanian upper class saw that the French were through and were all for appeasement with the Nazis—the Rumanian audience was made up of a newspaper owner who looked like Haile Selassie, a couple of well-known Rumanian journalists, a former Rumanian finance minister who was still in the race, and a sprinkling of Rumanian diplomats, officials, and society matrons.

The society matrons were reassured about the Nazi way of dealing with elegant women not only by the presence of Frau von Coler herself but by a princess, a gibson-girlish beauty, superbly dressed in something that spelled the Rue Cambon. This Serene Highness made no bones of the fact that, war or no war, her chief interest in life was clothes. Powdering her high patrician nose from a large, crested golden compact, she would say, with a trusting look at Nazi diplomats and journalists, "I do hope that now that we have Paris, I can buy at Chanel's and Molyneux with Reichsmark."

The Nazi diplomats and journalists would laugh and reply, "Don't you know, *Durchlaucht,* that for you to be able to buy at Chanel's and Molyneux with Reichsmark is one of the German war aims?"

Nothing seemed to distinguish the Nazis who sat with the Princess and me from any pleasant worldly young men one meets at parties all over the globe, except their sharper wit, greater conversational gifts, and a tendency to tell all the jokes about the Nazis before anybody else could tell them. They appeared to be perfectly at ease, and if they were afraid of the Gestapo they certainly did not show it.

Among them was a youngish German interior decorator

who looked like all the interior decorators the world over: refined in a peculiar way, and with horn-rimmed glasses and a haircut that emphasized a nonexistent intellectual forehead. He had done the interior of Hitler's chancellery and was now doing the interior of the Rumanian foreign office, just being constructed. To call in German artists was one of the delicate but indecisive attentions by which Carol so far had tried to keep the Führer happy.

Then there was Dr. Klaus Schickert, Bucharest correspondent of the DNB, the official German news agency. The corps-student type, he was blond and blue-eyed with scars on his chin, very bright and very conscious of the fact that he was. Another journalist, Count Anton Knyphausen, was handsome in the fashion of Clemens Brentano, the German romantic poet of the early nineteenth century, and had a very good-looking Norwegian girl for a wife. German correspondents, it would appear, were picked for their presentability as much as for their ability. Most of the German journalists spoke some French but little English. Dr. Schickert felt apologetic about it, but mixed apology with complaint about the fate of post-war Germany. "This is one of the results of the twenties," he said. "That's when we should have learned languages but then we Germans were too poor to travel abroad."

I said drily, "Well, you are able to make up for it now. Traveling has certainly become cheap for the Germans."

He grinned appreciatively.

There was another count, one of the "Kultur-attachés" at the legation. A thin, aristocratic Austrian in his thirties, he had a beautifully shaped narrow head, very nice dark blond hair, and the most remarkable face of all the men in the room—an ascetic, secretive face, the face of a young

sixteenth-century cardinal, who now and then delivered a
heretic to the stakes without fanaticism and without pity,
just because heretics were bad for the Church.

This count spoke French like a Frenchman and had
studied in Oxford. Looking over to the sofa where Frau
von Coler sat with the Rumanian newspaper owner who
looked like Haile Selassie, and the former Minister of
Finance who looked like a pasty-faced Rumanian, he said
cheerfully, "Dear Edit has her hands full making those
poor bastards forget they were ever pro-French. Until a
few weeks ago all these Rumanians were pro-French, and
we know it. Now they want desperately to be on the winning side, but feel embarrassed about switching so rapidly.
Dear Edit has to convince them that they have been pro-
German all their lives and that there is no reason for them
to be embarrassed. She is wonderful at such things." He
thought it all superbly amusing.

The Nazis that night, like the Jews, told jokes on themselves: jokes they would resent very much if other people
told them. They told, for instance, this joke about the
Führer: Hitler went to see a seeress and, in order not to
be recognized, went in the uniform of a chauffeur. "Ah,"
said the seeress to the alleged chauffeur, "poor man, you
are in a very bad way. The axis of your car will break.
You'll get no gas. And your driver's license will be taken
away."

Then there was this one about Goering: The Reichs-
field-marshal and his wife Emmy gave a party. After dinner, when the ladies had left the table, a tremendous crash
as of breaking glass came from the dining room. "Her-
mann," called Frau Goering, "did you hurt yourself? I told

you to leave that Venetian chandelier alone. You have enough decorations without it."

That night, too, I heard the jocose Nazi version of the reasons for their anti-Jewish policy. They could, they said, not tolerate real Jews when they were able to produce an ever-so-much-better synthetic Jew, as the person of Herr Dr. Goebbels proved.

That night, too, one of the Nazis imitated the speech the conquering Führer would make from Buckingham Palace. The speech began like this: "My Lords, Peers and Gentlemen, Europäer and Europäerinnen, my first greetings go to the Holy Father in Rome, Party Member Alfred Rosenberg. . . ." Then the Führer went on thanking "Gauleiter Pétain" and "Gauleiter Mussolini," and then proceeded to say that, now that a centuries-old ignominy has been rectified and "Sicily has been returned to the Fatherland," Germany had "no further territorial claims." Provided, of course, that "President Roosevelt did not interfere with Germany's justified desire for a place in the sun. . . ."

It was a lovely piece of satire on Hitler's way of speaking, and showed how too, too sophisticated the Nazi fifth columnists were. They were so sophisticated that they hardly mentioned the fall of France, or if they did, it was only in casual contexts. I wondered if these Nazis were pretending humbleness before foreigners or were spoiled by Hitler successes to the point of being blasé. I could not make it out, but I guessed that there was something of each in it.

In the midst of all this sophistication, only the German oil commissar stuck out from the subtle fifth-column crowd. He was a vulgar fellow, at the same time the kind

of handsome, strong animal at whose arrival a new anima-
tion comes over women. Forty-fivish, medium-sized, over-
dressed, small-featured face slightly puffed under insolent
veiled gray eyes, he did not look like a German. Rather,
I thought, like a Polish count who wanted to look like an
English lord. There was an incredible arrogance in the
way he made his way through the salon, one hand twirling
the black-rimmed monocle which hung from a black
string.

When this flamboyant man was being brought over
to meet me, the interior decorator said brightly, "This,
Madame, is the chief of the Gestapo in Bucharest," for
proof of which he indicated a black ring the oil commissar
wore which, he said, was one of eleven rings Herr Himmler
had given to his eleven closest friends.

Everybody laughed, as if this were a wonderful joke.
The oil commissar barked modestly, "Don't mention it,"
put his dark little mustache firmly to my fingers, then sat
down between the Princess and myself. The black ring on
the little finger of his left hand looked like all black rings
on men's hands all over the world, yet I wondered whether
the interior decorator was really as jocose as he sounded
when he presented the man as the chief of the Gestapo
in Bucharest, or whether he used the method, so effective
in Nazi dealings, of saying the truth in such a way that
nobody believes it.

The oil commissar jammed his monocle into his eye,
turned to me challengingly and said, "You are a journalist,
I am told. I give you good advice: don't distort things
you're cabling from here or you'll live to regret it." I was
fascinated; here at last was a Nazi who behaved like a Nazi
in a play by Clare Boothe.

I said innocently, "There is not much you could do to me here in Rumania."

The commissar barked severely, "Oh, isn't there? You don't seem to realize that the Axis is now on top in the European continent, and any foreign journalist who does not behave in one country will not be allowed into any other."

Before I could answer one of the smooth fifth columnists said something hastily, and the great moment when I saw a Nazi behave like a character by Clare Boothe was over.

Frau von Coler's secretary had begun to empty ash trays and put glasses together. It was late. I saw von Coler surreptitiously put her hand to her mouth to conceal a yawn. Then she sat again wakeful and upright in the corner of her sofa with her pale hair and her moonstones gleaming in the light and beckoned me to come and sit with her.

Frau von Coler admitted that hers were long days. She told me that she got up at seven in order to get work done before the press conference at the German legation at nine-thirty. From then on it was conferences and social obligations all day long. I gathered that there were all kinds of Germans who wanted to be brought into contact with all kinds of Rumanians: businessmen, scholars, scientists, artists, agriculturists. It certainly seemed no sinecure to be Hitler's agent.

Frau von Coler said quickly, "I don't mind working hard as long as it is useful for Germany." She told me that her husband, a German officer, had fought with the Finns against the Bolsheviks after the world war. She accompanied him and was enormously impressed with the gallant fight the Finnish people put up for their independence. And then she came back to Germany. "I can't tell you what that did to me," she said. "I was ashamed of my country. The great Germany had less pride and fight than little Finland."

She began then to work with the groups which worked secretly for German rearmament. And working with these groups she met with the people around Hitler. She had always believed in the Nazi movement and its leaders. "You can imagine what it meant to me that they are making Germany great and that I'm allowed to do my bit in all this."

From that night on the Count with the face like a cardinal was always around me. When I came down to the lobby of the Athene Palace at noon, he would be there, waiting over an amalfi, looking like a young cardinal of the Inquisition in twentieth-century clothes, his face always noble and impassive. He was, people warned me, an agent attached to me by the Gestapo, but I never could imagine that I rated my own private agent, though of course one never knew with the Nazis.

I once asked the Count, "Do you watch me or do you just love me?" He threw up his long elegant hands in the exaggerated gesture of Bernini's saints and complained, "Oh, don't go *literal* on me!"

Ours became a beautiful friendship built on mutual distrust, scientific curiosity, and a sort of wistful fondness—a friendship of two people talking the language of western civilization, but on different sides of the fence of a revolution. We were both vivisector and guinea pig to each other, trying to find out what made the other tick. And because we liked one another, and were both convinced that the other was on the losing side, we were generous.

Throughout my stay in Bucharest I could never get mad at the Count. He was once mad at me, because I told one of his tips to another journalist. It was the Count's low-down on the *Graf Spee* scuttling. Captain Landsdorf, his story had it, got a radio message, allegedly from the Führer himself, ordering the scuttling of the *Graf Spee*. Then, after Landsdorf had complied, he got hell from Berlin because, it appeared, the radio message was not from the Führer at all but from the British. That's why Landsdorf killed himself. . . . As an explorer in darkest Africa treasures his Woolworth wares because the savages swap foodstuffs for them, so the Count treasured such stories. They were his stock-in-trade to be bartered for pieces of information, and he frowned on anyone breaking his absurd monopoly.

The Count, descendant of a great Austrian Catholic family was, so he said himself, a 150 per cent Nazi. To which of the hierarchies of Nazi Government he belonged, I never attempted to find out. Once he told me that, though attached to the legation, he took his orders not from Ribbentrop but from the Brown House, which meant from the Nazi Party. He seemed to be especially interested in the Rumanian Volksdeutsche, the word the Nazis used for members of German minorities abroad. Before the war he was for a long time "on a mission," as he put it, in Paris.

One of his jobs seemed to be reading the American press, probably for Dr. Goebbels. His knowledge of all kinds of American publications was amazing; he would discuss by the hour the relative merits of Mr. Bliven of the *New Republic* and of Miss Kirchway of the *Nation*, and knew which columnist wrote in which newspaper. Only the *Saturday Evening Post* seemed to puzzle him. "Their editorials are most reasonable," he complained, "but in their short stories the villain is always a Nazi. Why?" I explained that to discuss the situation rationally in an editorial, which nobody read anyway, was one thing; but to have a Nazi hero in a short story was totally different, and not even the *Saturday Evening Post* could get away with it.

Like all Nazi intellectuals the Count was vividly interested in America. He was convinced that America would enter the war, but not in time or with sufficient men and material to change the outcome. In the long run, he was convinced, a people "sapped" by a national philosophy extolling the pursuit of happiness and the right of the individual did not, in spite of its riches and technical genius, stand a chance against a people which had gone through the steel bath of sacrifice and discipline. He thought that today's "total war" could be fought only by a people which believed in sacrifice and in death for the fatherland.

England, he thought, had a better chance to understand Nazi Germany than America, because England knew more of Europe, was less puritan, less self-righteous, and more cynical. America's short history had its roots exclusively in the ideals of the French revolution, which is why liberty, equality, fraternity, progress, and the essential goodness of man constituted her one-track belief. England, on the other hand, had memories of conquests, revolutions, and totalitarianisms, and could understand what was going on in Germany. This went doubly for France and the other continental countries. The Count thought America, in spite of herself, would develop toward totalitarianism, but would run along communist lines rather than along fascist ones, because there was no American race.

The Count made fun of the Nazi "cratoplutes" and their streamlined cuties who passed by our table in the lobby, and would even criticize certain measures and actions of the regime. Yet he lived for the Third Reich as much as the young cardinal of the Inquisition he resembled lived for the Church. Like a priest, he had given up all other loyalties for the one loyalty to Hitler. He was even afraid to acquire such an absorbing loyalty as love. When once I advised him to marry a beautiful and charming girl, who thought him wonderful, he said, "Good God, no, I wouldn't do anything after that but make love. What would become of my labors for the Third Reich?" He *would* marry one of these days, he said, but "a good healthy woman I can forget all about, who will have pretty, not too intelligent children."

Hitler's great merit was, so the Count thought, that he recognized man's need for an ordered universe ruled by absolute standards where sin was sin, and must be expiated, where you must sacrifice in order to get your reward, where paradise waited for the innocent and the guilty burnt in hell—an order that carried the principle of leadership through its entire structure and into its every phase. Equality never made man happy. For a man to look up to a superior, to respect his authority, and to believe in him, was as natural as sexual love. That's why the leadership principle and not equality was to him the natural state of affairs.

The trouble with liberalism was, thought the Count, that taking no account of human nature, it proceeded from the idea of a man who needed only to be free in order to be good, the élite man who existed only in very few samples in every society. Thus liberalism had set about to destroy the absolute standards of an ordered society which the simple human heart could not bear to doubt without losing his *raison d'être* even before himself. Liberalism destroyed the Church, sabotaged the comforting myths of right and wrong, good and evil, and submitted absolute truth to the corroding acid of doubt and skepticism. Doubt and skepticism, the Count thought, had their rightful place, but only among the élite, the "initiated" who bore the burden of knowledge, responsibilities, and freedom which went with knowledge, contrary to the "laymen" who followed and obeyed.

Thus the Nazi élite was allowed to do a lot of things which were entirely beyond the reach of the laymen, such as reading foreign books and newspapers and sitting with non-Aryan ladies in the lobby of the Athene Palace. The reason why they could do these things was that their Nazi creed was supposedly so firmly rooted in them that they were beyond temptation, intellectual and otherwise.

The Count was a violent antisemite, not on Streicher lines, though he thought that this kind of antisemitism of hate was justified as a dynamic necessity of the revolution. Actually, his antisemitism was more dangerous. Knowing the history of the Jews better than most Jews knew it themselves, and talking freely of "Jewish heroes," "really civilized Jews like Léon Blum," and so on, he considered the Jews intellectually and artistically altogether too seductive to be borne. "Do you know," he once said ruefully, "there is not one of us who has not a Gershwin record in the bottom of a drawer which he plays sometimes late at night."

The Jews, he thought, had brought oomph to the teachings of liberalism. Vitally interested in destroying the absolute in all its aspects—for only in a world where the values of Fatherland and Church were not absolute could they survive—the Jews had succeeded in raising liberalism and the relativity of all truth to a kind of new religion—Karl Marx in that he conceived a society outside of the natural boundaries of nation and country; Sigmund Freud in that he exculpated sin and guilt by the concept of an innocent unconscious; Albert Einstein in that he pulverized the concept of time.

If these theories, the Count thought, had come to the knowledge only of the élite they would have done a lot of good. Popularized, they created an awful disorder and alarm in the hearts and minds of the simple human beings.

Nor were the Jews the only ones whom the Count found too dangerous to be let loose on the unsuspecting Germans. A gentle young man, incapable of unfairness or cruelty in matters concerning his personal advantage, he would have gladly liquidated everyone who was dangerous for the Third Reich. Of a famous German beauty of great aristocratic family, whose loyalty to Hitler was under discussion, he said cheerfully, "One more picture of her for *Vogue* to remember her by and then off with her to Dachau for life!"

Once I reminded him that the world was really meant

to be many-colored with all kinds of men in it. I advised: "You better let them be, my good Count. Just imagine a universe with Nazis only!" The notion seemed to depress him slightly. But then his noble cardinal's face broke into a grin. "Maybe," he offered, "a reservation full of highly colorful people, regardless of race, would be nice." Here the Nazi élite could go and converse elegantly after work and here the kids of the Führerschulen (leader schools) could see for themselves what life had been all about in ancient times. I suggested instead that the whole of Europe should become a reservation full of colorful people. But this, unfortunately, was not what he meant.

*Among other evils which being
unarmed brings you, it causes you
to be despised.*

MACHIAVELLI

5 —BESSARABIA

Automobile doors banged in the early dawn of June twenty-seventh, outside the entrance to the Athene Palace. Sleepy porters piled a strange assortment of luggage on the floor of the bare white vestibule and placed with it paintings, silver chandeliers, rosewood café tables, Aubusson carpets, which the people in the cars had brought along. More cars arrived, mud-splashed and dust-covered, and more people whose worn-out children lay down between clothes baskets and objets d'art.

On the stone bench usually occupied by the apple-cheeked pageboys one lady gave her breast to a baby. Disheveled hair hung over her smudged, drawn face and a crumpled sports dress showed where her coat was open. The coat was a sable one, and as she bared her breast two large strings of pearls and several diamond brooches, pinned to her slip, were visible.

These people with their tired faces and the strangely assorted possessions were the big German landowners of Bessarabia and Bukovina, most of them princes and counts or barons at least. Their appearance at the Athene Palace

100

in this early dawn was the first evidence of events which were to shape the destinies of Rumania and the course of World War Two, first evidence that Stalin was about to annex two important Rumanian provinces—an area of 19,176 square miles, with a population of 3,464,952— and first evidence of the beginning of the end of Great Rumania which brought Carol's abdication and the Guardist revolution in its wake. First evidence, too, that all was not well between Stalin and Hitler, in spite of the pact of friendship of August 1939.

Word that Stalin was about to march had come to these German landowners in Bukovina and Bessarabia the afternoon before, from the German legation in Bucharest. No one else in the two provinces had an inkling yet that the Russians were coming. The German landowners had lost no time in getting out while the going was good. What made them flee in such a hurry was not so much fear of the invading Bolsheviki as fear that the people of the two provinces themselves, once they learned of the coming of the Russians, might get out of hand and begin to loot and kill. Though denied by Rumanian statesmen of all shades, it was nevertheless a fact that large parts of the peasantry and the city proletariat of these two Rumanian provinces were prepared to welcome the Soviets as saviors and liberators. There were various reasons for this lack of loyalty towards the status quo, the chief one being the bad politics which the Rumanian rulers had played in the two provinces for the last twenty years.

Both Bukovina and Bessarabia had been adjudicated to Rumania after the world war on ethnical grounds. Before that Bukovina had been part of the Hapsburg

Empire after having been part of the Principalities until 1774. Bessarabia, though always claimed as their province by the Rumanians, had been annexed by the Russians in 1812, and while a few Bessarabian districts were restituted to Rumania in 1856, the Russian domination of the bulk of the province was confirmed by the Congress of Berlin in 1878 and lasted until 1918. Perhaps the Rumanians never felt quite sure that they would be able to hold the provinces, or perhaps it was their way of doing things—anyway, they treated these newly annexed provinces as colonies for quick exploitation, investing little in roads and other living facilities for the population, while taxes and corrupt officials sucked the last farthing from the peasants.

At the same time the large Jewish city proletariat of these provinces, which increasingly antisemitic ordinances discouraged from any patriotism for Rumania, became more and more inclined to the conviction that they had nothing to lose and much to gain under the Soviet star. Communist propaganda played superbly on the discontent of the peasants and the despair of the Jews.

If this was the mood in the threatened provinces themselves, it was vastly different in Bucharest. Though the papers had carried no word of a Russo-Rumanian crisis, by noon everyone knew that there was one. A mysterious kind of telepathy, peculiar to all countries under censorship, had transmitted the news. At the Athene Palace we were even in the possession of details. A Russian ultimatum had arrived only last night, people whispered to each other in the lobby, and unless Rumania ceded Bessarabia and Bukovina, the Russian army would march by midnight. Stalin, it appeared, demanded Bukovina, which had never belonged to Russia, as "interest" on twenty years' "loan" of Bessarabia to the Rumanians. This part made the Rumanians especially mad.

Though there had been rumors about a possible Russian move for the last few weeks in every café in Rumania, and of course at the Athene Palace, few had believed in the immediacy of such a move. Stalin, even the best informed observers said, would not dare to grab such a large slice of Hitler's sphere of raw materials right under the nose of his hard-working economists and technicians. For in the two provinces to be ceded were 20 percent of Rumania's corn, 20 percent of her wheat and 32 percent of her sugar beets, 42 percent of her industrial plants, and all her caracul sheep, her main export article to America. Of course, there was the possibility of a previous agreement between Berlin and Moscow, which gave Stalin a green light, but this seemed improbable because the Germans had 100,000 out of their 140,000 soya-planted hectares in Bessarabia. The surest indication, however, that there was no such agreement between Berlin and Moscow seemed to be that some hundred thousand Volksdeutsche were still living in the two provinces, while Hitler had safely evacuated his Germans from the Baltic provinces before he let the Russians move in.

So Stalin's ultimatum came as a terrific shock to the Rumanians of the old Principalities, whose relations with the Russians, though slightly tinged with comedy, had in the main been grim throughout their history. There had been nine Russian invasions of Rumania since 1711, when Peter the Great taught the boyards to drink champagne and then proceeded to rob them while they slept it off. Each time Rumania had been "invited" by the

Russians to help them against the Turks, the Russians had, in return, annexed a Rumanian province or two. Russian invasion had become synonymous with broken promises, forced "contributions," purchases paid for by fake money, and all sorts of destruction and looting. "Wherever Russian armies passed," wrote a chronicler, "the soil groaned."

During the world war Rumania joyfully received a beautifully equipped and supplied Russian army, which never made a move when the Germans invaded and Bucharest fell. In 1917, when the Bolshevik revolution broke out, the Rumanians had to defend their front against the Germans and their rear against their Soviet allies. The Rumanian Treasury, containing the gold of the National Bank, the riches of the museums, the silver, jewels, and valuables of important persons, was sent to the Kremlin for safekeeping in the beginning of the war, and was promptly confiscated by the Bolsheviks. While a Canadian adventurer, Colonel Boyle, succeeded in getting Queen Marie's fabulous jewels away from the Soviets and returning them to the Queen, the Rumanians tried in vain to get the rest of their treasury back. Finally in 1935, shortly after the two countries resumed diplomatic relations, the first Soviet Minister to Bucharest, with a display of suitable pomp, brought the Rumanian Treasury to the Foreign Office. It filled only a valise. Gold, jewels, works of art were all gone; and the valise contained a few old Poiret gowns and corsets in which, twenty years ago, the Rumanian ladies had wrapped their valuables.

If thus, as a French historian put it, "The friendship of Russia has been more unfortunate to the Rumanians than the enmity of all the other peoples combined," Russian hostility augured even worse. So Rumanians today were unsmiling and intent when at noon on that twenty-seventh of June they lingered on the hot glaring Square instead of going home for luncheon and the long siesta, as they did on ordinary summer days. Silent groups watched the many cars parked in the courtyard of the Palace and those which swung into the driveway, discharging Carol's white-uniformed ministers and high officials. Footmen in white escarpins and white stockings held the door open for these newcomers and led them to a lighted elevator which took them up to the hall in the first floor of the middle wing. Here, the crowds on the Square could see, the big Venetian chandeliers were lighted, and they knew the Crown Council was in session, presided over by King Carol.

The Crown Council was a sort of board of older statesmen which gave advice to the Crown in ticklish political situations. All former prime ministers and the heads of the orthodox church were *per se* Crown Councilors, and lately Carol had added practically everyone who had ever played a role in Rumanian public life; the dictator's concession to democratic rule. But so far it had been only a nominal concession, for Carol still consulted chiefly with Urdareanu and the camarilla. Today, however, in extreme emergency, a matter of life and death for the country as well as for the throne, the Crown Councilors has been called in to advise their King and share the responsibility of his decision.

Under the big Venetian chandeliers, in the décor, part Italian, part Byzantine, of the vast hall, the Patriarch, head of the orthodox church of Rumania, his golden clothes veiled in black, would be sitting next to the King.

There would be the historian, Professor Nicholas Jorga, a former Prime Minister, and once Carol's tutor. Going on seventy, tall, handsome, with a long white beard and endowed with a fantastic memory, Nicholas Jorga was the Rumanian version of the "Goethean man," the last great humanist. Of an erudition both encyclopaedic and elegant, his ideas, projects, opinions, paradoxes, systems, stories, and memories had stimulated two generations of Rumanians. But the part he had played in Rumanian politics had been questionable. In a long life Jorga had been everything in politics once: leader of the liberal party, leader of the Peasant Party, leader of the anti-semites, pro-socialist, pro-fascist. Scheming in the great Byzantine manner, and a seductive teacher in his passing political whims, he had immense influence on his disciples. Now the liberals blamed him for having started the whole antisemitic-fascist business in Rumania, while the Guardists accused him of having sold them out to the King's camarilla, which accusation led to the terrible end he was to suffer at the hands of the Guardists in the forest of Ploesti a few months later.

At this meeting there would be Carol's old teacher of economics, Professor Cuza, eighty-five years old, the last of the patriarchs of European antisemitism. Fifty years of militant struggle against the Jews had strangely assimilated him to his victims. With his white goatee and a long beak of a nose he looked like a caricature straight out of the "Stuermer." Professor Cuza, who boasted that he made his first antisemitic speech in the Rumanian parliament in the year Hitler was born, was still going strong. Convinced that a world without Jews would be a perfect place to live in, and that the "Great Führer of the Great German Reich," as he put it, could never have achieved with the Jews what he achieved without them; anti-English because, as he put it, "the English have delivered the Holy Land into the hands of the Jews who betrayed our Lord," Cuza thought that the future of Rumania was with the Axis.

There would be also Georges Bratianu, grandson of Jon Bratianu who put Rumania on the map and smuggled the first Carol into the country, son of Jonel Bratianu who created the Great Rumania and was instrumental in sending the second Carol into his first exile. Throughout his young years Carol had resented the influence of the Bratianu family, which was closer to Rumania than the Hohenzollern dynasty, but had effected something like a reconciliation with the heir of this great name, third generation like himself. Georges Bratianu, a historian, was Michael's tutor. Leader of the neo-liberal group, he was for collaboration with Germany, no matter whether Germany won or lost the war. He considered collaboration an economic inevitability for Rumania.

There would be Juliu Maniu, leader of the once all-powerful Peasant Party, which had been instrumental in getting Carol back from exile and making him a king. Lupescu's return to Bucharest, by which Carol had flagrantly broken a solemn promise to his sponsors, estranged Maniu from the King. Though in the opposition for almost ten years, this fragile Transylvanian of sixty-seven was still the figure around whom the fondest hopes for a liberal Rumania centered. At every turn in Rumanian affairs the name of Maniu would pop up and make the friends of democracy, native and foreign, happy. Though the organization of his vast Peasant Party fell victim to

Carol's dictatorship, he was still very much loved, especially in Transylvania, and respected for his integrity in all circles, even among the Guardists.

There would be other men in the Crown Council: the acting Prime Minister, Tartarescu, whom the Germans detested; the present foreign minister, Gigurtu, whom Carol had put into the cabinet after the battle of Flanders, as his first concession to Hitler. And there would be the war minister and the chief of the General Staff.

They made a motley crowd, the men who sat in the Council today. Some were rotten, some were patriots. Some had a part in making the Great Rumania. There was little love lost among them, and they all detested Urdareanu, who even here was like a wall between them and the King, making it impossible to talk to the King as he should be talked to. Most had put great hopes in the King when he came to power. Some still held a sort of tenderness for him. All knew that he had made irreparable mistakes—mistakes for which the country was now going to suffer.

What would they advise the King? Could they advise him to fight the Russians with an army which at its best would be no match for the Red Army, but which graft and corruption had prevented from being at its best? Would they advise a last desperate stand? But then, would the Hungarians and the Bulgarians fall upon them too? Or would they advise to cede the provinces to Stalin? If they did, would the Bulgarians and Hungarians put up their claims, too?

Between Great Rumania and her totally hostile neighbor countries stood nothing but a British guarantee, entirely made of paper, and the hope of Hitler's protection, extremely doubtful because of the British guarantee and because of Carol's killing of Codreanu. Still, at this moment Carol and the Crown Council and the people down on the Square put their last desperate hopes on Hitler. Hitler might still dissuade Stalin from invading Bessarabia, or he might help Rumania to fight the Russians— or he might at least forbid the Hungarians and Bulgarians to fall on them while they were fighting the Russians.

This naïve hope of Hitler's good will for Great Rumania was based chiefly on a hasty gesture on the part of Carol, by which he hoped to prove to the Führer that he was a good boy. Only last Saturday Carol had decreed the existence of a fascist party; a party to end all other parties in the country, a party which was to out-Hitler Hitler in that membership was obligatory for anyone who wished to hold a Government office or post in private industry, or even in a shop. Jews were excluded from the new party, which meant that Jews were excluded from the entire public life of Rumania. This latter, the Rumanians had hoped, would especially please the Führer. They also had thought it shrewd of their King to jump on Hitler's wagon before the final victory, because Hitler, they hoped, would be more appreciative of this proof of pre-victory confidence than of any post-victory confidence.

Actually Hitler was not appreciative; he took Carol's little fascist set-up for what it was—a put-up job which did not deceive him. What Carol did not realize then was that the Nazis frowned upon the fascist quickies in general the way Mlle. Chanel frowns at the cheap copies of her models. Anyone who read the *Voelkische Beobachter* at the time, with its fulminations against the French-going-fascist, could see how emotionally resentful the Germans were against people who tried to go fascist overnight. Dr. Fabrizius and Dr. Neubacher advised Carol not to let himself in for a fascist party. The Führer, they reiterated, was not interested in a totalitarian Rumania but only in quiet in the raw-material sphere—any strong government which worked would be preferable to a fascist set-up which would not work. They tactfully explained that, in Hitler's opinion, the development towards totalitarianism, while unavoidable, must be organic and have a basis in the people themselves, instead of being decreed.

But Carol, feeling extremely insecure since the fall of France, had made up his mind that Hitler would be pleased with a fascist Rumania. Moreover, a single fascist party, obligatory to everyone, would effect a quasi-mechanical reconciliation with the Iron Guard and thus strengthen the inner unity of the country—which was, Carol felt, a very valuable by-product of his gesture. So he went ahead with the new party, against German advice. No doubt the cocky speeches made by him and various of his ministers over the week-end in connection with the big event had precipitated Stalin's action—a possibility of which, too, German diplomats had warned Carol beforehand. A showy move of this kind, they had explained, would make it appear to Stalin that Rumania was playing for German protection before he could get what he wanted.

So Carol's opportunistic gesture had backfired in several ways. But the crowds of the Square did not realize this yet. They thought that, because Rumania had gone fascist five days ago, the least Hitler could do was to help Rumania to preserve her territorial integrity.

By evening the tension in Bucharest was almost intolerable, though still no hint of a Russian move had yet been in the papers. The big news, whispered by Axis journalists and officials of the Ministry of Propaganda was that the "Palace" was waiting for a personal message from the Führer before midnight, which was before the Russian ultimatum would expire. The lobby of the Athene Palace was deserted and even the Old Excellencies, grimmer and more affected by what they called le désastre than I ever expected them to look, walked up and down the Square watching the crowds watching Carol's Palace. The crowd, pressed into the small space between the bronze Carol I and the Palace gate, was larger than at noon and there was more activity about the palace. Important-looking limousines swept into the driveway in a never-ending stream, while other important-looking ones swept out. The lighted Venetian chandeliers on the first floor showed that the Council was still meeting.

People in the Square were anxious and bad tempered. A few shouts of "Tareaska Regele Carol" sounded challengingly and then died down. From time to time police tried to move the crowds farther away from the Palace, but a few moments later they edged back on their favorite place between the bronze Carol I and the Palace gate. For want of concrete information all kinds of rumors filled the air: Russian troops were already fighting Rumanian troops on the frontier; Russian troops were already on their way to Bucharest; German troops were already on their way to Bucharest; somebody had shot at Lupescu, who hid in the Palace; the King in a fit of fury had slapped Urdareanu's face in the presence of the Crown Counselors; the Jews had called in the Russians to protect them against the new antisemitic laws; the communists (and the Jews) had called the Russians in to protect them against the Germans. . . . A moon came up over the Palace and, while the heat cooled off a bit, the bad temper of the crowd grew worse. A few tough-looking customers on the Square, among them some priests and officers, began to sing the national anthem in a sulky inflammatory way and to shout angrily for Carol.

As I went across the Square to keep a late dinner date at Cina's, I met Frau von Coler, looking very neat and cool in a gray linen tailor-made suit, showing the frills of a white organdy blouse. A white *canotier* sat on her blonde hair at exactly the right angle.

"Poor people," she said, looking out to the crowds on the Square, "they are so utterly unprepared for what is going to happen. It will be a terrible shock to them. You know," she added, "the more I see how badly other people are being ruled, the happier I am that we Germans have our Führer. We can feel safe." The conviction with which she spoke was staggering.

In the garden of Cina's one sat under big old trees in comfortable wicker arm chairs and watched the Palace and the crowds on the Square, while a little gypsy orchestra played the sad half-oriental Rumanian melodies. An old bent headwaiter said that today was the day to eat asparagus with hollandaise and Westphalian ham and fresh raspberries with cream afterwards. Headwaiters and porters around the Athene Palace never acknowledged catastrophe. They only admitted the pleasantness of elegant daily routine. It was very comforting. Yet one could feel that even at Cina's the guests only went through the motions of their own elegant routine. With their thoughts and fears they were up in the Palace, wondering about the decisions of the Crown Council, wondering still more about the méssage of the Führer.

There was only one gay party at Cina's: young Englishmen who celebrated what they called the "Russian diversion" with champagne. For unfathomable reasons the English in Bucharest had decided to consider the Bessarabian crisis as a British victory and a German defeat, happily oblivious of the fact that because of the British guarantee of Rumanian integrity the Bessarabian crisis was, to say the least, embarrassing; and oblivious, too, of the fact that any weakness shown anywhere on the European continent turned into Hitler's strength.

We were at the raspberries when an attaché of the Rumanian Ministry of Propaganda came up to us and said that the Führer's personal message had arrived at the Palace. Hitler asked Carol to cede Bessarabia and Bukovina without fighting. After the war, the Führer had said, he would settle things with Stalin, and Rumania would get the provinces back.

The attaché passed on to other tables and soon everyone at Cina's knew of Hitler's message, and that Carol would give in. Nobody at the time attached any importance to Hitler's promise that he would get Bessarabia back for Rumania. Even if the Führer really had said such a thing to Carol, which seemed doubtful, one felt it was all too much in the future to count for anything. Tonight the people took notice only of the fact that Carol would cede a big slice of their Great Rumania.

A strange mixture of relief, doom, and shame spread through the garden as the guests, food forgotten, talked in low tones of the disaster. In a vague way these Rumanians knew they had a right to something only if they fought for it, but they also knew that small countries had no chance to fight for themselves in Hitler's Europe. Throughout Rumania's history the country had survived because of clever pliancy rather than of the heroism of its people, but it certainly was not always pleasant to be a small nation and to be pliant. The songs that rose tónight from the gypsy violins under the trees of Cina's were old laments of oppression and of foreign masters. As they played, a woman in a silver fox jacket began quietly to sob, mascara running into the paprika chicken on her plate. . . .

That same night, while Carol, supported by the Crown Council, decided to give in to Stalin and worked at figuring out a face-saving formula, a man went into action who was to play a decisive part in the future destinies of his country. This was General Jon Antonescu.

Fiftyish, medium-sized, lightly built, General Antonescu had carrot-red hair and very blue eyes in a freckled ruddy face, the skin of which was tightly stretched over broad cheek-bones. There was no pose about Antonescu and none of the wordy, facetious, glitteringly concealing manners of the Rumanian upper class. Antonescu was simple, honest, and very much in earnest—qualities which would have made him vulnerable in a world of byzantine intrigue had it not been for his brutal frankness, an inclination toward violent rages, and a long memory for wrongs done him. All of these made him a redoubtable enemy.

For years the carrot-haired General had played the un-grateful role of Cassandra to King Carol. One of the ablest officers of the army and at one time minister of war, he exasperated the King by pointing out the graft and in-eptness prevailing in the army and denouncing the corrupt and sinister influence of the camarilla.

Inevitably disgust with the status quo, patriotic fervor, and hope for a new Rumania had thrown the General together with Codreanu. Sympathizing with the Guard's chief aims without, however, joining it, he had sold him-self to the followers and disciples of the Capitano by a gesture which was already part of the Rumanian fascist legend. At the high-treason trial of Codreanu, Antonescu appeared as a witness. While the courtroom waited with bated breath, Antonescu was asked whether he considered Codreanu a traitor. Standing erect, the General marched over to the accused Capitano, held out his hand simply for Codreanu's and pressed it. "Would General Antonescu give his hand to a traitor?" he demanded of the silent courtroom.

Antonescu's recognized military talents, his integrity and the following he had among the youth and the army, made him the most important man in the new Rumanian orientation. The Germans had immense respect for him, though he was by no means their man. Brought up in Saint-Cyr, the great French military school, a friend of General Gamelin, married to a French lady, General An-tonescu had always been pro-French and, in avowed con-trast to Codreanu, had viewed the future of Rumania in terms of collaboration with the democracies rather than with the Axis. The Germans were aware of this, but did not mind. They thought Antonescu, now that France

was beaten, would automatically come around to collaboration with Germany, sympathies or no sympathies. But
above all they took him to be the man to head that strong
government which would keep quiet in the raw-material
sphere.

Many months afterwards General Antonescu published
a statement about his activities at the occasion of the
Bessarabian crisis, activities which at the time were surrounded by all kinds of dark rumors. From the General's
own statement it appeared that, as soon as the news of the
Russian ultimatum had reached him that morning of
June twenty-seventh, he had made frantic efforts to get
the heads of the Rumanian nation to make a petition
before the King. Not divulging the exact goal of this
démarche, the General said that the gentlemen were to
demand that the King "understand that a nation cannot
pay for the faults committed by her leaders." Whether
this meant that they were asking the King to abdicate or
to fire Urdareanu, Lupescu, and other members of the
camarilla and army leaders, was not expressly stated. At
the time rumor had it that Antonescu already was out for
Carol's scalp, but his actions indicate rather that he was
only out for a Rumanian new deal with new collaborators.

Unable to round up the chiefs of the nation for con-
certed action, the General decided to ask the King for
an audience himself—a decision to which only the desperate emergency of his country prompted this proud
man. For the King had treated him badly as reward for
his criticism and for his attitude in the Codreanu trial.
A relative of Antonescu's carried this demand to the
Palace on the night of the great decisions, with the result
that the General was summoned to the Palace. But, in-

stead of seeing the King, Antonescu saw his arch enemy
Urdareanu who, as the General put it, had become "like
a dike between the throne and the fate of the nation."
After submitting the General to a real inquisition as to
the aims of his audience, Urdareanu refused him admission
to the King. Whereupon the two men, Bucharest rumors
had it, came to blows right in the Palace. General Antonescu, according to his own statement, flung at his ad-
versary, "Don't you dare establish yourself any longer
between the nation and the King!"

Twenty-four hours later the King called General Antonescu in, and again swallowing his pride—for one never
knew what Carol would do to those who criticized him—
the General went to the Palace. Now, according to his
own words, Antonescu told Carol of the sorrows of the
nation, "demonstrated to him all the dishonor of the
Rumanian army so near to his heart." And in order not
to leave a shadow of a doubt for history as to what happened between the throne and an old adviser to the
throne, the General left with the King a letter he had
written. This letter not only shows the state of affairs in
Bessarabia and Bukovina, when these provinces were
ceded overnight, and the mood in all of Rumania after
the ignominious cession became known, but the state of
mind of a great patriot who hopes nothing for himself
but fears everything for his country.

"Majesty," the alarmed General began urgently, "the
country crumbles. Heartbreaking scenes take place in
Bessarabia and Bukovina. Big and small military units,
abandoned by their chiefs and surprised without orders,
let themselves be disarmed at the first menace. The officials and their families and the families of the officers

are abandoned to terrible disaster. Immense matériel,
military supplies accumulated by carelessness and main-
tained to the last moment by order are all in the hands
of the enemy. This, Majesty, paints one chapter of the
nation's tragedy and its Calvary which is only beginning.
People and army are disarmed without fighting. The de-
moralization has no limits. The lack of confidence in the
leader is complete. The hate against the guilty, all the
guilty of today and yesterday increases by the hour." It
was no use crying over spilled milk, the General continued—this would only precipitate the catastrophe inside
Rumania. Instead, he urged closing the ranks and making
a supreme effort. This supreme effort, he added significantly, could not be made by those who unleashed the
present catastrophe. An immediate change in system and
men was inevitable.

"For years," he wrote bitterly, "I have informed the
Governments and responsible chiefs of the army and Your
Majesty yourself on the catastrophe of today. . . . But I
was treated as a rebel." And here the letter becomes as
hard and challenging as a letter to a king can be. The
General wrote: "Now I am ready to give my support,
but my honest conduct must be answered by honest conduct. I am not looking for revenge. . . . I only want to
save what still can be saved of the Crown, of the order
and of the frontiers."

At the end Antonescu used the tender, urgent tones of
a worried father: "Majesty, you must listen to me in
this hour. I never was an enemy of Your Majesty. I always was a fanatical servant of this nation. I have been
thrown aside by the intrigue and calumny of those who
have led the country where it is now. Don't lend them

your ear any more, Majesty. They are those who got you where you are and where we find ourselves. This is my last cry of alarm, Majesty." It was a cry in the wilderness.

Instead of answering this passionate letter, Carol ordered Antonescu arrested and sent to Monastirea Bistrita, a prison which Carol himself knew well, as he had been held there for a time after his flight with Zizi Lambrino into enemy country in the middle of the world war. Everyone knew this was another victory for Carol's camarilla, and especially for Lupescu. It was the last they had, while Carol lost his great opportunity—probably his final one—to save what remained of Great Rumania and to save his throne.

The Germans considered the harsh treatment of General Antonescu one of Carol's most disastrous blunders. "It's always a mistake to alienate a good man who is close to a radical movement, but does not belong to it," Dr. Neubacher sagely observed. But, what was more, the Germans knew now what they had expected all along: that Carol did not mean his new totalitarian orientation seriously enough to make sacrifices for it.

Outwardly the Nazis were very smooth about Stalin's grab of Bessarabia, but for the first time, in a roundabout way, they began to express doubts as to the possibility of keeping Russo-German relations on a friendly basis. Did the Germans consider the Russian move as provocation, one would ask German diplomats, and they would smile and say, "The Führer never lets himself be provoked. He proved that in Austria. He was sick with fury when his followers were hanged and put in concentration camps by Schuschnigg, but he did not make a single move *before the time was ripe."* It was these last words that counted.

Germany, they said, had declared her disinterest in Bessarabia when the Russo-German pact was concluded in August 1939. At that time Rumania, having accepted the British guarantee, had put herself into the opposite camp. However, it was agreed between Ribbentrop and Molotov that Russia would keep hands off the Balkans during the war, in order not to disturb the German raw-material sphere. The reason why Stalin did not stick to his agreement was the fall of France.

The fall of France, the Germans felt, had made Stalin nervous. He realized that, with the danger of a two-front war gone, a strong Germany could fight Russia at any moment. While he knew that eventually he would have to face Germany alone, he had hoped to face a Germany weakened by a long war.

There were three reasons why Stalin was making this grab of Bessarabia and Bukovina now. One was that he did not wish to owe these provinces to German bounty, but wished to take them on his own steam. Another was that he was afraid Germany would become difficult to deal with after the full victory. The third reason was that he wanted to complicate things just enough to keep the war going and to postpone the inevitable final settlement between Germany and Russia. This third reason was the most significant. Here, the Germans felt, was the rub. Stalin's nervousness, his desire for a long war, made him an unreliable partner. It might lead him to double-cross Germany with England and America, and maybe with Japan—or maybe just to blackmail, extracting a province from them for every million tons of oil.

The Nazis would say: "The Führer has already sacrificed the Baltic States to the Russian friendship, and now Bessarabia and Bukovina. He will not let more parts of Europe fall into Russian hands. He wants to reestablish the European solidarity which had been lost since the end of the German Kaisers of the middle ages."

Beginning with Stalin's grab of Bessarabia, I heard the Nazis talk about the "unavoidable final settlement with Russia." Not that all of them saw it in terms of war. The German economists and diplomats emphasized the scrupulous way in which the Russians kept their side of the trade treaty and were inclined to wish for a diplomatic settlement. But the others, most of all the military men whom I was to meet later on, held that a military decision—as soon as possible—was far more desirable. They said: "A modern army is trained like athletes. Why send them home and let them get soft and in the meantime let the Russians arm? Now is the moment."

In many talks with high German military men about a war with Russia I found none who had any doubts that they could win this war, nor did I find anyone who had any illusions as to the strength of the Russians. After all, no other two armies had known each other better for twenty years than the Reichswehr and the Red Army. In a way they grew up together after the treaty of Versailles, the two pariah armies. German officers spoke with respect of the Russian soldier's standing power, his courage and indifference to death, the excellent equipment of the Red Army, the difficult territory. I never heard any one of them say: "This campaign will be over in three weeks." But I heard them joke: "For this campaign we will not need generals. Non-commissioned officers will do the trick." Evidently they thought little of the leadership of the Red Army.

The aims of the final settlement with Russia—or war aims—as the Germans saw them at the time were in the main these: limitation of the Red Army, the only land army which was the match of Germany; economic domination of the Russian territory to the River Don which, regardless of their conquests in the West was, together with the Balkans, the really essential part of the German Grossraum; political adjustments inside Soviet Russia necessary in order to make the economic organization feasible; adjustments of Russian foreign policy necessary in order to liquidate the Comintern on the European continent.

This program really amounted to the liquidation of the Soviet regime, but this the Germans at the time would not admit. They said if only Stalin would be reasonable, everything could be managed in peace and friendship. Maybe they believed it then. Months later, after Molotov's visit in Berlin, even diplomats and economists began to doubt openly a peaceful solution—of course only in informal conversation—for the Molotov visit was a perfect flop from the first moment on. Hitler and Ribbentrop, it appeared, tried on Molotov some of their ideas for Russia, but Molotov would not even listen. In fact, he wanted to go home immediately. The Germans forced him to stay by refusing him a train. Both parties used Molotov's forced stay in Berlin to smooth the first unpleasantness over a bit, but there could be little doubt from this visit on that the parting of Russian-German ways which had begun with Stalin's grab of Bessarabia could not be put off much longer.

> *. . . What an extraordinary pic-*
> *ture, if one could paint it, of*
> *human power and weakness, as*
> *that of this impatient and mobile*
> *genius (Napoleon I), incessantly*
> *making and unmaking his own*
> *work and driving the nations and*
> *princes to despair, less by what he*
> *made them suffer than by the eter-*
> *nal incertitude in which he left*
> *them as to what remained for*
> *them to fear.*
>
> TOCQUEVILLE

6—TRANSYLVANIA

In three months," the Nazis at the Athene Palace boasted in July, "nobody will talk about the war any more. It will be all over." Never before and—as this is written—never afterwards were the Germans so on top of the world, so sure of the irresistibility of their armed forces.

To the Rumanians there was nothing in the performance of the German armies so far which did not justify this belief. France was gone. There was on the Continent no army left to take up the battle. Talk in the cafés said Britain would surely capitulate or, if she would not capitulate, she would be bombed off the map and invaded.

After the inglorious cession of Bessarabia had made it shockingly clear that Rumania was no match for a really great power and the self-determination of small nations was the bunk, surrender-to-life-with-Hitler filled the air everywhere. In and around the Athene Palace you could cut it with a knife. Sick and tired of playing Great Power when she was not, Rumania decided to go realistic and took an almost frenzied delight in being told by Hitler what to do and how to do it, thereby duplicating what happened all over the European continent that summer. The fall of France formed a climax to twenty years of failure of the promises of democracy to handle unemployment, inflation, deflations, labor unrest, party egoism, and what not. Europe, tired of herself and doubtful of the principles she had been living by, felt almost relieved to have everything settled—not satisfactorily but in such a way that it absolved her of all responsibility. Freud talks somewhere about man's subconscious longing to get away from light and back to the stuffy warmth and safety of the womb. The European man's surrender to Hitler seemed to be the translation of this longing for the mother-womb. Hitler, Europe felt, was a smart guy—disagreeable but smart. He had gone far in making his country strong. Why not try his way? That's how Europeans felt in this summer of 1940.

What really made for surrender to Hitler was people's distrust of freedom because of the weaknesses in its wake and people's fed-upness with their ruling class; and the ruling class' fed-upness with itself. The celebrated fifth columns gave merely the circumstantial fillip, as the right lamp shining over the right divan does for seduction.

The flag on the roof of the Palace still flew at half mast in mourning for Bessarabia when Carol, fearful of Bulgarian and Hungarian moves, and of further Russian activity, took another turn at appeasing Hitler and formally repudiated the British guarantee, which was no great help anyway. A few days later the pro-Ally liberal Premier Tartarescu was replaced by his pro-Axis Foreign Minister, Jon Gigurtu.

Gigurtu was fiftyish with graying hair and a graying mustache emphasizing his small, very black eyes, bushy black brows, and a monocle. Originally an engineer, he had worked up to being the boss of the Mica, Rumania's biggest mining concern, and his admiration for Germany sprang from his admiration for her technical and economic achievements. The same could be said of Manoilescu, the new foreign minister.

Manoilescu, tall, endowed with intellectual charm, had quite a political past. Formerly connected with the Peasant Party, he had been instrumental in bringing Carol back from his first exile. In 1927, on one of his trips to Paris for a clandestine meeting with the King, he was arrested at the frontier. At the treason trial which followed the arrest his words, "My great crime is that I love my country too well, and love the father of a certain little blue-eyed boy . . ." brought the audience to tears. He was acquitted. Manoilescu became Governor of the National Bank, was the first Balkan economist to catch on to the Grossraum-and-barter theories of Hitler's economists, wrote scholarly books about the economy in the cooperative state.

Through these two men, Gigurtu and Manoilescu, the accent of the new cabinet was on out-and-out economic collaboration with Germany, which was a significant feature. Even so, the lobby of the Athene Palace was more excited by the presence in the Cabinet of Horia Sima, leader of the Iron Guardists, as Minister of Culture.

Thirty-four, small, hollow-cheeked, with wild black hair, mouse-sharp black eyes, Sima looked like a story-book revolutionary. A friend of Codreanu, and one of the few surviving intellectuals of the Guardist movement, Horia Sima had been more in than out of jail, and had finally escaped to Berlin for safety. Rumor had it that Malaxa, friend of Carol and Lupescu, persuaded Sima that now was the time to return to Rumania. The industrial-ist always played the whole political field and had dis-creetly financed the surviving Guardists all along. And Carol undoubtedly felt that putting Horia Sima and a few minor Guardists and semi-Guardists into the cabinet gave an extra convincing touch to his out-and-out Axis policy.

The first thing the new Government did was to expel British oil engineers, some of whom had lived in Rumania for twenty years, and then issue a series of decrees pre-venting the British from selling their oil shares to parties undesirable to Germany. The Germans had learned that the British intended to sell them to the Russians. Another series of decrees excluded all Jews from the press, theatre, and the management of big business pending the practical organization of the new party and the drawing up of a Jewish statute which was to decide who was a Jew and who was not.

The Old Excellencies in the lobby of the Athene Palace were languidly amused about these new laws. Things "written on paper," they said, had a shorter life in Ru-mania than anywhere else. After a few weeks the best laws were forgotten or lost their zip because everybody had learned to get around them. This, the Excellencies said, was the Rumanian way of life. The Jews, they said, were too important in the economic life of Rumania to be liquidated in a hurry. Moreover, they said, "Though we are antisemites, we are somehow unable to live without Jews. A Rumanian never trusts another Rumanian. Only to a Jew he can confide his sordid little affairs."

But the Jews themselves took a more serious view of the situation. The Jewish population of Great Rumania was claimed by the antisemitic leaders to be as high as 2,000,000; government spokesmen placed it at 1,200,000; and the Jews themselves estimated it to be 900,000. Anyway, several hundred thousand Jews, even though after the cession one had to deduct some 250,000 Jews in Bessarabia and 120,000 Jews in Bukovina, were trapped in Rumania. Their danger was more immediate here than in middle Europe, because the Rumanian people, after the Poles, have always been the most violently antisemitic people in Europe, and pogroms come easy to them, especially if the law gives them a green light. All day, every day, long lines of Jews stood before the American legation, in the Strada Dyonysie, hoping against hope to find a refuge in America, though the Rumanian quota there was filled for years to come.

In Rumania, antisemitism was a very old story. Even the liberals of the nineteenth century, the Bratianus and Rosettis, pursued an antisemitic policy; eminent writers and intellectuals like Eminescu, Goga, Jorga, and others were first and last antisemites. This antisemitism was the reaction to the fact that the Jews had succeeded in forming the middle class between the boyards and peasants, and in creating the only bourgeoisie in Rumania.

Without enjoying civil rights the Jews exercised a financial monopoly in the early Rumanian capitalism, between 1830 and 1880, when there existed only Jewish banks and credit institutions, and the most important bank, Marmaros, Blank and Co., the Rothschilds of the Balkans, financed the young Rumanian kingdom, complete with the first railway and the Russian-Rumanian war. Not before 1880 did the liberals succeed in establishing a national banking system, nestling around the National Bank; but Jewish banking was still going strong until the crisis of 1931, when the National bank, under its governor, Manoilescu, helped the Christian houses, but forced Marmaros, Blank into liquidation.

It was one of the ironies of history that it was the German victory over Rumania in 1916 which first brought full equality to the Jews. Until then there existed an "exceptional equality," a concession to Bismarck who championed the Rumanian Jews at the Congress of Berlin. But only 2000 Jews—Jewish statistics say only 700 Jews—had been naturalized in Rumania from 1877 until the world war.

As soon as the German domination over Rumania disintegrated, Rumanian statesmen hurriedly canceled the German-made equality laws. But under the pressure of the Allies they reluctantly promulgated a satisfactory citizenship law in 1919 and thus the hundred-year-old struggle of old Rumania's Jews for civil rights ended and the struggle to retain these rights began. For sentiments towards the Jew remained the same. The moment the new Rumanian constitution became effective, the antisemitic national movement took on momentum. This was when Codreanu, joining hands with old antisemite Professor Cuza, made his political début.

A campaign to deny citizenship to the Jews, beginning as soon as the new constitution was validated in 1923, suited the liberal Government of Jonel Bratianu and all following governments. By intricate legal trickery thousands of Jews were stricken from the citizenship lists, even before the short-lived Goga Government issued its law for revision of Jewish citizenship in 1938, and thus deprived about 225,000 Jews of their citizenship. This law, while never voided, affected the economic existence of the Jews less than one would expect, for, as the Excellencies said it, "things written on paper" had a short life in Rumania and could be easily overcome by greasing the right palms. It was only tough on those who did not have enough money for this backshish.

Rumanian antisemites had not yet caught on to racial antisemitism. With them it was the religious brand and the economic variety. The most popular grievances against the Jews at the present time were Madame Lupescu and the Jewish middlemen.

According to the Rumanian antisemites the Jewish middlemen had built up a devilish system to enslave the peasant. As to Lupescu, she would probably have got by if she had been the natural daughter of an orthodox Catholic streetwalker, but being of Jewish extraction was too much for her to overcome. The Rumanian people felt humiliated that their King had dropped his Queen for a Jewess. And now they were blaming her for the misfortune which had befallen the country—and they blamed the entire Jewish race for Lupescu.

In this atmosphere of abject surrender and superstitious hate the scene was set for new and greater disaster. For, before the hot glaring heat of this summer had subsided, Carol would have signed away about 22,000 square miles more of his country's territory, and Great Rumania would have shrunk almost to her pre-world war proportions.

The cession of Bessarabia acted, as everyone expected it would, as a come-and-get-it signal to Hungary and Bulgaria, who between them wanted the return of Transylvania and Dobrudscha, a large and fertile slice of Great Rumania. In July the battle of pressure for these territories began in earnest, when Count Teleki and Count Czaki, the Hungarian statesmen, suddenly set out for Munich to see Hitler. Hearing this, Rumanians in and around the Athene Palace became frantic at the thought that the Hungarians had Hitler all to themselves, with no one around to present their side of the case. Then, as in all good tragedies, came a moment of respite when things seemed to brighten. The Hungarians had seen Hitler, and left—and nothing had happened. For forty-eight hours every piccolo in the hotel, every shampoo girl at Jonica's, the hairdresser, everyone in the lobby, said that the Führer did not really like the Hungarians and that he had sent them home empty-handed. Surely, they added optimistically, Hitler was far too busy planning the invasion of Britain to bother about the Balkans.

But this optimism was of short duration. On July twenty-sixth Rumanian statesmen were summoned to Salzburg, where they were ordered by Hitler and Ribbentrop to confer at once with the Hungarians and Bulgarians and find a solution for their frontier problems. Somebody who was present told me that the meeting between Gigurtu and Manoilescu and the Führer was pleasant. Hitler was gracious and patient, listening attentively, making no promises but insisting that he was not interested in Balkan politics; only in Balkan economics. He even gave a fleeting glance at the papers which the Rumanians had brought along, but pushed them aside with a lazy hand, saying, "First come to an agreement with the Hungarians and Bulgarians. As to the future I have much better ideas for you than you can ever hand me here."

Rumanians were furious at the results of Salzburg, being sick and tired of playing Great Power and eager to submit to Hitler's fatherly decision. But no fatherly decision was forthcoming. Hitler declined to decide anything and threw the responsibility back to the Rumanians, who felt cheated. I asked the Count what seemed to be Hitler's idea in this. The Rumanians and Hungarians would never come to an agreement when left to themselves. The Count replied cynically that nobody expected them to. The Führer just believed in keeping the Balkans busy until he got around to dictating something.

A high Nazi official of the German Foreign Office, coming from Berlin, put it differently. He sighed and said: "As long as there are negotiations, there is no shooting." Who would shoot at whom? The Nazi official answered: "The Hungarians would begin to shoot at the Rumanians."

I asked: "But why don't you just tell the Hungarians to hold everything until after the war?"

"Oh," said the high Nazi official loftily, "we don't wish to play nursemaid to all of Europe."

This gave me my first inkling that Nazi diplomacy was not as smart as I had thought. Germany *had* to play nursemaid to the Balkans if she wished to fulfill her chief aim of quiet in the raw-material sphere. It was a grave mistake for a power such as Nazi Germany, which had achieved the domination of Europe by being dictatorial and totalitarian, to relapse suddenly into a *laisser-aller* policy. But that became German policy in Rumania, no matter what people thought.

The more I saw of the way the Nazis handled the Hungarian and Bulgarian revisionist claims against Rumania in the course of the next weeks and months, the more I modified my views about Nazi methods. Up to Salzburg I believed the Nazis had blueprints for every phase of the establishment of their new order in Europe, blueprints just waiting in the files to be used. But this, I noticed now, was not so. The Nazis did not plan so much as muddle through. They might have a very clear idea of what their new order was to be in the end, but they certainly did considerable improvisation on the way. They left whole phases to chance, fumbled and experimented, made decisions on the spur of the moment, retracted decisions and took other tracks. Muddling through, it seemed, was no specific attribute of British imperialism, but was the human side of any imperialism. Not even German efficiency and thoroughness were able to plan to meet the infinite vagaries of life and man and to cope with the dynamic unexpectedness of conquest. This was a hopeful thought.

In Rumania, German muddling through worked this way: the Germans had a beautifully detailed blueprint for the economic organization of the country, which they followed religiously, but their political plan was a mere appendix to this economic plan. "Quiet in the raw-material sphere in wartime" was the general idea, and "Any good strong government which can assure this quiet." But the Germans were very half-hearted and contradictory in their efforts to assure it; certainly the worst way to achieve their aim was to tear the whole country apart and thus discredit the powers-that-be.

In view of their desire for quiet in the raw-material sphere in wartime, the only sound German diplomacy would have been to make every effort to put the whole matter of Hungarian and Bulgarian revisionist claims on ice until after the war. Then the new Hitler order would make state frontiers nominal anyway, and thus rob the whole issue of the passion which it now aroused in people's hearts. But the Germans made no such effort. They let the most ticklish of Balkan problems take its untimely course, and what a mess they made of it!

There was nothing brilliant about the way German diplomacy blundered along, surprised at every turn by events shaping up in some quite unexpected fashion. Even the Führer's warmest admirers had to admit that the famous Hitler touch was lacking in Rumania, but if anyone pointed out to the Nazis the wastefulness of their methods in their material, emotional, and psychological aspects, they would say airily, "Oh, we always take mistakes and miscalculations into account beforehand."

But this was not the reason why their muddling through had not come out too badly so far. It was just that nothing can come out too badly for the one who holds the monopoly of power—as long as he holds it.

The passion which surrounded the issue of Rumanian revisionism was chiefly centered around Transylvania. Nobody got very excited about the Southern Dobrudscha, which Rumania had annexed after the Balkan war in 1913 for chiefly strategic reasons. Carol could have ceded it— 2,983 square miles with a population of 380,000—without much loss of face had it not been for Queen Marie's heart, which was buried in her castle in Balcic in Southern Dobrudscha. The Queen had been charmed with this country, where the tombs of the Scythians formed little round hills surmounting the wide bare plains, where the minarets still rose in the villages and Tartar women in wide trousers veiled their mouths in Islamic modesty. Marie built a Palace in Balcic which was all terraces and an English garden descending right to the shores of the Black Sea, and savage desert winds and African sun made seeds from Surrey bloom forth in fairytale sizes and colors. But this was not the only reason why the Queen wished her heart to be buried here. The beautiful Queen, who in spite of her weaknesses took a deep and ambitious interest in Great Rumania, had a knack for symbolic gestures. This one was meant as a reminder and an obligation for her heirs never to give up this province. In 1938, when she died, the Queen could not imagine that by 1940 fear, weakness, and defeatism would black out her country so that her people would not think of fighting for the soil to which she had given her heart, but would only argue where to move it.

Contrary to Dobrudscha, Transylvania was sheer dynamite. The treaty of Trianon had adjudicated Transylvania to Rumania in 1920 and this province had represented the most glittering piece of spoils Rumania had got out of the world war. Though since 1868, Transylvania had belonged to Hungary and before this to the Austro-Hungarian monarchy as far back as 1690, the Allied Powers had justified the transfer of Transylvania to Rumania by the large Rumanian minority living in Transylvania.

Hungary never recognized the treaty of Trianon, and for twenty years never allowed Hungarians or anybody else to forget the unfairness of the treaty. Flags on official buildings in Hungary were hoisted at half-mast all this time, and Hungarian family fathers said "Nem Nem Soha" (which means "No, no, never will we submit to the dictate of Trianon") as they sat down to eat their goulash. When Hitler had just begun to make the "shackles of Versailles" familiar in Munich beer halls, tons and tons of propaganda had already carried Hungarian protests against the shackles of Trianon to the remotest corners of the earth. Thus Hungary had been the first have-not country to make a relentless revisionist policy and to stick to it without compromise.

When finally Adolf Hitler rode to power and success on the wave of his revisionist policy against Versailles, he became the natural champion of all revisionist claims resulting from the world war, and the Hungarians expected him to support them in undoing Trianon as soon as he himself had succeeded in undoing Versailles. At the dismemberment of Czechoslovakia in 1938 and 1939, Hitler got back for Hungary 4600 square miles of territory. But the big prize still stood out: the big prize was Transylvania.

Unfortunately there was no fair solution to the Transylvanian question in terms of state frontiers. The Rumanian minority was settled to a large extent near the Hungarian frontier and large batches of the Hungarian minority were distributed inside the country in parts not even the Hungarians themselves could hope to get back. No frontier could make for a satisfactory peace between Hungary and Rumania, so it would have been only rational to postpone the whole matter until after the war. With the uncontested authority which Hitler at this time enjoyed such postponement would have been easy to manage. Nor was there any wholly satisfactory explanation why Hitler did not resort to this postponement.

There were only two motives discernible which might have prompted this strange chapter of Nazi diplomacy: one was that to Hitler the treaty of Trianon was emotionally so closely tied up with the treaty of Versailles that its revision became a symbolical obligation to him, more important than any practical consideration. The second motive, which probably strengthened the first one, was Hitler's growing distrust of Carol.

Carol of Rumania, I found from my first day in the Athene Palace, was a most controversial figure to the Germans in Bucharest. There were those who thought that Carol, in spite of Lupescu, his killing of Guardists, his pro-Allied past, and his doubtful pro-Axis loyalty of the present, was the only person to hold the fickle Rumanian flock together. All the Germans who had known the Rumanian set-up for a long period were pro-Carol—Dr. Fabrizius, Frau von Coler, the old-time German bankers, the German industrialists and businessmen in Bucharest. They said that in spite of everything Carol was the only man to hold Rumania together, that he was amenable because he was so corrupt, that there would be a hole where Carol had been if he were forced to go. But the *nazissime* Nazis and those who did not know Rumania saw in Carol only a double-crossing so-and-so, detested by his people, who could be of no possible use to the Fatherland.

This second group had begun to overshadow the first

just when foreign journalists cabled stories about Rumania's English-baiting and Jew-baiting totalitarianism under Gigurtu's new government. But more than anything else it was Carol's way of handling totalitarianism which made him suspect even to his German champions. The German consensus was that Carol was far from putting his heart into totalitarianism. To them the best proof was the imprisonment of General Antonescu, the only man who, in their opinion, could form that much-desired strong government, and the fact that Carol had not discarded the detested camarilla of his pro-Ally, Guardist-killing days. There were still Urdareanu, Moruzov, the chief of the Secret Police, Marinescu, the Chief of Police. Even Georges Tartarescu, the former pro-Ally Premier, still came to the Palace for luncheon. And there was always Lupescu, who, the Germans were sure, was on the payroll of the wise men of Zion.

In a system of personal dictatorship, the Germans insisted, only the King and his immediate entourage counted, and this was as anti-German as ever. To them Carol's pro-Axis cabinet was just window-dressing, a phony combination of various groups which controlled each other and canceled each other's influence. Carol's attempts to appease Hitler in a hurry appeared equally unsatisfactory to the Germans. On the day the English oil engineers were expelled from Rumania, Dr. Neubacher said sarcastically, "The ruthlessness with which Carol is now treating the British shows how he would be treating us if we had lost." And the German reaction to the new antisemitic legislation was almost comically negative. A precipitated dejudaization, they protested, would disrupt the whole Rumanian economy, and they hinted broadly that they were less interested in a pure Rumanian race than in the functioning of the economic machine.

On July twelfth, German journalists told me, Carol had called in the German military and air attachés, requesting them to ask Hitler to dispatch a military mission to Bucharest. Carol's idea was, of course, to frighten off the Hungarians, Bulgarians, and Russians from planning any land-grabs. The Germans felt outraged at this request. "Why should our men fight for Carol, who does not even believe that we'll win the war but just tries to kid us along until a British victory?" they asked.

It all sounded very ominous for Carol, and often when I looked over at his white Palace, I wondered whether he would be here to see the annex finished.

In the midst of this situation Edit von Coler was recalled to Germany. One day in the middle of July the court circular reported that Mme. von Coler had been received in audience by the King. Later people said that this very audience (obtained, they said, without the knowledge of Dr. Fabrizius) had caused her disgrace. However that may be, a few days after this audience Frau von Coler said goodbye, first saying that she would leave only for a few weeks. But then she paused and said, "My people in Berlin seem to think that my usefulness here is over. So I might not come back." She made no further comment, but she was depressed. The Rumanian newspaper owner who looked like Haile Selassie patted her hand and said: "I wish, *ma chère*, Rumania would become a German protectorate with you as Führer."

Frau von Coler made a helpless little grimace and for a moment looked as if she were going to cry. Instead she smiled a stiff little smile, which she held as we shook hands. The sun was on her blonde hair and on the moon-stones in her ears.

Afterwards the Negus said: "I do hope *chère Edit* will not be put into a concentration camp. To be down and out is no fun in a totalitarian country."

"Why should she be down and out?"

"Because she has been friends with all the wrong people: the King, Malaxa, Tartarescu, Gafencu, Bratianu, Maniu."

"But these people have been the most useful to befriend, and certainly Frau von Coler has made a good job of weaning them from the French."

The Negus laughed. "They were useful, but now they are goners. And Edit's enemies will say that *chère Edit* has always played around with the anti-Nazis, anti-Guardists, and internationalists." The Negus wagged his pointed black beard and said, "Don't tell anybody, but Edit's recall means that this is the twilight of the gods—especially Carol."

If the information of the guests of the Athene Palace was scant in these days of quick developments, the people outside the Athene Palace wandered in a jungle of the most conflicting rumors and conjectures. The newspapers never mentioned the coming negotiations with Hungary and Bulgaria, or that they were undertaken at Hitler's insistence. Buried among lengthy reports on the invincibility of the Axis there were now and then terse official statements that all rumors of new cessions of territory were bloody lies. . . . Never, it would seem, was a crisis more ineptly handled than this one.

Hundreds of people were put into concentration camps

for spreading false rumors. Most of them were Jews and communists, but a few of the nicest princes who used to sit with the foreign journalists in the Athene Palace were fetched by police as they were having their cocktails in the lobby. In all the shops of the Calea Victoriei you could hear wild rumors that Hitler had given Rumania to Stalin as a present; that Hitler had promised Carol to leave him Transylvania provided he sent Lupescu abroad; that the Hungarians were already marching into Transylvania and the Bulgarians into Dobrudscha, and that Hitler was making a protectorate of the rest. Though official statements were sadly lacking, unofficial ones made the rounds. There were Maniu's memoranda protesting against any kind of negotiations, which were circulated all over town. Maniu was a Transylvanian himself and he felt especially passionate about the matter. Some of the memoranda were co-signed by Georges Bratianu and other distinguished liberals and Peasant Party leaders. They came out for fighting for every foot of Rumanian territory.

"But if you fight the Hungarians and Bulgarians, the Russians will come and swallow you up," a foreign correspondent said to one of these leaders.

He answered bitterly: "Better to be all Rumanians united under the Soviet star than to live apart in a Hitler-dominated Ostraum."

This was an astounding statement for a Rumanian liberal statesman to make, one who had always been more anti-Russian than anti-German and who lately seemed so resigned to collaboration with Germany. But such was the Rumanians' despair about the threatening loss of their most beloved province that any solution, even wholesale annexation by Russia, seemed preferable. Which showed to what extent, by just unrolling the question of Transylvania, German diplomacy lost the good will of Rumanian statesmen.

Then suddenly the Rumanian Government decided to interest the world in their side of the Transylvanian question, and invited the foreign journalists on a trip to the disputed area around the Rumanian-Hungarian frontier. In view of the fact that the Hungarians had endeavored to influence the world in their favor for twenty years, the belated Rumanian effort was pathetically futile. But then the haves are always more careless about propaganda than the have-nots.

The party of foreign journalists who gathered in the sleeper for Cluj on August fifteenth were mostly Americans, with a sprinkling of Swiss journalists. The German journalists had not got permission from their legation to come on the trip; it could have been interpreted as German interest in Transylvania at a moment when Germany wished to keep on the sidelines. Italian journalists followed suit. British and French were not invited. The Americans had turned out in almost full force.

The idea underlying the trip was to prove to us that the majority of the population in this frontier region was Rumanian and that the Hungarians were only in the cities. This fact was well known to us without the trip, for during the last fortnight we had been bombarded with maps showing the distribution of the Hungarians, Germans, and Rumanians in Transylvania. Nor would the sight of a Hungarian have changed our sentiments. We were all pro-Rumanian, partly because we really liked the country and the people and partly because we were against a Hitler-made or Hitler-suggested world. But the gentlemen of the Rumanian Ministry of Propaganda who escorted us thought differently about this matter. They never let us out of sight for a moment and discouraged any personal initiative. One of them sat in every car, issuing a steady flow of propaganda and listening in on our conversations.

We stopped in the cities only overnight, for owing to the fact that the cities were prominently Hungarian, they were considered dangerous ground. Instead we drove for hours through a beautiful countryside with mountains on the horizon, sampling Rumanian villages. This would have been nice had not the roads been so terrible. The millions of leis which, the gentlemen of the Propaganda Ministry insisted, had been invested in these roads, certainly did not show, and it was not surprising that the graft in Transylvania had been such that a few months before all the civil prefects had been replaced by military prefects.

Every few hundred yards the roads were blocked by barricades of barbed wire and wooden logs, and the soldiers stopped our caravan. Rumanian soldiers looked nice and dumb and a little hungry, for, as with the money for the roads so with the food for the soldiers: it was caught somewhere between the Treasury and where it was supposed to go.

There were innumerable Rumanian villages and we stopped in most of them. Then the peasants in their Sunday best would gather around the cars and shout *"Tareaska Presidentele Roosevelt,"* which, the gentlemen of the Propaganda Ministry wished us to believe, was a spontaneous ovation.

The Old Excellencies at the Athene Palace and everybody who loved Rumania had always told me that I should not judge the country from the people I met in Bucharest, but that it was the Rumanian peasant who counted. And really the Rumanian peasants were handsome in a lean, clean-cut, sunburnt way, very different from the pasty-faced gents in town. They worked hard and were humbly resigned to poverty; their eyes were kind and trusting, like children's.

I liked best seeing them working in their sunflower fields, moving in their heavy white linen shirts between the high golden flowers, smiling at us from far. We smiled, too, and shouted *"Sanatate,"* which means "Heil." And one wished there would never be a war or any disturbance to take these men away from their fields.

I found out on this trip that the Transylvanian peasants were quite satisfied with their Rumanian rulers, even the Hungarians. Through land-reform 540,000 Transylvanian peasants who had had no land before had received some, and they were afraid of losing it once they returned to Hungarian rule. For not only had the Hungarians no land-reform themselves, they had also repealed the Czechoslovak land-reform in the regions they received in 1938 and 1939.

Hungarians in the cities were a malcontent, sullen lot, relations between Hungarian intellectuals and Rumanian authorities being especially bad. The Hungarians were just biding their time, waiting Der Tag when Transylvania would become Hungarian again. The large Jewish city population of Transylvania, faced with an unhappy choice of Rumanian antisemitism or Hungarian antisemitism, preferred Hungarian antisemitism. Having been the backbone of pro-Magyar sympathies for twenty years, the Jews now figured that Hungarian antisemitism could never be as bad as Rumanian antisemitism. The Hungarians, they argued, were numerically too small a people to fill all the space they wished to conquer. They could do it only by assimilating other minorities. So by force of habit the Hungarians would change their antisemitic policy and relapse into their old custom of magyarizing their Jews. While it was doubtful that things would come about this way in Hitler-dominated Eastern Europe, it showed that the recent Rumanian antisemitic legislation certainly was no help in Transylvania.

I heard many atrocity stories about the methods of magyarization which the Hungarians had applied while in power here. One Rumanian gentleman told that when his mother brought him to the principal of the high school, the principal said: "What, a Rumanian boy? Doesn't have to go to high school. Shall guard pigs." The Hungarians had certainly made it tough for the Rumanians, while the Rumanians were more easy-going.

But more terrified of Hungarian domination than the Rumanians themselves were the Transylvanian Germans, who all wore black tight-fitting gabardine suits with high boots, very much like a chauffeur's uniform, the costume they had worn when they had settled in Transylvania in the eighteenth century. They were convinced that nothing worse could happen to their minority of 250,000 than to come under Hungarian rule. Because of the Roman Catholic Church, which was a main instrument of magyarization, the Germans, they explained, were much more exposed to magyarization than the Rumanians, kept apart by their Orthodox faith. Innumerable Germans had completely merged into the Hungarian people, but this time, they said, "We'll fight to the knife for our *Volkstum*." The young Germans said they wished nothing better than to fight the Hungarians.

"What if your Führer should decide that your district should become Hungarian?" I asked one of the leading Germans in Transylvania.

"I can't believe that the Führer will do this to us," he said. But on second thought, he added, "Of course, his word goes, though it would be the worst that can happen to us."

Evidently the Germans in Transylvania had no quarrel with the Rumanians. They detested the Hungarians, but were first of all Germans.

Transylvanian statesmen, among them the Royal Resident, Tataru, a friend of Maniu, were bitter. "We have two enemies," they said, "Budapest—and Bucharest." They wished to fight for Transylvania were it only to save their honor and the respect of their people. But they felt in their bones that Carol would back down once more.

A Hungarian military and diplomatic delegation met a Rumanian delegation in Turnu Severin, on the Danube, while we motored through Transylvania. This was done only to please the Führer; actually there was such a wide abyss between Rumania's offer and Hungary's claims that there was no basis for negotiations. The Hungarians asked some 60,000 square kilometers (out of 62,229), and Valer Pop, the Rumanian delegate and a Transylvanian himself, answered this staggering demand with a vague offer of an exchange of populations and territory in proportion to the Hungarian surplus. Followed a few days of mild bickering, and the negotiations were broken off.

After a last session, in which both parties agreed that they had not found anything to agree upon, the Rumanian delegates felt confident because they had "showed the Hungarians." But they did not feel good for long. When they telephoned to Bucharest about the breaking off of negotiations, they got hell from the King and were told that the negotiations had to be resumed at any price. So the Rumanians had to go to the Hungarian diplomats and ask them please to reopen negotiations. The Hungarians, sparing the Rumanians nothing, said that this time the Rumanians would have to come to Hungary, and off the Hungarians went.

Two days later both the Rumanian and Hungarian statesmen were asked by Ribbentrop and Count Ciano to come to Vienna immediately. Now everybody felt with relief that at last the question would be settled once and for all and, strangely enough, the Rumanians felt extraordinarily cheerful about the prospect. Though they had joined the Axis only a few weeks ago, they felt like full-fledged little partners, bound to be treated as such. And even the Germans admitted that the ethnical claims of the Rumanians would fit better into the Führer's new order than the revisionist passions of the Hungarians. The Germans, they said, did not want the Rumanian space to become too small, and they got on more easily with the amenable Rumanians than with the Hungarians who somehow were always offended because they were not the Germans and the Germans the Hungarians. The Germans believed that the Rumanians would have to give up a few frontier districts, but nothing like the 60,000 square kilometers the Hungarians claimed.

It all sounded quite reassuring for the Rumanians until Friday, the thirtieth of August. In the afternoon I met Dr. Neubacher, looking pale. He told me Hitler had decided that the Rumanians would have to cede 45,000 square kilometers.

I said, "Good God, how will they take it?"

Dr. Neubacher shrugged his shoulders and looked depressed. "Believe me, this comes as unexpectedly to me as to anybody else. As far as I knew Ribbentrop went to Vienna with a proposal for the Rumanians to give up four frontier districts. Something I don't know yet must have happened these last four days."

If the Vienna decision came as a shock even to the Germans, anything might be expected from the despair of the Rumanians themselves. Throughout the night from Thursday to Friday the chandeliers of the big hall in Carol's Palace had been lighted while the long line of limousines again waited at the Palace courtyard. Nobody got excited about it that night, for with the censorship everybody thought the Crown Council was deliberating over proposals coming from Vienna. They didn't know there were no proposals.

Ribbentrop and Ciano, it appeared, had not even bothered to go through the motions of arbitration, but had faced the Hungarians with a take-it-or-leave-it proposition and the Rumanians with an ultimatum to the effect that German, Hungarian, and Russian troops would march in unless they accepted within six hours.

So that night from Thursday to Friday the Crown Council had debated acceptance or non-acceptance of a

Hitler-made destiny. It was a dramatic session. The King, beside himself with despair and humiliation, his eyes bloodshot, his beautiful blond hair rumpled, trying to steady his nerves with whisky, talked of suicide. With all his autocratic self-assurance gone, unable to form a thought and even less a decision, crushed by the first impact of Rumania's disaster and the realization of his own guilt in it, he looked for comfort to the sorrowful advisers whose counsel he had so often disregarded—honest men like Maniu who had brought him to power and for whom the loss of Transylvania was an almost unbearable heartbreak; the other Transylvanian leaders who wanted action; and the older statesmen who had seen the Great Rumania rise.

But there was no comfort to be found from them in this dark hour. The Patriarch, so it was said later, made an impassioned speech against acceptance of the Vienna terms. So did old Professor Cuza. There was something pathetic about this "grand old man" of European antisemitism, who had thought so highly of the "Great Führer of the Great German Reich," as the fulfiller of his boldest antisemitic dreams who now had to hate Hitler for tearing his country to pieces. Maniu, of course, came out for fighting for Transylvania. So did most of the older statesmen, who had seen Great Rumania rise. But for acceptance, so it was said, were Georges Tartarescu, the former pro-Ally Prime Minister whom the Germans detested, and the military men present. They knew that the Rumanian army was in no position to fight. For acceptance also was the brother of Codreanu, who attended the Crown Council as representative of the Guardist movement, which was by tradition pro-Axis. Georges Bratianu, once a champion of the German-Rumanian rapprochement, who would certainly have voted against acceptance of the Vienna terms, was mobilized and could not get to Bucharest in time for the meeting. Nor could two Transylvanian statesmen who would also have voted against acceptance. A narrow vote came out for acceptance.

All this became known much later. Throughout Friday everything was serene. Newspapers said nothing of developments in Vienna, and the people passing by the Palace watched the long line of limousines without foreboding.

August thirtieth was a lovely night, warm but with the first tinge of autumn. On this night, with awful suddenness, the Rumanians learned of the Vienna decision from the German and Hungarian radio. The shock on the people was terrific. I dined that night at the Athene Palace in the little courtyard off the green salon. It was crowded, but the guests conversed in subdued voices and nobody laughed. Foreigners looked serious and the Rumanians cried openly. Even the hard-boiled waiters had red eyes.

No one could see that the Vienna award did anything to reverse the injustice of Trianon. It seemed a blatantly uncreative, unimaginative, sterile decision, without a spark of an organizing idea in it. It could only create ill will against Germany all around, embittering the Rumanians and leaving the Hungarians still unsatisfied. It was the kind of decision which made one doubt whether Hitler really had the stuff for creating a new order. If he had, this first stab at it certainly did not show it. The Vienna award was no better than anything that had come out of Versailles. Without saying it in so many words the Germans glumly agreed. They hinted that Ciano had forced

Ribbentrop's hand, for the Italians had always been partial to the Hungarians and resentful of the Rumanians who had cooperated in the sanctions against Italy. But this was a poor explanation. Ribbentrop was not the man to let himself be cajoled into changing plans just to be nice to Ciano.

Later that same night a German diplomat gave an explanation which seemed more plausible. The verdict of Vienna, he said, was the immediate consequence of a last-minute attempt by Carol to conclude a military alliance with Russia—of course against Germany—through his envoy in Moscow. Ribbentrop was informed by Molotov of Carol's attempt at the double-cross shortly before his departure for Vienna and, finally convinced of Carol's congenital illoyalty, Germany decided at the last moment to give Ciano his way and award the Hungarians the lion's share of Transylvania.

This was a good story, though one could hardly imagine Carol being stupid or desperate enough to try double-crossing Hitler at this juncture. Yet when I brought this story to the censor, it was passed with some minor changes. The censor said bitterly: "It does not matter whether the story is true or German propaganda. It shows that the Axis wished to punish the King and that we, the people, have to suffer for his sin." Long pent-up hate of Carol could not be restrained any longer, even by his officials.

After dinner that Friday night the Square again had the familiar crisis-look. People again crowded on the space between the bronze Carol I and the Palace gates and watched the lighted chandeliers in the big hall of the first floor and the courtyard overflowing with the limousines of ministers and Crown Councilors. It was an angry crowd this time, with officers, priests, and communists walking around haranguing people about the "betrayal by the Axis." Talk ran through this crowd, and it was interesting to observe how, from one day to the other, the cruel blow they were suffering at Hitler's hand made many Rumanians change their opinion about his chances of winning the war. While only a few days ago they thought that the British defeat was a matter of weeks, now even people close to the Iron Guard said, "Well, the Germans don't seem to make much headway with their air attacks on England." Or, "Hitler has to conquer Rumania because he can't conquer England." There were even those who said that it was not worthwhile getting excited about the Vienna award, as they would certainly soon get everything back from the British.

In Brasov, Transylvania, Gauleiter Hühnlein, who had come from Berlin for the auto races that day, had the swastika flag torn from his car and trampled under the feet of an angry mob.

Gigurtu and Manoilescu, the Rumanian delegates, returned from Vienna on Saturday and Manoilescu made one of the strangest speeches ever made by a statesman in trouble. He talked of the "terrible hours in Vienna" as if he had seen the Gorgon's head but did not dare to describe it. He said that the acceptance of the verdict had been unavoidable, without saying why. And he shrouded the events preceding the verdict in even deeper mystery by admitting that the conversations of Salzburg had not let him expect such a terrible blow. After he was through, everybody was sure that Carol had tried to double-cross Hitler, maybe by an attempted military alliance with Stalin, and had thus upset the apple-cart. So

the people turned their fury away from Hitler and Mussolini and turned it full force on Carol and the camarilla.

At five p.m. on Sunday there was a demonstration on
the Square as protest against the cession of Transylvania.
A large crowd of students, joined by people of all ages
and classes gathered, shouting, "We don't want to cede
Transylvania. Give us Transylvania back. Down with the
traitors who sell Rumania out. We want Maniu." The
President of the University made a speech and so did a
few liberal politicians and Peasant Party leaders. Everybody cried! The Rumanians cry easily. Then there was a
sudden commotion and the gendarmes began to shout and
jostle the crowds. The prefect arrived in person and with
him a company of what I took to be tanks, menacing be-
hemoths painted sky-blue, with muzzles turned at the
crowd. A gentleman from the Ministry of Propaganda
grabbed my arm and rushed me quickly to the other side
of the Square just as the "tanks" began to let loose—
sharp jets of water. In less than a minute the Square was
empty; I never could figure where the people disappeared
to so quickly.

The man of the Ministry of Propaganda looked back
and said bitterly: "*That's* the way the Rumanian Government shows courage."

> *At all times the kings were toys*
> *of their own passions and of the*
> *intrigues of everyone close enough*
> *to them to find out their weak*
> *sides and shrewd and wicked*
> *enough to abuse them.*
>
> WIELAND

7—THE KING

Jonica's, the chromium-glittering, streamlined beauty parlor of the Athene Palace, is the lobby and the bar and the restaurant of the Athene Palace in negligee. In Jonica's you see your favorite military attaché, Gestapo agent or oil man, collarless and swathed in white with soap on his face looking a far cry from the finished product. And he sees you with wet hair sticking unbecomingly to your head.

At Jonica's men were done over downstairs and women on a gallery upstairs. There are mirrors everywhere at Jonica's, but no curtains. Head tipped back into the basin, you watched in the mirror as one of the Old Excellencies had his mustache touched up in black and next to him the ex-envoy of some South American country who was now smuggling drugs and money in and out of Rumania on his diplomatic passport got a shave. The female employees at Jonica's were pretty things who had every secret and every intrigue of Bucharest at the tips of their fingers and played a part in many of them; they all were supposed to work for one secret police or other. Since all the foreign diplomats and diplomats' wives and the whole Bucharest Who's Who frequented Jonica's, it was quite a likely place for secret police to be interested in.

Jacqueline, the red-haired shampoo girl, rubbed the soap vigorously into my scalp and asked, "Does Madame think that Mr. Popescu can stay on?"

Everybody knew who was meant by Mr. Popescu. Popescu, a name as common in Rumania as Jones in the United States was the pseudonym which the Rumanians used for Carol. If bad came to worse, one could pretend to mean any of the innumerable Popescus.

"Popescu must go and *she* must be quartered," Jacqueline went on, pouring too-hot water down my neck.

Since last Friday, when the Vienna verdict had been sprung on them, Bucharestians, no matter what their jobs, were bad at them. There was too much tension in the air, a passionate tension radiating hate and revenge and apprehension of worse to come. It was now Tuesday after the fateful Friday and in the lobby of the Athene Palace the odds against Mr. Popescu staying on were 3 to 1. But they were fluctuating. The Germans, it was said, after having Carol properly chastised, were now for keeping him on the throne.

Jaqueline wound a towel around my hair and whispered, "There will be a revolution unless he goes at once. He cannot treat his people like this."

She led me over to a dressing table where Monsieur Robert, Jonica's star hairdresser, was waiting for me. Rumor at the Athene Palace had it that Monsieur Robert was really a German Colonel in disguise planted here by the German Military Intelligence—a rumor to which his unusual tall blondness gave weight, but which one was nevertheless inclined to discount, for no matter how good the German army, it was improbable that she could produce an inspired hairdresser like Monsieur Robert.

"Did Madame see the article in *Universul?*" Monsieur Robert bent closely over to me, as he began to pin up little curls. All around the dryers were buzzing full force, but one could not be cautious enough. I nodded—it was not necessary to ask which article. Yesterday's was in everyone's mind, a savage article against Carol, talking of ten years of corruption and theft and ineptness, topped off by collapse. And *Universul* was the official paper. People said that General Antonescu himself had dictated that article. The General had been set free after the Vienna decision.

Yet the article was nothing compared to a leaflet which Monsieur Robert now put between the open pages of my *Vogue.* Signed by Horia Sima and distributed all over the barracks, it flatly called Carol a traitor whose double-cross caused the Vienna disaster. The story of how Carol had tried to conclude a military alliance with Stalin was described in detail. Lupescu's name figured prominently and in the most unflattering contexts. Plainly this was a call to revolt!

Monsieur Robert said, "Madame is ready for the dryer," and he arranged the helmet over my head. As he worked, a gentleman passed and bowed politely.

"Monsieur Barbu Jonescu—I wonder what he is thinking these days," Robert whispered.

Barbu Jonescu, in his fifties, had a yellow, heavily lined face and wide loose mouth of a tired *bon viveur.* He carried himself with a slightly used but jaunty elegance. From under the dryer I watched him sit down at a manicure table. I, too, wondered what he thought, for this was the man who had actually financed Carol's exile and comeback.

In the twenties and early thirties Barbu Jonescu was a man about many European capitals, who made quite a social splash in Brussels, Paris, and London. "A rich Rumanian" people said of him, and flocked to his hospitable house. He was married to a girl of good French family and had a pretty daughter who, already as a child, was an outstanding rider. At that time few people knew or remembered how Barbu Jonescu made his fortune, and he himself was too snobbish to tell. It came about this way: one day a group of exacting guests in a Soho restaurant in London complained about the coffee, and the lowly dishwasher, hearing them, offered to make them coffee such as they had never tasted before. This dishwasher was Barbu Jonescu, who served that day the thick syrupy Turkish coffee he knew from Rumania. Barbu's brew became a sensation. Coffee lovers rushed to Soho. Barbu was made waiter, then manager, and finally partner. Soon "Jonescu's coffee" became a trade mark all over England. He enlarged the Soho restaurant, built up a chain, all featuring the Jonescu coffee.

With the wealth made from his coffee Barbu branched out into other more profitable financial fields and in an amazingly short time was a rich man with a country estate and political ambitions. These and a romantic adoration for his exiled King prompted him to offer his support to Carol, then living in Paris with Lupescu. Carol and Lupescu were practically broke when they began to stay for months at a stretch with the Jonescus in London and Brussels, and later in a little Belgian château which Barbu had fixed up for them.

Soon the Rumanian Government got wind that on Jonescu's English country estate Carol was secretly meeting the envoys of Maniu. And Barbu Jonescu's sudden interest in aviation frankly alarmed them. Jonescu, their spies had found out, had a plane constantly waiting for him at Croydon, which could mean only one thing, the Rumanian Government rightly surmised: that this plane was to take Carol to Bucharest. On pressure from Queen Marie, the British Government advised Carol to leave England. So Carol had to make his return flight from Le Bourget instead.

The sums Barbu Jonescu spent in financing Carol's exile and his return to Rumania were said by some people to have gone into millions of dollars. Anyway, they sufficed, together with other reverses, to ruin Barbu Jonescu. Characteristically Carol never thought of paying Barbu back in money. Instead he gave him the Order of the Thorn, a high Rumanian decoration held by only eleven people.

Barbu Jonescu and his wife and daughter went to Bucharest to live, hoping that something might turn up in the shadow of the throne. For a time Barbu really had entrée to Carol, remained his trusted friend and belonged to the first camarilla, the one headed by the notorious Puju Dimitrescu. Then Barbu was thrown to the dogs, the way Carol and Lupescu threw most of their friends.

There was some excuse for this, really. Barbu committed the thousand and one tactlessnesses that go with poverty. He sold a watch Carol had given him to an impossible person who went around boasting that the King had given *him* the watch. Barbu used his friendship with the King in a desperate effort to regain some foothold in business life again. Finally he began to write Carol's biography.

The story of Barbu's biography of Carol is a typical Rumanian story. The Government authorized the writing of the book, on which an English journalist began to collaborate with Barbu. The Government even financed the work. But at the same time the secretary of the two authors was on the payroll of the Ministry of Interior and, of course, without Barbu's knowledge brought a copy of every chapter to the then Undersecretary of the Interior Titeanu. As Titeanu had feared, the book was sensational. The first chapter was titled "Marriage and Love" and was all about Carol's first marriage with the Hungarian Zizi Lambrino. The second chapter, called "Marriage without Love," was all on Carol's marriage with Queen Helen. The third chapter, "Love without Marriage" was on Carol and Lupescu. At this point Titeanu went into action, confiscated all copies, shipped the English co-author home, and took away, at a search in Barbu's home, all evidence of his friendship with the King and Madame, such as letters, photos, jewels, and bric-à-brac.

Barbu never quite understood what had been wrong about the biography and in spite of the King's ingratitude he still adored Carol and wished him no harm and never blackmailed him, as some people suspected. He thought Carol's love story beautiful, and his co-author, who knew the British market, told him every day that the book would be a best seller. So what could be wrong? However, what friendship and gratitude had not done with Carol, fear of embarrassment accomplished. Barbu now got a small pension and a job of sorts manufacturing boxes for Malaxa. And from time to time His Majesty would most graciously deign to ask Malaxa how Barbu was getting along. Carol did not go in for gratitude.

I never heard what Carol's horoscope was like, but it must be a most remarkable astrological chart if it really describes a king who possessed to the highest degree qualities which destined him for a royal success, and at the same time all the weaknesses which destined him for a royal flop. King Ferdinand, Carol's father, once put it this way: "Carol," he said, "is a very good boy, very intelligent, too. But he is like a Swiss cheese: he has so many holes."

These qualities destined Carol for royal success: first, his blood, which came from three of the greatest rulers and ruling families of Europe—Queen Victoria, the Russian Czar Alexander II, and the Hohenzollern. Second, the superb training for royalty which he had received from the strict first Carol of Rumania. And third, an excellent, cultivated mind and an unprejudiced intellectual curiosity rare with reigning princes. When, during his exile, Carol was thrown into the company of artists and writers, his natural eagerness to learn and understand enchanted these people, who otherwise had little use for run-away Balkan princes. Reading much, with the pedantic thoroughness which was his Hohenzollern inheritance, he was surprisingly well informed about the intellectual trends of the Western World. And exile itself, with all its vicissitudes, broadened his experiences.

There is no doubt that Carol, as he descended from the skies over Great Rumania in 1930, hoped ardently to make a good king for his people. When he arrived in Bucharest, looking like a demigod, tall, slender, elegant, and charmingly affable, his people forgot all about the divorce from Queen Helen and about the hated Jewish mistress for whom he had forsaken them. Such was their joy and relief at having their dream prince back that they knelt in the dust before him. Only a few short years later his people were so fed up with Carol that he scarcely dared show himself on the streets without elaborate police guards. Carol's weaknesses, the many holes in the Swiss cheese, canceled the effect of his good will, intelligence, capacity for work and his still considerable personal charm.

Though he was the first Hohenzollern king born in Rumania, Carol did not escape the strange fate which befell this essentially German dynasty in Rumania—they all went a bit haywire under this violent sun and the deep blue skies. They could not take it. They overdid everything, especially their greed for money. All three generations of Rumanian Hohenzollerns had a passion for wealth and were incredibly stingy besides, Carol more so than the others.

The King's key weaknesses besides his extraordinary greed for money, coupled with an extraordinary stinginess, were a violently suspicious and jealous temper, a streak of cruelty and disloyalty which shot up luxuriantly in the byzantine climate of Bucharest Palace intrigues. To the Rumanian people all these weaknesses were personified by one person. She was Elena Lupescu, who for more than fifteen years had shared Carol's destinies.

When in 1930 Maniu and his friends called Carol back, it was on one condition—that Lupescu stay abroad and that the affair be ended once and for all. Carol solemnly agreed to this condition; then, to the horror of the leaders who had arranged the coup, Lupescu stepped, so to speak, out of Carol's luggage. This flagrant breach of a solemn promise estranged his most fervent champions and marked the beginning of the ever-growing void which surrounded Carol.

The people took it even harder. They had hoped that Carol and Queen Helen would be reconciled and live happily ever after. Instead Queen Helen departed in a huff leaving the field to the other Helen.

Elena Lupescu—Duduja to the King—had been a beautiful girl with natural red hair, a skin of magnolia white, lovely hands, and a figure not bad but not graceful. For lack of money or lack of taste, or both, she was, in her first years with Carol, a mediocre and uninspired dresser. This changed, however. Lately her chic and sophistication made up for the waning bloom of youth. At times she would put on weight but dieted it down again. Rumor had it that Professor Voronoff, her cousin by marriage, had operated on her legs to make them slender. She dressed exquisitely, mostly in black Chanel dresses which brought out the white of her skin and the flame of her hair. She telephoned, it was reputed, every day from Bucharest to her dressmakers, milliners, and corsetières in Paris. Bucharestians added that these calls went over the telephone line of the Palace, and thus were made on the people's money.

There were many stories told in Bucharest as to how Carol met Duduja. One story had it that she was really out for King Ferdinand but was instead noticed by Carol. Another was that Carol met Lupescu at an officers' party when she was married to an obscure lieutenant in the army. The most intriguing version had it that Queen Marie's all-powerful favorite, Prince Stirbey, threw Carol together with Lupescu in an attempt to discredit him with the people. Or at least that he built the affair up as the great public scandal which led to Carol's exile. Carol hated Stirbey from early youth on and Stirbey knew that once Carol was king he would deal ruthlessly with him and his family. So Stirbey had good reasons to wish to get rid of him.

But the most interesting part of the story is that they met at all, so great is the abyss between this son of the noblest blood of Europe and the daughter of the ghetto in Yassy. Lupescu's grandfather on her mother's side was a Bessarabian rabbi. Her father, alternately described as a small manufacturer and as a small dealer in jewels, was very poor until his daughter became the Rumanian Pompadour. He lived in Bucharest until his death a few years ago, and his daughter used to see him every day. In order to please her, the camarilla had to pay him visits, too. Talking of his daughter and Carol, Papa Lupescu would cutely call them "the children," as if it was an ordinary case of daughter and son-in-law. And realizing the hate which engulfed his daughter, he would sigh and say, "Really, one should not blame the child for the company she is forced to keep."

Lupescu, it was said, was blatantly uneducated when she met Carol, but Carol, with the pedagogic streak inherited from his great uncle, was only too pleased to play Pygmalion. Lupescu was ambitious. In their exile Lupescu learned languages and everything a lady is supposed to know. She acquired a quiet, dignified, society manner, reserved, untalkative, and observant. She never developed much taste for the intellectual and the artistic, which may be one reason why her conversation and appearance always lacked a certain spark, a certain *douceur*. Another might be that her complete self-centeredness precluded all real warmth for anything outside herself. Come to think of it, Lupescu was rather a dull woman.

In a way Lupescu reminded one of "La Paiva," the great Paris demimondaine of the nineteenth century, as the Goncourts have described her in their *Journals*. At that time a cold, rather disagreeable woman with only the remains of a great beauty, La Paiva staggered the Goncourts by the admission that, at one juncture of her life, she had locked herself up in a room for two years doing nothing but just willing her destiny. One could imagine that Lupescu was this kind of woman, though her friends said that with the King she was kind and motherly, creating a friendly and *gemutlich* atmosphere in her little red brick house in the Avenue Vulpache. But this was no contradiction: the King was herself.

Hated as Lupescu was by the Rumanian people, she was never really isolated. There were always enough statesmen and diplomats who knew where their bread was buttered, and a good many society people, too, to fill her days. Prime Ministers and generals, society matrons and ambassadors appeared as petitioners at the house in the Avenue Vulpache. Only a few, like General Antonescu and the Princess Cantacuzino, ever really snubbed her. Until a few months ago Lupescu went out to dine at the Thierrys', the French envoys', and at some Rumanian houses. She did this rarely, spending most evenings with the King. Since the killings of the Iron Guardists she had completely stopped going to the theatre or dining at

Capsa's—both had become too dangerous. Day and night guards were posted before her house, but it was not true that she paid her visits to Carol hidden in a delivery truck, entering and leaving the Palace by the back entrance. Nor did she have any doubles. Lately she stayed much in the late Queen Marie's palace in Cotroceni or in one of Carol's country places, and the King used to come to her rather than she to him. Since the Bessarabian crisis he never let her out of his sight and she stayed at the Palace with him. Lloyd's would not have insured her life for a dime that summer.

Lupescu never talked politics with Carol, but indirectly, through Urdareanu (and before him through Puju Dimitrescu), her influence was omnipresent. She discussed people with Carol, and being of a suspicious and fickle nature transferred her swift likes and dislikes to the genuinely distrustful King, thus strengthening a dangerous weakness.

Lupescu's very existence in Carol's life tended to isolate him. In the beginning of his reign he tried to put her over with the court as his *maîtresse en titre*, as Louis XV had with Madame Pompadour. Lupescu appeared at official court events, but Carol was unable to put her over with the friends of Queen Marie and of Queen Helen. The consequence was that Carol held no court to speak of; there were no balls, drawing rooms, or concerts at the Palace any more, as in the times of Ferdinand and Carol I. More and more the King relied on small functions, stag most of the time, with the gentlemen of the Crown Council, high officials, and officers and occasional foreign diplomats.

This lack of social representation weakened the royal prestige with a society accustomed to brilliant court life headed by the beautiful Queen Marie. Society drew away from a king who refused to be the head and center of society, and increased the void around Carol.

The King began to live more exclusively with Lupescu and the notorious camarilla, and while the names of the camarilla changed it was always the same: a court marshal, a cabinet minister who knew how to flatter madame, a chief of the secret police, rounded out by the inevitable rich men. It was the most corrupt and most unscrupulous company which ever set about bleeding the people in the shadow of the throne, even in Rumania, which is saying a great deal, for Rumania had always been ruled by camarillas rather than by political parties or cabinets. Even Carol I had a camarilla, old men and women, who intrigued against the then "Young Court," dominated by the Crown Princess Marie. The Crown Princess, later Queen Marie, was in turn surrounded by a camarilla which was headed by Prince Stirbey. An extraordinarily handsome, tall, Rumanian aristocrat and a business genius, Stirbey belonged to the Bratianu clan and was for many years the Eminence Grise of Rumanian politics, the most powerful man in the country, and the most hated.

Still, compared to Carol's present camarilla under Urdareanu, Queen Marie's camarilla under Prince Stirbey appeared like shimmering knights out to make the good people of Rumania happy. They certainly had better style than the awful company which Carol dominated and, after all, they accomplished the Great Rumania and practically nobody was murdered under their rule, which was something. Carol's camarilla boasted figures like Gavrila Marinescu, the chief of police to whom every streetwalker in town was said to pay tribute, as well as every night club

and restaurant owner and who was said to be chiefly responsible for the Guardist killings; and Moruzov, the all-
powerful chief of the secret police who, people said, began
his career as a Russian spy, sold out to the Rumanians, became Carol's bodyguard and man of all dirty work. He too
was reputed to be in on the Guardist killings.

The most important man of the present camarilla was
Malaxa, the big industrialist. Of Greek descent, intelligent, incredibly devious, Malaxa played the whole political field, financing socialists and Guardists, pro-French
and pro-Germans, but since Hitler had come to power
veering cautiously towards the Germans and the Guardists. It was he who had tried to reconcile Carol with
Codreanu; it was he who was reported to cut the King
and Lupescu into his big business deals and transferred
their money abroad. It was he who contributed heavily to
Lupescu's household expenses, as both the King and
Lupescu were very stingy. At the poker parties at his house
the players, frequently including the King and Lupescu,
found 100,000 leis before every chair.

Indicative of the way the King and Malaxa operated
was the fashion in which they got rid of Max Ausschnitt.
This disagreeable, ugly, intelligent Jewish boy from
Galatz, who had created the Reschitza—the largest armament and steel trust in Rumania, comprising everything
from the output of ore to ready-made products, mostly
armaments—had been even closer to Carol and Lupescu
than had Malaxa. Only a few weeks before his fall, he
escorted Lupescu to the Bal des Millionaires, one of the
great social events of Bucharest. And suddenly he was in
jail on charges ranging from crimes against the exchange

law to fraud. Speculation ran high as to the real reasons for such sudden and complete disgrace.

One rumor had it that Lupescu was jealous of the beautiful young Madame Ausschnitt, with whom Carol was supposed to have had a flirtation. But another version, told to me by reliable source, appeared more plausible. Malaxa, so this version ran, at a visit in Berlin got written proof from his German friends that some Rumanian industrialists in their business deals with the Germans always added large sums supposedly destined for the King. This Malaxa brought to the King, who got very mad, not because his name had been used in disreputable context, but because he had never got the money. That is why Carol, according to my story, believing Ausschnitt one of these, had him thrown in jail, and how Malaxa had eliminated his fellow-tycoon.

Ausschnitt was offered an opportunity to leave the country but chose a trial, being angry at the camarilla and out for blood. His revenge fell flat, however, at least for the moment. The trial was held behind closed doors and nothing at all leaked out except that Ausschnitt was guilty and that he was being kept in a damp cell, chained to the floor like the Iron Mask—which picture rather appealed to the demimondaines in the lobby of the Athene Palace who said that Ausschnitt was the kind of man who made the girls return his presents when he tired of their charms —at least so the girls told me.

The camarilla got cuts on every Government contract; and the King himself was there with them, up to the neck. People said that it was Lupescu's Jewish greed which had had a contagious effect on the King, but here, too, she only strengthened an existing weakness. Carol's taste for money had already set tongues wagging in Potsdam when, before the world war, the young Prince served in a regiment there. His mother used to send him Rumanian rugs and embroideries to give as souvenirs to his comrades. Carol found it more profitable to sell them at auction. The poverty Carol suffered in exile strengthened his determination to make the most of his royal opportunities. Madame's instincts were not against this; moreover, she had a good head for business, so that after entering the royal business penniless ten years ago, financial circles estimated Carol's fortune to be £20,000,000. Carol was a big stockholder in every worthwhile company in Rumania and had large funds abroad. There was, people felt, something shocking about a king who got rich quick.

There was no evidence that Lupescu ever gave a damn for her country, except at times indirectly, inasmuch as she wanted Carol to make a successful king. Nor was there, on the other hand, evidence that Lupescu, as her enemies insisted, stuck to Carol only for his money. Lupescu has been a wealthy woman for years, with money safely invested in American banks. Had she been out for money she could have got out long ago. Almost anywhere her life would have been safer than in Bucharest. No matter what her sentiments for Carol in the beginning of their relations, she seemed to have become entirely devoted to him in the course of the years. This summer, when friends warned her to get out while the going was good, she insisted on sticking it out with Carol in Bucharest, saying they would only go together. The lady would have done better for Carol to get out, though. Even after the cession of Bessarabia, and even after Transylvania, her final exit, together with Urdareanu's might have turned the tide in Carol's favor.

Barbu Jonescu said Carol and Madame had been married in exile, shortly after his divorce from Queen Helen. According to German and Italian diplomats they had been married by Rumanian law on their return to Rumania. There was a story that Carol stayed with Lupescu because some seeress had prophesied that he would die when he let her go. There were many stories by which people attempted to explain Carol's loyalty to a woman who was no longer young but as embarrassing as ever. Carol, everybody knew, had a roving eye but always returned to Duduja, who did not seem to mind his escapades. *"C'est une artiste,"* the old Rumanian Excellencies would say and look knowingly wicked. "All of Carol's money is invested in her name," the Germans would say and look severe.

But sex and money were not enough to explain why two people, both cold, selfish, and fickle, hung together against all odds and at great sacrifice. One is tempted to believe that here was real love.

Yet in spite of her devotion to Carol, Lupescu certainly messed up his life. Not that Carol had ever stopped working with a sort of dutiful fury at being a king. He kept long hours, making it a point to see every document of importance, amazing everybody who worked with him by the thoroughness and originality of his marginal notes. And he had something to show: among other things a youth movement which was one of the best in Europe, a real capital, beautiful and on a large scale, which he had created from scratch in ten years.

The trouble with Carol was that the harder he worked at being king the more hopeless became the void in which he moved. He became too dictatorial for collaborators who were not yes-men. He jealously insisted on being the master of his country, the sole figure to whom his people owed everything, the sole figure they loved. This was the strangest thing about a king who unscrupulously enriched himself, surrounded himself with the most corrupt, played everybody against everybody else, was disloyal to all except to Lupescu and his son Michael: he still wanted to be loved by his people and be the source of all the blessings given them. Carol's jealousy about any other figure the people might love more than himself was as strong as his greed. It explained the persecution of the Iron Guardists and the hardness against his mother.

If one looked deeply into Carol's life one could probably trace the profound influence his mother had on him. Carol as a boy had loved this beautiful goddess, and when he discovered that she was only human, began to mix his love with hate. He never stopped being preoccupied by her personality, the love she could arouse in people's hearts in spite of her weaknesses, the immense influence she exercised on a whole generation. Many of the things Carol did in later life, he did to spite Queen Marie or to steal her thunder. His pro-Ally policy, for instance, was by way of stealing Queen Marie's thunder—only the Queen, with her uncanny sixth sense, was already very much aware of the Third Reich and ready to play ball with the Führer for all he was worth, when Carol was just at his policy of sanctions against Italy. Rumanian newspapers were forbidden to mention Queen Marie. But when she went to Switzerland, where Prince Stirbey, exiled by Carol, lived, editors got word from the Palace that Queen Marie was "visiting with Prince Stirbey." Carol hoped that Queen Marie's connection with the much-hated favorite would sour the people on her.

When at his mother's sixtieth birthday, the female organizations of the country planned a big celebration for the Queen, Carol put his foot down. All celebrations for his mother were to come from him and nobody else. She should have access to the people only through him, and the people whose destinies she had shared for almost fifty years should be allowed to love her only through him.

But, with all this, any $50-a-week American publicity man could have saved Carol's throne, even after the Vienna verdict—and could have saved Lupescu all along. Rumanians would say to this that Lupescu's Jewish origin created insurmountable odds against her because the Rumanian people, deeply antisemitic and deeply religious, could never forgive a Jewess for breaking up their King's home. But not even the slightest effort was made to present the lady in a more acceptable light. Her name, so unfortunately familiar in connection with graft and corruption, was never mentioned in connection with charity. In a country where poverty is so great and so universal it was not known that she ever gave a generous gift to the poor, the ill, or, lately, to the refugees from Bessarabia. Her name was never connected with art or science. Any American publicity man could have built up Lupescu as a clandestine Lady Bountiful who spent her spare hours establishing soup kitchens and kindergartens—certainly an improvement over the picture of a woman piling up money and practising witchcraft on the King.

As to Carol, there seemed to be no excuse for his losing

the throne unless he was sick and tired of the whole thing —an impression one was bound to get watching him handling himself in the crisis which began with the cession of Bessarabia. After the Bessarabian crisis Carol never appeared in public. During the tense weeks which preceded the Vienna verdict the Palace remained silent. Any American press agent could have drawn up a plan showing him how to prepare his people for this severe trial, how to make himself more appealing in his very helplessness. Instead, nothing was heard of the King except reports of a very small donation for the refugees from Bessarabia, counteracted by another report in the official *Monitor* to the effect that he had sold Queen Marie's Palace in Balcic to the community of Bucharest for a huge sum—a most objectionable deal in view of the imminent cession of this province.

The Rumanians, passionate, religious, and mystical, do not necessarily view national disaster in terms of politics. They were just as prepared to view a disaster in terms of sin and expiation. They only needed leadership, a king who included himself in this process of sin and expiation. Even after the Vienna award a fireside chat in Carol's beautiful radio voice would have done something to the people. But Carol did nothing at all. "How To Lose a Throne in Ten Easy Lessons" should have been written all over Carol's performance of these last two months.

> *Beware the Prince! For, he can never rob a man so completely that no knife is left to him to revenge himself.*
>
> MACHIAVELLI

8—ABDICATION

On the evening of September third there were no cars in the courtyard of Carol's Palace, and only on the third floor, where the court minister had his office, were the windows lighted. On the roof the Rumanian flag, now at half-mast because of Transylvania as well as Bessarabia, flapped in the mild breeze. People walked slowly through the Royal Square, faces and clothes making dim white splashes in the swift-falling dusk. They walked slowly that night because a spent, hollow feeling had taken the place of the passionate grief of the last few days. Gingerly the Bucharestians were trying to pick up the threads of their normal life.

Then suddenly a shot sounded near the Palace, and another, and a third. With each detonation a flash of light blazed up near the tall iron fence around the Palace, and somehow one got the impression after the last shot that something had fallen. The people walking in the Square ran toward the sound of the firing. From everywhere, seemingly, soldiers and police sprang up, blocking pedestrians from the Palace and ordering automobiles to detour around the Royal Square. Then all life died down on the Square; there were no more shots.

In the Athene Palace, where everyone jammed the windows facing on the Square, word spread that the gunshots in the Palace courtyard were part of a putsch engineered by Maniu's Peasant Party and the army, to oust Carol, and that already they had succeeded in seizing the telephone building and the radio station. This last seemed to be true, for all telephone lines were cut and the radio seemed to be dead. A threatening quiet hung over the city, a tension that seemed gradually to lessen only toward midnight when the telephone service came on again. Soldiers lined the walls of the Palace the night through, while others patrolled the sidewalks, and only the white-uniformed dignitaries who approached the Palace in their limousines were allowed to pass. At the Athene Palace people talked, but knew nothing; this was the most tantalizing kind of crisis, the sort about which one was not told a thing.

Next morning the papers, which everyone grabbed breathlessly, minimized the abortive putsch. No names or parties were given, but through the day it leaked out that the putsch had not been engineered by Maniu's Peasant Party and the army; this had been just one of the many false rumors in this rumor-ridden city. The putsch was by the Iron Guard. In the night the Guardists had also seized the telephone stations in Brasov and Constanza, and still held them. Clearly the Guardists felt their time had come. They were out to get Carol.

By noon word spread that the Gigurtu Cabinet—Carol's sop to Hitler—had resigned and that Antonescu had been called in to form a new one. It came as no shock to the Rumanians that Antonescu stepped from jail to the cabinet; in Rumania jail served so frequently as antechamber to the cabinet that no one got excited about it. But in other respects the person of the General now taking over the dominant role in the Rumanian political scene gave rise to all sorts of speculation.

Antonescu, everybody knew, had been raging mad about the cession of Bessarabia. The question was, what would the General, now that he was in power, do about Transylvania? Antonescu's position was not completely clear. He had friends and admirers among the Germans, and by the efforts of the German minister his imprisonment had been changed to *arrêt de domicile*, an infinitely pleasanter status. Still, this was not sufficient to sell Antonescu on collaboration with Germany, especially after the verdict of Vienna and since his up-bringing and connections had always inclined him toward France. It looked, people said, as though Antonescu would do a De Gaulle rather than a Pétain, would defy Germany and fight Hungary. He would have the army behind him and the Iron Guard. But what would the Germans do if Antonescu decided to fight? They would probably march in and establish a protectorate, which they undoubtedly could do in a few hours. At their legation the British were already packing their boxes.

For a few hours everything hung in the balance. At the cocktail hour in the lobby of the Athene Palace the odds on Carol's abdication grew higher as the minutes ticked off. Yet this abdication, which a whole people wanted, now seemed unimportant in the light of the events of the morning. What people wanted to know now was, what would Antonescu do? Would the General fight the Hungarians and thus provoke German interference, or would he form a strong military dictatorship which might satisfy the German cry for any strong government in the raw-material sphere?

By dinner time it seemed ominously as though Antonescu would not be a Rumanian De Gaulle. For it became known that he would keep Manoilescu, the man of the Vienna award, on as foreign minister, at least until the evacuation of Transylvania was completed. This act was indicative of peaceful intentions and the German journalists and diplomats who dined in the courtyard of the hotel looked cautiously pleased that evening. They were looking forward, they said, to an Antonescu dictatorship, provided the General was able to keep order. They were not sure whether the General would establish a military dictatorship, keeping the two important ministries—interior and war—himself and putting a few generals in the other ministries, or whether he would take the Iron Guard into the cabinet and make a mixed military and Guard cabinet. The British and Americans continued to hope against hope that Antonescu would form a cabinet with Juliu Maniu, the Peasant Party leader, and Georges Bratianu, head of the neo-liberals and young Michael's tutor. Anyway, the British and Americans consoled themselves, it would be impossible for the Iron Guard to have much influence in the new set-up. It was, they said, with the Iron Guard as it was with potatoes: their better part was under the earth. The thousand top men needed to fill the key positions had been killed. Now the Iron Guard was only riffraff.

That night there was another crisis-crowd in the Square, a quiet, good-natured, not-too-anxious one, waiting for the new cabinet to be formed. The person of Antonescu at the helm of the state had inspired confidence, for people knew he was an honest man. This was such an unusual and interesting feat for a public figure in Rumania that it amounted practically to a sensation. Beyond this, Antonescu was known as the prophet of the present disaster, scorned and mistreated by the King, and as a good hater who never forgave his enemies. People thought that by calling in Antonescu, Carol had called in his hangman.

Late that night came the first definite sign of crack-up in the Carol government. Sitting in the Athene Palace we learned that Urdareanu, Antonescu's arch enemy, had resigned as court minister. This was already almost as good as if the King had abdicated, for Urdareanu was the most powerful man in the country and, after the King, the most hated. Having disposed of Urdareanu, Antonescu asked the King to sign a series of decrees canceling the Constitution of 1938, which vested dictatorial powers in the King, and gave Antonescu these dictatorial powers. This Carol refused under violent protest, whereupon Antonescu said that he could not be responsible for Carol's safety; the Guardists were out to get him and would not relent unless they learned that in the future Carol's part in the government would only be window-dressing. The King raved, and shouted that Antonescu was committing high treason. Antonescu, the story is, answered quietly, "So far, Your Majesty, only one of us two has committed high treason," which was alternately interpreted as a reference to the trip of Carol's to Odessa in the world war in the uniform of a Russian officer when he secretly married Zizi Lambrino or, in a more general way, to Carol's behavior throughout the years of his reign.

Enraged, the King ordered Antonescu from the Palace and Antonescu marched off. But Lupescu, who sat listening in the next room through the whole stormy night, hurried to Carol and urged him to call Antonescu back. Pale, shaken, and humiliated, Carol told Antonescu he was prepared to sign the decrees.

Next morning the new decrees were published in the newspapers. They left Carol merely the right of amnesty and to give decorations. Antonescu was dictator. In the afternoon the Germans began to say: "The story is over, as far as Carol is concerned. He is rendered harmless and may as well stay on." The odds for abdication among the foreigners went lower and lower. Some people tried to get out of their bets by saying that this decree really amounted to abdication. But the Rumanians who knew their Carol said that Antonescu could never afford to leave him on the throne; as long as Carol was in the Palace, with Udurianu and Lupescu around, he would contrive to win ascendancy over the General. Antonescu, they said, knew this; and so did the Guardists.

At eight that evening, quite unexpectedly, the Gendarmes began to block all the street exits from the Royal Square. Nobody was allowed to go in or out of the hotel. A few moments later the Square was empty, except for the troops streaming by from all sides. Dead silence descended on the Square as the troops posted themselves in readiness before the Palace gate, the hotel, everywhere. Machine gunners lay on their stomachs all across the Square; and one of the big sky-blue tanks stood in the background. In five minutes the Square had acquired the menacing look of a modern civil-war scene in an expensive movie.

At the Athene Palace the Gendarmes went from room

to room ordering the blinds down, for protection. The Iron Guard, they said, was marching toward the Palace. If they got through, there would be shooting. Then suddenly the stillness was cut by the steps of marching feet, belligerent songs, a few shots. They came from the Boulevard Elisabetha, nearby, where a troop of Guardists tried to break through. One could hear them shouting in chorus: "Give us the King! Don't let him get out of the country with his money! Don't let him get out with Lupescu! Give us Udurianu!"

It sounded genuine; it *was* genuine. The Guardists were after Carol's scalp. Yet that night the Guardists were, without knowing it, marionettes dancing on General Antonescu's wire. For it was Antonescu who directed this civil-war scene tonight. His own part in it was complicated and apparently contradictory. On the one hand it was he who gave the Guardists a go-ahead for a march on the Palace. On the other it was he who organized the armed protection and defense of the same Palace.

What was the General's game? He wanted to force Carol to abdicate by demonstrating to him that the Guardists meant business, and that he could not answer for Carol's life. Carol, he suspected, accepted the humiliation of the decrees which reduced him to a puppet king only as a temporizing device to tide him over until the moment when he was again strong enough to take action. Such a risk Antonescu could not take with a prince mistrusted by all and connected with every misfortune which had befallen the country. He had to get rid of Carol for his own sake and the sake of Rumania. The only way to do this was to show that death was just around the corner. Carol was a coward and these dangers were real: the Guardists would not stand Carol on the throne any longer. So tonight's play was not entirely put up by the red-haired General after all. Only its timing—tonight of all nights—and the happy ending were by Antonescu. He did not really want the Guardists to get to the Palace or to have troops shoot at them. He knew that the shouts and songs were enough to convince Carol that his time was up.

We ate our dinner looking through the cracks of window blinds. There still came the shouts and songs of the Guardists, but they did not come nearer. For the first time I heard the Guardist song of the *Capitano*, which was to be heard so often in the months to come. Sad and fierce, the song is the most stirring revolutionary song of its kind.

Towards midnight the sound of Guardist songs and shouts from the Boulevard subsided. Machine gunners in the middle of the Square scrambled up from the asphalt and disappeared. Only the sky-blue tank remained with the troops guarding the Palace and the exit streets. Antonescu's demonstration for the King was over, and the whole third floor of the Palace was lighted now.

We hung out of the hotel window and watched the long limousines swing as so often before into the courtyard of the Palace, white-uniformed, black-coated passengers shadowy in the uncertain light. One of the limousines was the German minister's. He came to the Palace at 11 p.m. and at 3 a.m. was still there.

We learned next morning that Carol had abdicated. After the Guardist demonstration Antonescu had found it easy to make Carol understand that he could not answer for his life any more. The German minister had backed him up. Carol signed the abdication, so a gentleman of the Direction de la Presse told foreign journalists, at 4 a.m.

Characteristically, the hours before were chiefly spent on vigorous bickering about Carol's pension.

Everyone believed next day that Carol had left in the early hours of the morning. At the Direction de la Presse it was said that because General Antonescu could not answer for the ex-King's life for another hour, Carol had been spirited away to Constanza in a German legation car, escorted by the German minister. At Constanza Carol, joined by Lupescu and Urdareanu, would board his yacht, which was, incidentally, the same yacht on which Edward Windsor had made that famous holiday cruise with Mrs. Simpson. This plausible story was put out to deflect people's attention from an implausible reality. Actually, Carol, Lupescu, and Urdareanu stayed in Bucharest at Catroceni Palace for more than twenty-four hours after the abdication. Why, no one could figure, for it was an immense risk to take.

Even greater was the risk taken in leaving by train instead of by airplane. This train was a special one with a salon car for Carol and his companions, and it carried hundreds of pieces of luggage, among them famous works of art such as the Grecos which Carol I had acquired, and which, some people said, belonged to the state. As the train was slowly picking its way to the Yugoslav border on Saturday afternoon, it was machine-gunned by Guardists at its arrival at Temesvar. But instead of stopping the engineer put on speed and got away with a few unimportant holes. Carol, one story had it, ducked into a bathtub for shelter before the shots. And another story had it that he flung himself on Lupescu to protect her.

The adjutant who escorted the ex-King to Switzerland returned to Bucharest and told that the three refugees had been dejected and tired all along the trip and blamed each other in turn for everything that had happened. When finally Urdareanu began to attack Lupescu, Carol snapped at him: "Lay off her, for God's sake. Whatever she did, she could only do because of my weakness."

Yet it appeared that even in the hours of greatest vicissitude Carol faced his abdication as though it were a temporary nuisance. On the eve of his departure he jotted down on the menu of his presumably last dinner, "Auf Wiedersehen!"

Abdication Friday rose gloriously over Bucharest. The sky was very blue and the air had the dry cool quality of air in the high mountains. It was St. Michael's day. St. Michael was not only the Saint of the new King, but also the Saint of the Iron Guard. And today was very much the day of the Guardists, too.

At 10 a.m., when the crowds began to gather on the square, I could see the first green shirts of the Iron Guard, so long forbidden in Rumania. They must have been kept for years hidden in drawers and chests, waiting for Der Tag. The Guardists came marching in long columns. Priests in their black garb marched with them, and white-robed nuns, and youngsters in rags. It was a motley crowd, a young crowd, which had come to greet a young King. Singing the national anthem and *Capitano*, they drew up on the space between the bronze Carol and the Palace, and this time there was no police force to keep them away. Instead two greenshirts mounted guard at the Palace gate, together with the usual soldiers, and some of the youngsters climbed up on the tall iron fence. Shouts rose in urgent crescendo, *"Tareaska Regele Michael."*

After a time the glass door to the terrace of the middle wing was opened by lackeys, and the young King appeared, escorted by Antonescu and several ministers of the Gigurtu cabinet. The others kept in the background, while Michael stepped forth to the middle of the balcony and raised the arm in salute. He was very tall in khaki uniform, his young face set and unsmiling, giving the salute patiently again and again in a beautifully precise movement, looking handsome and pathetically lonely. The people broke into wild shouts and yells. All hands were raised and the national anthem rang out full and triumphant, miraculously dissolving all gloom and humiliation into new hope and enthusiasm.

To become King was no new experience for this boy of nineteen. In 1927, at the age of five, he had succeeded his grandfather Ferdinand in place of his father Carol, who had renounced the rights to the throne and was in exile. When the little child showed surprise at the servants suddenly calling him "Your Majesty," his mother told him, "It's just another nickname, darling."

Michael was proclaimed King in parliament then. Frightened by shouts and screams of deputies and senators acclaiming and cheering him, he all but crept into the black veils of his mother and whispered: "Why do they all scream so loud?"

"For you, Michael, to show you their love," Queen Helen whispered back.

"Mummy, tell them never to shout so loud for me again," he begged.

Did Michael thirteen years later like the screaming any better? One wondered. One wondered what this boy really thought of his people who seemed mad with joy and relief over him. Did he remember the times not long ago when the people gave his father similar ovations?

Michael adored the father who had lived closely with him so as to make up for the loss of his mother, for Carol had made a good father and a reasonable one, as far as this was feasible under complicated circumstances. By all standards the boy got an excellent education. Together with twenty-four others picked from all walks of life he went through the private equivalent of Junior College and had only a few weeks before taken his final examination. While Carol himself was brought up in the internationalist tradition of ruling houses in Europe he saw to it that the "Great Voivoda of Alba Julia"—this was Michael's title as crown prince—was first and last a Rumanian. Even Carol's enemies admitted grudgingly that he did an intelligent job in bringing up the future King of Rumania. Of course, the boy was torn apart in his feelings, as children of divorce are the world over. Michael spent his vacations with his mother in Florence or Venice and probably wished that his parents would get together again. But habit and a wide range of common interests attached him more and more to his father.

Michael enjoyed comparative liberty. He could be seen driving up the Chaussée in his roadster at breakneck speed alone or in the company of the Malaxa children. The Malaxa boy was his closest chum, and he was devoted to the Malaxa girl, a pretty thing about his own age. Rumor had it that Lupescu had engineered this friendship between the Crown Prince and Malaxa's daughter so as to strengthen her hold on everyone concerned. Anyway, young Michael had had as good a time as a boy who had been made King at five and whose parents were divorced could have. That is, until the night before. . . .

Then Michael went practically on his knees before General Antonescu to let him go with his father, and got so distracted that even the severe General took pity on him. But Dr. Fabrizius raised objections. Hitler, he remembered, was very keen on preserving the dynasty in Rumania. Finally they decided to put a phone call through to the Führer and hear what he had to say. They could not reach Hitler; instead they got Ribbentrop, who said, "Nothing doing. The little one must stay."

Later General Antonescu made a public statement to the effect that in the night Madame Lupescu, appearing dramatically on the scene of the negotiations, had declared that Carol and she would leave with Michael or not at all. This Antonescu interpreted as an attempt at blackmail and as a devilish scheme to rob the Rumanian people of their rightful King. Such an interpretation would seem rather harsh. Madame was very fond of the boy she had known from early childhood and who played such a large part in Carol's life. People close to the court used to say that Michael turned to Duduja when he had tough going with his pedagogical father and that Duduja indulged him. So it seemed plausible that in this extreme emergency Michael turned to Duduja for help and that she acted out of pity for the boy and because she knew how miserable it would make the father to leave him behind.

Michael was still saluting patiently and beautifully with the roars of his people rising enthusiastically up to him. His people for the moment had forgotten all about the disaster and terrible losses they had suffered and were simply beyond themselves with joy to be rid of Carol and what he stood for—and to have a new King. From time to time Michael's other hand went quickly up to his eyes, probably to wipe a tear away. Then he turned and, followed by Antonescu and the ministers, disappeared into the quiet Palace.

9—REGINA MAMA

Sunday morning, ten days after the abdication, Queen Mother Helen entered Bucharest. For her arrival the Royal Square was covered with three-colored flags and streamers traveled down the façades of the buildings. The Square itself was lined with people: peasants in their white Sunday best and their women dressed in apple-green, raspberry, rose, or lemon-yellow embroidered splendor, looking for all the world like vari-colored candy sticks; the Knights of St. Michael in their long white capes with the long crosses; the city officials, morning-coated and high-hatted; and the nuns in their chaste white veils. The Square that morning looked like the dream of a Hollywood director gone technicolor mad.

For hours the Guardists marched by, thousands of them winding an unending stream of green. For hours soldiers marched, too, a steady stream of muddy brown. For hours the air rang with the National Anthem and Guardist songs, and with the rolling of drums.

And now the orthodox clergy in golden surplices and dalmatics in sharp green brocade marched down the Calea Victorice on their way to the Cathedral. As they came, the cannons in the city boomed forth to tell that

187

the Queen Mother and Michael, who had met her at the frontier, were leaving the train. Presently the air was filled with silent expectancy and everybody looked in the direction from which the royal party was to come. The cheering came nearer and nearer and the hussars of the Fourth Rosciaris galloped by with their high busbys. They were Queen Helen's old regiment and rumor had it that its horses had never got enough fodder in these last ten years, by way of punishment. Then the air reverberated with cheers and the fore-riders with white aigrettes on their helmets came galloping down the Calea Victoriei. And at last the gilded carriage, drawn by four horses and covered with roses, was here for one moment and gone the next.

The Regina Mama, a small chic toque of pink flowers over a delicate profile, bowed to the right and to the left, a narrow, white-gloved hand acknowledging the enthusiastic salutes and cheers with a simple but superbly done gesture which would have enchanted Marcel Proust as being one of the few professional secrets of royalty. A slender shoulder outlined in a dark printed silk brushed against the khaki shoulder of the handsome sulky-looking King, and they were gone, while the cheers faded away in the tolling of bells which accompanied the royal party on its way to the Cathedral.

No princess could have fewer illusions about the risky business of being a queen than Helen of Greece, daughter of Constantine, King of Greece, three times exiled and dead in exile; granddaughter of Georges I, King of Greece, assassinated at Salonica; sister of the twice-exiled King Georges II of Greece; niece of the dethroned Emperor of Germany; second cousin of the massacred Czar of Russia; abandoned wife of the twice-exiled King Carol.

Yet the dynastic troubles the Princess had seen were nothing compared to her domestic misfortunes. Her marriage had started off with high hopes. Young, handsome and charming, there was no reason why these two great grandchildren of Queen Victoria should not live happily ever after. True, the marriage had been arranged by Queen Marie chiefly in order to wean Carol from his passion for his erstwhile wife, Zizi Lambrino, yet there was evidence that Carol soon held something more than warm affection for his bride. "My very-much-in-love son" was how Queen Marie referred to the bridegroom in newspaper interviews, and according to Carol's own remark at the time of the betrothal, Helen "has considerable understanding for my battered heart and shares completely my views of life."

But in spite of such good signs, and the birth of Michael, the marriage for some reason went quickly on the rocks. For awhile Zizi Lambrino again loomed on Carol's horizon, then there were less important ladies—and finally there was Lupescu.

Opinions about Queen Helen's handling of the Lupescu affair varied greatly. The same people who took the meeting of Lupescu and Carol as a plot cooked up by Prince Stirbey in order to further his own ends felt that Helen never gave Carol a chance. If Helen, they argued, had not fallen hook, line, and sinker for Stirbey's plot, she could have had Carol back. He had even asked her to come with Michael to Paris and join him in exile. The same people also blamed Helen for leaving Bucharest at Carol's return with Lupescu in his luggage. After all, they put it, she was the Queen and should have put the King's mistress in her place. By leaving Bucharest she practically delivered Carol to Lupescu on a silver platter.

The Rumanian people at large did not share these views.

They had taken to their hearts this young forsaken princess who led a difficult and lonely existence between the
intrigues and affairs of altogether too many crowned female in-laws, this mother of their little King, who had
never been a Queen. Now more troubles faced the Queen
Mother. For all General Antonescu expected of her was
to be a severe governess to the young King.

Michael in the short days of his reign had put up a sort
of sullen resistance which Antonescu found trying. The
young King missed his papa, detested his job. The night
after his father left, he asked the General whether he
could have the young Malaxa boy stay with him at the
large resounding Palace, which seemed so terribly empty
after his father's departure. Antonescu curtly refused; to
him nothing seemed less desirable than a close companion-
ship between the young King and the son of Carol's evil
spirit. He did not wish to have to cope with a new camarilla. But the General's "No" and other evidence of the
severe new order to which he intended to submit the
Court, stiffened Michael's disgusted resistance. When the
General wanted him to talk over the radio, Michael refused. He would not, he declared, talk over the radio until
the vile newspaper attacks on his father were stopped.
Even Queen Helen, asked by the General to return immediately to the country, to take up her rightful place at
the side of her son, had made the condition that the attacks, so detrimental to the dynasty, should be stopped.
And the Queen took more time than was expected to
leave Italy where she had made her home these last ten
years, as if hesitant to give up the very gracious way of
private living which she had built up for herself.

Now the tolling of the bells died away and the Royal

Party had entered the Cathedral. Soon the Holy Mass began, heard on the streets by loudspeakers. On the Square and streets as far as one could see people knelt down for prayer: soldiers and Guardists and peasants and the guards before Carol's sprawling white Palace and the taxi drivers all scrambled down from their seats and knelt. People cried as they crossed themselves and those who did not cry were visibly moved. The little English girl in the window next to mine said, "My governess had told me that people get very wicked in a revolution, cutting each other's heads off and that sort of thing. But it was just a fib to frighten me. Revolution is very much like church, isn't it?"

The first act of the Rumanian revolution, when Antonescu stepped into Carol's place, had really been by way of religious revival. General Jon Antonescu—or, as he was now called, the Conducatore, which is the Rumanian for leader—had done an extraordinarily neat job so far. His radio and newspaper proclamations and public addresses were given in the monosyllabic language of the soldier and the peasant, a soothing language which went right to the hearts of simple people, and at times reached an almost Biblical emphasis and beauty. What Antonescu said, and the way he said it, seemed to belong definitely to a feudal Slavic and half-oriental world rather than to the Latin world. Such language had not been heard in modern Rumania except in the utterances of the Iron Guard, and it appealed to the imagination of the people. In a week Antonescu had lifted the spirit of the country from the blackest despair to a new confidence in its destiny, recasting a sense of loss and humiliation into new hope and self-reliance. It bordered upon the miraculous, for he had to do it without any help from events.

While the Hungarians were swarming over the ceded part of Transylvania, while the cars of Rumanian officials and other refugees still choked the roads to Sibiu and Brasov, the cession of the southern Dobrudscha to Bulgaria was signed without much ado. The valiant heart of Queen Marie, exiled from its last resting place in Balcic, traveled northward. Yet, discouraging as all this remained, the Rumanians had been happy during this first week under Antonescu.

It was not only that they were pleased to be rid of Carol and Lupescu and thought themselves at the beginning of a new era, but in masterly fashion the General had played on the religious mysticism and nationalism so peculiar to his countrymen, and on their readiness to view national disaster in terms of sin and expiation rather than in terms of bad politics. Thus he had begun his revolution with a Sunday of Atonement following on the heel of Carol's abdication. On that day at 11 a.m. every Rumanian, in accordance with a proclamation by Antonescu, had knelt down wherever he was to expiate for his country's sins and to pray to the martyrs who had suffered and died for a strong, pure Rumania. Such religious demonstrations had taken place all week long, and the return of the Regina Mama was their climax. For to this mystically religious people the return of the much-wronged Queen, who in the popular imagination was the personification of Good —in the same way in which Lupescu was the personification of Evil—symbolized in an eminently gratifying way the purification of national life and divine forgiveness for their dynasty's and their own sins. . . .

When, a little later that Sunday morning, the Queen
Mother and her son drove to the Palace through the tolling of the bells and immense cheers—in an open motor-
car this time—General Antonescu stood up in a car all by
himself and received tremendous cheers, too.

These cheers came from everybody, but most of all from
the green-shirted Guardist crowds which lined the streets
and the Square. For this Sunday, September fifteenth,
when the Rumanians had awakened to the happy expecta-
tion of the Regina Mama's return, they had also awakened
to General Antonescu's proclamation of a Guardist state.
Thus life began for the Guardists this morning and they
were happy and grateful to the General.

To the last moment British and American newspaper-
men had clung to the hope that the General would base
his government on the army and on collaboration with
Juliu Maniu and Georges Bratianu, who still had a great
following in Rumania. Yet it was in the cards from the
beginning that Antonescu could only rule with the Iron
Guard. Even if he had preferred to rule with the army,
this was for the moment out of the question. An army
can afford to be beaten and still remain a decisive force
in the state, as one could see in the Germany of the
Weimar Republic. But an army could not afford to do
nothing on two occasions of large-scale national emergency without losing its prestige. This was what had
happened to the Rumanian army in July and August 1940.
Thus, devoted as the army was to General Antonescu, it
was not sufficiently strong a basis on which to build his
regime, which precluded a purely military dictatorship at
least for the time being.

Considerations of foreign policy were against combin-

ing with Juliu Maniu and Georges Bratianu. Maniu, because of his long pro-Allied past, and Bratianu because of
his violent new anti-Axis sentiments, the result of the
Vienna award, were suspect to the Nazis. Their presence
in the new cabinet would have presented serious obstacles
to the road of strict collaboration with the Axis on which
the General had decided, in the hope of saving at least
the independence of Rumania.

So everything seemed to point to ruling with the Guard.
Nor was this only because the abdication of Carol and
Antonescu's own coming-to-power were largely due to the
menacing shadow of the Guard and because Antonescu
owed the Guardists a debt of gratitude for their support.
It was much more important that the Guard at the
moment was the strongest force in the country. This
party, which had lived underground for several years, and
had lost its entire élite, held a miraculous attraction for
the youth of the country. In these last ten days the flow of
would-be members to the newly set-up party centers had
been such that the membership lists had to be closed.
Though many of these new followers of the Capitano were
opportunists, it was evident that the sufferings which the
movement had had to undergo and the martyrdom of its
leaders made it almost irresistible. Nothing sells a revolutionary party like martyrdom, especially to a mystical people like the Rumanians.

Another advantage of collaboration with the Guardists
was that they were staunchly pro-Axis, blaming the verdict
of Vienna on Carol's double-crossing policy, and more
anti-English than Hitler, so that General Antonescu could
feel safe in this direction. Yet it would be a mistake to
think that the Germans had insisted on the establishment

of a Guardist regime, for they had not. Eternally worried about the quiet in the raw-material sphere, official Germany was rather afraid of these young Guardists' revolutionary zeal. Even the *nazissime* Nazis, while believing that a fascist regime in Rumania with a vested interest in the German victory would have its advantages, candidly doubted the ability to rule of these left-overs of the Guardist élite. However, realizing that at this juncture of the game there was nothing else to do, the Germans crossed their fingers and hoped for the best—an attitude which, while not running true to expected Nazi form, they adopted more often than not. It was a sort of uneasy wait-and-see attitude, part of their muddling through.

So Antonescu, after temporizing for ten days under the pretext that the former Gigurtu government should wind up the Transylvanian affair, but in reality because he was still haggling with Horia Sima about the Ministry of Interior, key ministry in any revolution, finally came through handsomely with a Guardist state. The General himself was the leader and Horia Sima the vice-president. And the Guardist Party with Horia Sima as commandant was the only recognized party.

A new cabinet was established which was preponderantly Guardist, but with a sprinkling of military men and experts. The only survival from the Gigurtu cabinet was Leon, the minister of economics, a concession to Dr. Neubacher, who had made it clear that he could not bear to explain the German economic theory all over again. Horia Sima had not got the Ministry of Interior, which reassured the bourgeoisie—but mistakenly so, for it had gone to General Petrovicescu who, it later turned out, was entirely the man of the Iron Guard and went through thick and thin for Horia Sima. But this important dénouement was kept for the last act of this tragic revolution.

The noblest Rumanian names were among the new Guardist dignitaries, such as the new Foreign Minister, Prince Michael Sturdza, a career diplomat and former minister to Copenhagen who had lost his job for his Guardist sympathies and whose wife had even been put into prison. A Ghyka—with a "y," which for some reason was ever so much more fashionable than a Ghika with only an "i"—became chief of the state police. A Grecianu became minister to Berlin. There were many more Rumanian aristocrats who got jobs with the Guardist state, which showed how many of the so-called best people had been followers of the Capitano.

Often in the course of the next weeks I looked at the gigantic woodcuts of the Capitano which, put before some background of green, decorated the background of the big Guardist demonstrations. These words were always written below the Capitano's picture: CORNELIU ZELEA CODREANU PRESENT. And indeed at these demonstrations, attended as they were by bemedaled Rumanian generals and ministers, and by emissaries from Hitler, Mussolini, Franco, and the Emperor of Japan, nobody was quite so present as the dark-haired young man who died at the age of thirty-nine, with the black fiery eyes and the happy smile, who used to wear the thick white linen shirt of the peasant. I know of no other political movement so completely dominated by a figure from beyond the grave as the Guardist movement. In the imagination of the Rumanian people Codreanu stood as a martyred prophet and as the real leader of their revolution.

While thus the Capitano still dominated the Guardist

scene from beyond, little Horia Sima, with his long black mane and his small quick eyes, ruled as his vicar-on-earth. Horia Sima never pretended to wield power on his own steam, but made it clear that his authority rested on divine mandate. Which was smart of him, for actually in the Capitano's lifetime Horia Sima never belonged to the top rank of Guardist leadership. However, he was the top of what was left after practically the entire élite of the movement had been killed off.

Yet from the beginning Sima's "divine mandate" was seriously contested by the Codreanu family, father and two brothers. Codreanu père was a former high school professor, a wild-eyed, red-faced, long-mustached old man, clad in the white linen shirt of the Rumanian peasant, and not a very convincing figure. Still, he was the father of the dead leader, and when he said "My son said," of course it carried weight. Codreanu père was a wily old gentleman. He ventured his little "my son said" at highly psychological moments and let them explode as bomb-shells around Horia Sima's ears. The day before the establishment of the Guardist state the old man gave an interview to the effect that the Capitano never wanted the Guardist movement to come to power before it was well organized and strong, neither of which it could be after years of underground existence. This crack was especially directed against Horia Sima, and was violently resented.

Old Codreanu's game never became quite clear. Maybe he wanted power for himself. Maybe he wanted the power for one of his sons. Maybe he just wanted to be a nuisance. Anyway, it was clear that there existed at least two distinct Guardist groups when the party came to power: the

one around Horia Sima and the other around the Codreanu family. Even then there was already a rumor about
a third group, said to be communistic and terroristic, but
nobody could tell anything definite about this group,
either as to its size or as to its influence or leadership.
It all went to prove that the movement was strong but
not united in its leadership when it came to power and
that Horia Sima faced opposition, or at least competition,
in a party in which he never really was the leader but
only the commandant.

When the Regina Mama had disappeared into Carol's
white unfinished Palace, which she had never seen until
today, the important-looking limousines once more swung
into the Palace Courtyard and once more the white escarpined lackeys opened the door to uniforms and morning
coats as in the crisis-ridden days which ended Carol's
reign. But this time the dignitaries brought their ladies,
for it was an elegant occasion, with the Queen Mother
receiving the congratulations of officials and the diplomatic
corps.

I did not know then that this was the last time that I
would see life centering around the Palace, but it was.
From now on the people of Bucharest would not watch
the lights in the third floor any more to check up on their
King, nor would they count the limousines in the courtyard to see whether the Crown Council was meeting and
big political events were going to break. From now on nobody bothered about Carol's white unfinished Palace—not
even the crane before the raw red brick annex. General
Antonescu found that there was more urgent work to do
than building royal palaces. Antonescu, too, discouraged

the Queen Mother from reviving a court life at serious times like the present, and from forming a camarilla of her own. The poor Queen began to live a dull life, managing her handsome sulky boy, who smarted under the General's severe regime and longed for his father and the good times Duduja had given him.

Once at noontime the Queen Mother, flanked by Antonescu and Michael, strolled up the Calea Victoriei, just the three of them, looking at the shop windows. They made a pleasant enough picture: the pretty slender woman in a beautifully made blue striped suit and a little blue sailor hat, between the two good-looking officers. This picture was by way of demonstrating the difference between the new and the old regime, for Carol during the last years would never dare to set foot on the street without a police cordon. It was also by way of demonstrating that the Conducatore and his King and the King's mother were just one happy family. The General, contrary to Carol, did not need a fifty-dollar-a-week publicity man; he had all the little tricks at his fingertips.

But anybody who saw Michael on that occasion observed the muscles working continuously around his sullen mouth, as if he could hardly suppress his contempt and rage, probably for the General who forced him to go on with the show, and for the cheering crowds which, he knew, might heap dirt on him tomorrow as they did on his father.

The royal family resided in Sinaia most of the time that autumn, and at the end of November the Queen suddenly left for Italy. It appeared that she too, like poor Frau Dr. Fabrizius before her, had succumbed to the temptations of Neumann's in Brasov, the smartest dress shop in Rumania, but Jewish. Also, needing treatment for her eyes, she had insisted on seeing her Jewish eye specialist. Her sudden departure was interpreted as a gesture of protest against Horia Sima's reproaches on this score. It might also have been a gesture of protest against the tactless way the Rumanian newspapers dealt with the Greek side of the Greco-Italian war, so dear to her heart; but it might just have been that she needed a little change after the boredom to which she was condemned in her life as Regina Mama of Rumania. Helen's sudden departure made quite a splash at the time, but she returned before Christmas and stayed.

Carol's Palace remained quiet at daytime and dark at night. Political interest retreated from the Palace, to the Presidency, further down in the Calea Victoriei where General Antonescu worked and even slept in a small room next to his office—not even taking time out for his meals, so that Madame Antonescu had to carry him his food— and to the squares and streets where the Guardists held their gigantic demonstrations and where their motor-cycled police squads shot by on some awful raid; and to the cemeteries where the Guardists exhumed and reburied their martyrs; and to the prisons which had become so crowded that the surplus could be absorbed only by whole-sale murder.

The return of the Queen Mother to Bucharest ended the first act of the Rumanian revolution. It was to be expected that, once these frustrated little Guardists were in the saddle, they would not be content with expiating the sins of the former people by prayer alone. Religious revival could not possibly satisfy their long pent-up hate and lust for revenge. They would not stand long for a *revolu-*

tion à la pastorale, a revolution "which was like church,"
as the little English girl had put it. There was bound to
be violence and bloodshed.

So while the Square was still ablaze with the gay three-
colored flags gleaming in the sun, Jews and "the former
people" already began to brace themselves for such long
nights-of-the-long-knives as the greenshirts might choose
to have. It was obvious that one could not call in the most
cruelly persecuted nationalist movement in Europe, hungry
young men who had seen all their leaders and many of
their comrades brutally murdered, and still have everything nice and respectable.

10—BLOODLESS REVOLUTION

Revolution must be consummated as quickly as possible. No smart revolutionary leader suppresses bloodshed until it rises to an evil and long-drawn-out crescendo, but rather permits the revolution its night- or nights-of-the-long-knives in the beginning, knowing that the sooner revenge is satisfied the quicker life settles down to normal, and that this procedure costs less blood in the long run.

This seems a callous thing to say, and I personally dislike taking my revolutions raw; for that matter I should prefer to live in a world altogether without revolutions. But as revolutions seem to be as unavoidable as birth and death and love, I like them at least done in a technically flawless manner.

There are revolutions which can do without a program of immediate and tangible revenge because the winners find bread and circuses at the end of the road or because the suffering en route is comparatively little. But when a persecuted, decimated nationalist movement is lifted to the saddle, human nature has decreed that explosions of hate and violence are unavoidable and the best thing to do is to have done with bloodshed at the start.

This point became clear to all those who watched the Guardist revolution in Bucharest. It began too respectably and ended up by drowning the country in a flood of blood and terror.

The trouble with this Guardist revolution was that Antonescu did not make up his mind in time to deflower it. Clever politician though he was, he knew nothing of revolutionary dynamism and was afraid that the Germans would make a pretext of any violent happenings to interfere with Rumanian independence. So he tried to kid the Guardists along by slow legal measures against the culprits of yesterday, whom the Guardists wished to see burned at the stake, and gave genteel demonstrations instead of violently absorbing fun. It was like feeding tigers on broccoli.

As to the Germans, whose program for quiet in the raw-material sphere was considerably endangered by this badly done, long-drawn-out revolution, they watched from the sidelines, doing nothing and saying indecisively that a "revolution needs to run hot," which meant that one had to let the revolution pick up its own appropriate speed and intensity as it ran along. And while there may be some wisdom to the German attitude, their do-nothing policy jeopardized at least temporarily their chief objective in Rumania, quiet in the raw-material sphere.

My first inkling of the technical flaws of the Guardist revolution came while I stood in line to see Lupescu's house, which the Guardists had thrown open to the public.

An oversized bird cage stood in the little courtyard of the red brick villa in the Avenue Vulpache—the kind of

bird cage you see in zoos. This one was of brass and looked
very new. The door of the cage was open and the cage
itself empty. It was the Guardist way of saying the bird
had flown.

A hungry-looking greenshirt waiting in the line before
the notorious house looked grimly at the cage and mut-
tered, "Would it not be fine to have *her* carried through
the streets in a cage stripped for all to see?" His colleagues
agreed fervently. "They should never have let her leave
the country alive."

During the next few months I often thought of this
snatch of dialogue, and that having Lupescu carried
around in a cage or some such strident and unsavory
amusement in the first days of the Guardist revolution
would have saved much terror and bloodshed later on.
Not that I wished any evil on the lady, but from the point
of view of revolutionary technique what the Guardists
really needed was some fun. Instead, the nearest they got
to having fun was a look inside Lupescu's house.

The Guardists borrowed a leaf from the Bolshevik book
and had opened the Lupescu house for sightseers, taking
twenty leis from outsiders and nothing from party members, school children, and other privileged groups. The
Bolsheviks had done the same with the Nicholas II villa
in Tsarskoye Seloe, presenting it as Exhibit A of the former people's way of life. The Czar's dingy villa had had
nothing royal about it, but looked like the house of a
well-to-do family with a very sick boy, whose braces and
medicines still filled the shelves of the nursery. One never
knew what the Bolsheviks tried to prove by showing this
modest, somewhat stuffy home; certainly not the wanton
splendors of the murdered autocrat. Rather it showed a

sense of insufficiency and distrust of his power which prompted the Czar to camouflage his inherited grandeur behind petit bourgeois contentment.

What the Guardists tried to prove by exhibiting Lupescu's villa was evident from the excited newspaper stories describing "priceless" silks, laces, and brocades and the "unique" perfumes and soaps by which the scarlet woman had surrounded herself while the people starved.

From the street the villa in the Avenue Vulpache by no means gave the impression of luxury. It was the kind of one-family house you find in any American middle-class suburb, but sullen looking and not too well kept up. Two-storied and narrow, lack of architectural beauty chastely hidden by ivy, it was dwarfed by newer and more elegant villas all around it. Lupescu's was a dingy place, which, one could see from the smallish windows, must be dark inside.

It *was* dark inside, and not luxurious at all. Walking through the little dingy first floor, crammed with indifferent furniture and bric-a-brac like a second-hand furniture shop, this exhibit of the sins of the former regime really proved only one thing,—that sin did not pay. Madame Pompadour would have turned in her grave could she see what her profession had come to. Here was the house of the most successful royal mistress of the 1930's, and a discouraging place it was.

The green-shirted guide led the way first through a number of little salons. In one of them he stopped, turned solemnly around to his flock and intoned, "This is the room where Elena Lupescu used to sleep with Puju Dimitrescu." Taking in the room, which looked as disconsolate as a rainy Sunday afternoon, an outsider felt sympathetically that such was probably the best use one could make of it. But the greenshirts, who had never seen an issue of *House and Garden,* and were devoid of any sense of humor, were grimly impressed with the combination of red velour and extra-illegitimate sin.

True, Lupescu had a few good badly hung paintings, said to be "stolen" from a state museum. There were a few pieces of very good jade, said to have belonged to the collection of Queen Marie, and among the mass of commonplace bric-a-brac were one or two amusing eighteenth-century pieces in china, with little pornographic twists. Madame also went in heavily for ikons covered with silver or gold, except for the saint's painted faces and hands, and for a small collection of Bibles, old and new testaments, in the midst of a library which chiefly consisted of French mystery stories. The Guardist guide specially pointed out the David's Star on the old testaments, conveying the impression that this proved Madame's close connection with the authors of the Protocols of Zion.

Nowhere was the house better than indifferent, and even this distinction was only achieved in the so-called studio and in the bedroom. The studio was a little room with light wood furniture in modern-art style and a life-sized portrait of Carol in mufti, one hand patting a Pekinese and the other hand holding a long black cigaret holder. In the studio the guide had a field day. Here on the floor was a heap of black, green, red, and white jewel-cases with the gold-pressed names of the great jewelers of the Rue de la Paix and the Place Vendôme on their lids. Their beds of velour and silk still showed the imprints of pearl necklaces, diamond parures, brooches, clips, and rings. The guide intoned again, "This is what remains of the jewels which Carol bought with the tears and the sweat of the Rumanian people for Elena Lupescu." Everyone looked very grim, except the ladies in the party who looked wistfully envious.

"And here . . ." the guide made an eloquent gesture in the general direction of a bedroom, and left the visitors to their own thoughts. The bedroom was in conventional French taste. In speculative silence all eyes went to a wide upholstered bed covered with gray silk. There were a few good Empire chairs, said to be a present from Professor Voronoff, and many photos on tables and chests, most of them of Madame herself: walking in a park in a summer dress and a wide hat, with her father and friends, with the King in a white car before the background of the Exposition of Paris a few years ago. On the table beside the bed was a telephone with several buttons. This was the direct line to the Palace. The buttons read *Studio, Office, Bedroom*—one read *Bath*.

Unlike the family of the late Czar, who had to leave in haste and could take nothing along, Madame or her maid had done a thorough job of packing. Wide closets yawned emptily except for a few shoe-trees and hangers. Only a green silk dressing gown still hung on the door to the bathroom, which was done in green. The hungry little fascists were fascinated with the splendors of this green bathroom, but except for a lovely green marble bidet with gilded taps there was nothing one could not buy at Sears Roebuck.

I was very curious about the much-advertised "unique" perfumes and soaps, and examined the cabinets in the bathroom with great care. There were still half-filled or empty bottles and pots of Elizabeth Arden's cosmetics and

a few boxes of Guerlain soaps, but there was nothing ex-
travagant about them. The only puzzling item was a staggering amount of alum. It looked as if the lady had lived
in the deadly dread that Hitler might buy up all the alum
in the world, so bought it up herself. What she did with
all this alum aroused much speculation among foreign
journalists. In medical dictionaries one could read that
alum had many uses and was for its astringent qualities
known as an arcanum by the ladies of the seventeenth
century.

When the Guardists first entered Lupescu's house, they
found the last practical joke Lupescu played on Rumanian
society: a large box filled with letters, in the middle of
her bedroom. It was a bitter joke, this, for in these letters
from the greatest ladies and gentlemen of Rumania, the
writers fawned in the most abject terms upon "Darling
Duduja." One internationally known Rumanian princess
even went so far as to address Lupescu as *"Ma souveraine,"*
going on to say that "the moment today when you allowed
me to kiss your hand was the happiest of my life." And
one high dignitary of the former regime addressed her as
"Your Majesty," following up with assurances that he had
only one wish in this world, namely, to see her crowned
as the rightful Queen of Rumania. These letters, now in
the hands of the Guardists, hung over Rumanian society
like the sword of Damocles, their existence being specif-
ically painful to some ladies and gentlemen who were
now making a frantic effort to align themselves with the
new order, professing a complete horror of the "dirty
Jewess." Madame certainly had left this box behind inten-
tionally, knowing very well that these opportunistic little
notes made the authors eligible for the twilight of the gods.

This twilight of the gods was in full swing anyway. On the Chaussée, Bucharest's fashionable quarter, there were guards before every second house, which signified that the owner was under police surveillance pending investigation as to the ways and means by which he afforded his house. The Guardists were investigating anyone who had held office during the last ten years. Transfers from the National Bank to foreign countries were investigated, too, and so was the use of the funds of the army, navy, air force, and youth movement.

Sidorovici, leader of the youth movement in Rumania and a close friend of Carol, had only a few days ago received a high Hitler decoration; now he committed suicide because he could not account for the origin of some eleven million leis. Even the Old Excellencies in the lobby of the Athene Palace were uneasy for a few days, but then got over it with a flourish. They really were quite poor. But the Negus, Frau von Coler's admirer, who had prophesied so correctly the twilight of the gods (all the while including himself out, because of his friendship with the Germans) was put into Vicaresti prison. He was put in the cell next to Max Ausschnitt, who was reported to have said after Carol's abdication, "And now a nice big cell for my friend Malaxa." But he was disappointed, at least for the moment, for Malaxa once more triumphed over destiny. There is little doubt that he was the key figure to all of Madame's and Carol's money transfers and business transactions, and that General Antonescu hated Malaxa. Yet for the moment Horia Sima held his hand over Rumania's industrial tycoon, who gave in return a stadium and canteens to the Party. Also, while the Germans made a point not to interfere with the course of Guardist justice, it seemed they found Malaxa too important in the scheme of Rumanian economy to have him rot in jail.

Police officers and cabinet ministers connected with Guardist killings, and the generals connected with the martial court which convicted the Capitano of high treason, were put into prison pending trial. Most important among them were Marinescu, the minister of police and member of Carol's camarilla; Moruzov, chief of the secret police; former Prime Minister General Argeseanu, who revenged the assassination of Calinescu, his predecessor, with the awful mass murder of Guardists in September 1939; General Jon Bengliu, the chief of the police, who was instrumental in this murder—all these and many others were thrown into Fort Jilava where the Capitano's corpse still lay under the thick slab of concrete. Writs were prepared for a monster trial of these men, to be held before a kind of people's court and broadcast all over the country, a grandiose action of belated vindication of the Capitano and condemnation of the former regime.

Horia Sima and his boys got very excited about this plan, but unfortunately it was all wrong from the point of revolutionary technique. It was too legal and too slow. One had only to attend Antonescu's demonstrations at the big "Square of September Sixth" to know that demonstrations alone could not possibly make the Guardists happy. They were pretty and colorful enough, Antonescu's demonstrations. The square was at the foot of the lovely hill, Dealu Spirei, a sort of Bucharest Kremlin crowned by the white churches and buildings which form the Metropolie, seat of the Rumanian orthodox church, and the Parliament. The square itself was an immense sea of greenshirts and white-shirted peasants before a background of green draperies and the flags of the Axis and Spain and Japan, together with the Rumanian flags. Detachments of uniformed SA and SS, Italian fascists, and Spanish falangists bordered the enclosure, with its high green painted platform dominated by woodcuts of the Capitano. What took place in this enclosure was an Axis family party, complete with the diplomats and special emissaries of the Führer, Mussolini, Franco, and the Emperor of Japan. Clad in a green shirt, Antonescu spoke from the high green platform, and then little Horia Sima got up and spoke, too. The two then stood hand in hand for a long moment, looking into each other's eyes. Everything would look fine and hopeful, and people in the enclosure sniffled, while the Axis diplomats watched benevolently over the performance, the way Maurice Evans would watch a high school performance of *Hamlet*.

What one remembered of these demonstrations was not the important emissaries of great powers, or even the white-clad peasants from all over the country and the thousands of young greenshirts who lined the square, but the hundreds of people in mourning who were admitted to the enclosure. These people, most of them humble folk, poorlooking beside the bemedaled dignitaries, were the relatives of the Guardist leaders killed by Carol's police. The pools of black which they formed amidst the glittering color struck an ominous note: there were altogether too many mourners of too many killed Guardists. Looking at them you knew that there could never be a bloodless revolution when so much blood cried for revenge. Codreanu's mother and wife were there, invisible behind their heavy widow's weeds, and the widows and mothers of the so-called "Nicadorii" and the "Decemvirii," the thirteen comrades murdered with the Capitano in the forest of Ploesti, and many more who had sons, husbands, brothers killed by Carol's police.

The most distinguished mourner in the enclosure was old Princess Alexandrine Cantacuzino, small, stout, with a set, impenetrable face, reminiscent of Queen Victoria in widow's weeds, but with something orientally enigmatic and at the same time sharply latin in her eyes. The mother of one of the murdered Guardists and one of the great ladies of Rumania, she was prominently displayed at the functions of the new regime. After her year imprisoned in one room of her palace Antonescu had freed her the day he came to power. Unbroken, with a sort of detached serenity, she took up the threads of her incredibly active life, looking after her schools and the Women's Club she had founded after the example of the American Women's Club, and her vast and varied charities. Around the fireplace of her salon, a light, long room where the eighteenth-century Aubusson chairs formed inviting little groups in the classic style of the great salons of the Faubourg St. Germain, one met the social cream of the Guardist movement. On the walls the mysterious gold and brown splendors of a Rembrandt would gleam near the gold and red of a Florentine master and the whites of a French impressionist, and a superb ancestor, a turbaned hospodar, with his long black beard growing up to the eyes and the bejeweled sword stuck in his bejeweled belt, haughtily watched this brave new world.

Over delicate petits fours from Capsa's the Guardist nephews and cousins of the old lady and their friends expounded their plans and theories for the New Rumania: economic, literary, artistic, educational plans, theories for the "pure Rumanian race," which gave even the Germans a good laugh, for there was no race more hopelessly a mixture of all races than the Rumanian. They were in a fever of creation, these young men, their rather effeminate looks forming a strange contrast to the tough terms in which they were accustomed to consider life, terms of prison, flight, and murder.

The Princess herself was no Guardist. "I know," she would say of the young men, "that they will destroy everything I love and everything I stand for, but God, how I prefer them to the young men in France who would not fight for anything at all."

The old Princess was a passionate patriot and a politician, too. As such she was skeptical of Antonescu's bloodless revolution. The General, she would warn Axis diplomats, needed a quick success, or the revolution would become very, very bloody. The former regime, she pointed out—and she spoke from experience—had set standards of violence which the revolution could be expected to surpass. By quick success she meant that the Axis should return part of the ceded Transylvania to Rumania, something Hitler and Mussolini could not possibly do even if they wanted to, because of the Hungarians. So the Guardists, the Princess feared, would find another violent outlet.

There were several reasons why General Antonescu tried to make his revolution genteel. One was a soldierly sense of discipline and decency; another was a mistaken notion that he could substitute reform for revolutionary dynamism. But the chief reason was fear that the Germans would make disturbances of any kind a pretext of setting up a protectorate. This fear of German interfer-

ence was shared by Horia Sima, which is why he fell in
with the Conducatore's idea of a bloodless revolution. At
least in the beginning.

The strange part of this was that this fear of Germany
was the most unjustified fear of all. The Germans at this
juncture wished nothing less than to establish a protectorate or anything of this kind in Rumania. A new phase
of the most contradictory ad-libbing on the part of German diplomacy had set in. Was "quiet in the raw-material
sphere" still their major objective? It certainly was. But
they did nothing decisive to achieve it. Instead they
seemed set to wash their hands of the whole Guardist business. They were evidently as disgusted at the thought of
having to play "nursemaid to the Rumanian revolution"
as would a bachelor asked to hold an unhousebroken baby.
One never knew whether this was just a passing mood, or
a policy, or camouflage.

But evidently there were a few weighty reasons why
outright domination of Rumania in the form of a protectorate over Rumania did not suit the Germans at the
time. They did not want to alarm the Russians by a show
of open domination of any Balkan country. The Russians,
so high German diplomats explained, had more or less
explicitly recognized that the Balkans were the sphere
of German economic interest, but had not relinquished
their pan-slavistic ideas, which included the Balkans in
the Russian sphere of political interest. Then also, like
rich old men who want to make the world believe that
some pretty young girl married them for their personal
charms, the Germans wished to show the democracies
that they were irresistible without conquering by force.

This was not, however, altogether a question of vanity,

but also a question of expediency. By now the Nazis were beginning to have tough going in the Netherlands, Norway, and other conquered areas, while they were getting on quite well with the Swedes, the Swiss, and the Bulgars, who had preserved at least a nominal freedom. German economic experts, harried by their negotiations with businessmen and economists in the occupied countries or protectorates and their passive resistance, came back to the Wilhelmstrasse and advised their bosses against any form of direct domination in Rumania if it could possibly be avoided. So the Germans let the Guardist revolution take its course—and after four weeks of it there was not a shred left of "quiet in the Rumanian raw-material sphere."

The Guardists were not altogether the reason for this. Evacuation of Transylvania had disrupted the transportation system to such a degree that it practically nullified the agreement concluded in August by which Germany would get all of Rumania's exportable grain surplus. Nor was it the Guardists' fault that there were no means to transport the Rumanian exportable oil, estimated at five million tons per year, to Axis countries and countries friendly to the Axis, though Rumanian reservoirs and tanks were full of oil with no place to go. But aside from these difficulties of a purely technical order, the Guardist revolution decidedly prevented the Germans from doing business as usual.

First of all the Germans were stopped by the consequences of the twilight of the gods. Young Stinnes, son of the German industrialist who controlled German economy during the inflation, told foreign journalists that at the Reschitza, Max Ausschnitt's former firm, and at Malaxa's, all the directors and managers were out—in prison and under *arrêt de domicile*—or too afraid to take the responsibility of negotiating business deals. This brought business practically to a standstill. Much as this hindered Rumanian business, however, it was not as serious as the new anti-Jewish legislation. The Guardist masses, deeply antisemitic and violently resentful of the Jews, really wanted a pogrom in the Jewish quarters to start their revolution.

Antonescu, however, with his fear of violence, tried to compromise instead on new antisemitic legislation which went far beyond that recently issued by Carol. Starting off with the expropriation of all rural Jewish property, in return for worthless bonds and for a nominal price, this new legislation provided for the elimination of Jews from the economic life of Rumania within one to two years. Meanwhile "commissars" were put in charge of important Jewish businesses: young Guardists who knew next to nothing of business, but a great deal about terror, blackmail, and corruption. If the Conducatore had set out to establish standards of honesty in a country where everyone has a price, it was evident that he failed where these commissars were concerned. They were the worst hold-up men imaginable, terrorizing the Jewish businessmen out of their motorcars and villas and ruining their businesses. When the tortured Jews dared complain, the Guardist police descended upon them at night, fetched them to the Prefecture on some trumped-up charge, and left them there until they were ready to sign away everything, including their factories.

This handling of "Aryanization" dismayed the Nazis because of its disrupting effect on business. One German economic expert asked Horia Sima how he could attempt to achieve the de-judaization of Rumanian business in one year when it had taken the Germans six or seven years, and they were even now still holding on to individual Jews whom they called "WW-Jews," (meaning *wirtschaftlich wertvolle Juden*: economically valuable Jews). In Rumania, the German pointed out, a much greater percentage of business was in Jewish hands than in Germany and while in Germany there were ten efficient Germans to every efficient Jew, in Rumania there was hardly one efficient Rumanian to ten efficient Jews. Horia Sima replied with a levity which disgusted the German economist, "This only proves that we can do ever so much better than you." A quick de-judaization was, Horia Sima felt, the only fun which the Guardists could offer their followers. But this fun was not quick enough or general enough to save the revolution.

In order to keep the industries most vital to them from going altogether to pot, the Germans evolved a plan of buying up the shares of the Jewish enterprises, putting Rumanian and German businessmen on their boards of directors, and—this was the most important part of it— keeping the former Jewish owners on as business managers. So German businessmen by the dozens began flocking to the Athene Palace, intent on snatching a mine or a factory for practically nothing at all. They were less hand-picked a lot and more boche-looking than the batch of German businessmen who had come here last summer before the fall of France and before Rumania turned totalitarian. The Nazis evidently thought that after conquest they did not have to seem as seductive as before.

These businessmen from Hamburg or the Rhineland

arrived convinced that everything would proceed according to plan. The Jewish owners would be only too willing to sell and to stay on as managers for a year or two, for they had no place to emigrate, anyway. The German would be in a self-congratulatory mood. "Have you already got the okay of the Rumanian government?" we would ask such a German businessman. "We have sent the papers to the ministry for signature, but this is only a formality," the German would reply. But it was not just a formality, at least not the way the Guardists handled it.

In almost five months of the Guardist regime I did not see one German "Aryanization" deal go through. The Guardist authorities, without being caught on a point-blank "No," found ways and means to prevent the Germans from getting any foothold in Rumanian business. Their motto became "Rumania for the Rumanians and to hell with the Jews *and* the Germans!" And while they never said this in so many words, they drove the businessmen from Hamburg and the Rhineland crazy by their vague, slippery methods.

The German businessman would sit around the Athene Palace waiting for the signed papers, cheerfully first, then slightly puzzled, then bit by bit impatient, then angry, then furious. From there on he might either fly back to Germany, leaving his interests in the hands of the lawyer of the German legation, or he might stay on in Bucharest, sitting gloomily at the bar in between visits to the Strada Wilson, from where Dr. Neubacher and his young men were supposed to bring pressure on the Rumanian authorities. Dr. Neubacher, his tired eagle's face looking more tired than ever, could promise no quick results. "The Rumanians," he would say, "are so very, very oriental."

Dr. Neubacher knew how Guardist resistance worked. It was slippery and intangible, never amounting to outright refusal. Instead Guardist authorities would temporize, sending papers back because of technicalities, then sending them back again because there had been new decrees. Finally they would promise a decision for the end of the week. But then, when the German businessman at last thought everything was settled, the Guardist put the Jewish owner into prison and kept him there while his business was quietly ruined by the commissars. Or they would torture him into selling the shop for nothing to some Guardist. In either case, the Germans lost out.

"Why don't the Germans take Rumania over before the Guardists have ruined everything?" I asked the Count. "It's the story of the goldfish bowl," he replied, and told me the story: At the peace conference Hitler, Churchill and Pétain, between negotiations, got to watching a goldfish in a bowl. Which of us can get it first? they wondered, and all three tried their luck. Churchill made a noose out of his watch chain and threw it after the fish, but did not catch it. Pétain let a fly down into the bowl as bait, but the fish did not respond. Finally it was Hitler's turn. He took a spoon and began patiently to ladle all the water out of the bowl, until the goldfish lay quivering helplessly on its dry bottom. "Now you fry him, Adolf," Pétain and Churchill suggested. "Oh, I wouldn't do that unless the goldfish asks me to," Hitler answered virtuously.

But there was one foreigner who could do business with the Guardists. His name was Dr. A. A. Tester. Half German and half English by blood, and a business genius, he knew enough of the oriental turn of mind to understand the Rumanians. A sucker for nationalist movements (at home he was a follower of Sir Oswald Mosley; in fact one of the co-founders of the British Fascist party), he professed an enthusiasm for the Guardists which delighted them. Of all the amazing things which happened on the turbulent Rumanian scene the most amazing was that one of His British Majesty's subjects was the one man who could ease the way of the Germans into Rumanian business.

In his middle forties, fat, medium-sized, dark, bemonocled, Tester, who dwelt in his roomy Bond Street clothes as in a house, would waddle through the middle aisle of the lobby like a one-man procession. Laughing easily and speaking in a booming voice, he was considered the most sinister character washed against the shores of the Athene Palace by the war. British and Germans both distrusted him. The British accused him of being a traitor and doing business with the Nazis. The Germans, with less assurance, hinted that he was using his business contacts and his fascism only as a cover for his work for the British Intelligence.

I met Dr. Tester at the end of July shortly after his arrival in Bucharest. In the course of weeks and months I got to know him very well, and to like him. To me he never seemed to be a sinister character, probably because there is always something pathetic about a fat man in plum-colored dressing gowns who trails a wife, six children, assorted sons-in-law, governesses, maids, and pet dogs behind him through a war-torn world.

Son of an English businessman and a German singer, Tester was born in Stuttgart and educated in German schools and universities. He would modestly say, "I went by stuka through school." But this had not kept him from being a well-read man; he could recite all the German classics by heart in the manner of various great German actors, and could do the same with Shakespeare in English and the French classics in French, speaking both English and French with a German accent. If he felt like it, he could also sing any Wagner, Verdi, or Mozart opera complete with text, or whistle Beethoven's Fifth without a stop. He used to say that what he would have really liked to be was director of an orchestra. Instead he became an international lawyer and financier.

Tester told me that he had been completely wiped out three times, the first time in Germany when Dr. Schacht stabilized the mark. Tester took his young wife to Paris then and told her not to worry, because in six weeks she would again have her Hispano Suiza with two white-uniformed chauffeurs. In six weeks she had them. Since then Tester had never taken the trouble to tell her when he was broke, because before she got used to the idea, he had made a nice new bankroll again and everything was fine.

Tester would announce in his booming voice that he was "the last British fascist in freedom," and the contact man for "my leader, Sir Oswald Mosley." At big occasions he put on his black shirt, made the fascist salute, shouted "Heil Mosley." After having lived in England for the last fifteen years, Tester decided to take a year's cruise on the yacht he had given his wife. The war surprised them cruising in the Mediterranean. Tester gathered his wife and his children around him on the deck and pledged them to forget all about fascism and to think only of being good Englishmen. He was always very much affected by the memory of this scene and, because he had a hunch that the followers of Sir Oswald would have a tough time of it at home, he first set sail for Port Said, where he gave his yacht over to His Majesty's Navy and cautiously settled in Greece. Determined to do his bit for England, he traveled up and down the Balkans trying to make important contacts for buying foodstuffs for England. But the official English were exceedingly cool to all his patriotic efforts; to them he was still fascist and half German.

This was enormously distressing to Dr. Tester, for like most people who are of divided loyalties and conflicting talents, Tester had a passionate desire to "belong" and to be taken at face value by respectable people. He also had the understandable desire to be used in accordance with his extraordinary abilities. To make big money everywhere and under any circumstances was so simple that it bored him; he wanted the smell and the excitement of the political stage. If Tester could not be in the cast, he wanted at least to be the wire puller, scene shifter, prompter, and confidant of the stars.

So when the official English at Athens and Belgrade refused to treat him as an English patriot who had just delivered a yacht to His Majesty's Navy, but rather as one of Sir Oswald's wayward boys and a half-German in the bargain, Tester decided sulkily that he really was a fascist at heart and began to act accordingly. This, at least, was Tester's own story.

Tester would never admit that he worked for the Germans. Rather, he said, he worked for British totalitarianism. Believing that the Germans would win the war before the winter was over, Tester was sure that only a fascist regime in England could get an honorable peace from Hitler, a peace which would leave the British Empire intact. But aside from the question of peace, what fascinated Tester most about the new fascist world order were its economic possibilities. "Don't believe that the era of big business is finished. It's just beginning," he would explain, and he would expound his idea of a European clearing house for goods on the basis of barter: a gigantic enterprise which would direct the totalitarian European economy much more thoroughly than the City ever directed private capitalist Europe. This gigantic clearing house would, of course, be in London. To skeptical objections that such a clearing house would be managed in Berlin by the German Government itself, Tester would reply that, first of all, such deals can only be brought about by businessmen and not by officials, and secondly, English fascism would be ever so much more efficient than German fascism and ever so much more acceptable to other nations.

"You see it yourself right here in Rumania," he would say. "The Germans even now, with all their power, are tolerated but not liked. Not that they are overbearing. It's just that they haven't got the great English manner. These Rumanians are used to Englishmen who come here with a fat checkbook, write a check for £100,000 and get themselves an oil company with no questions asked. They just can't stand these German businessmen, who first send their experts, then want a guarantee, then want a mortgage on the plant, and finally want to have it as cheaply as possible. It just does not work this way."

Tester, or as his friends called him "A. T.," attributed his unique success with the Guardists to the fact that he always dealt as an Englishman and was such a good fascist. But I myself believe that the secret of his success was that his style of life corresponded to the oriental traditions of the Rumanians and appealed to their oriental turn of mind. Tester lived like a hospodar and the Rumanians loved it. They loved the way he had built around him a miniature state which comprised his blood relatives, his in-laws, his purveyors, clients, and *Hausjuden* (Jews belonging to the family), and finally an amorphous legion of hangers-on whose only visible job was to be present, to form a chorus, to fill the void of space and time. Out of their own Turkish past the Rumanians have a nice Turkish word for these hangers-on. They call them the Mossafiri, the invited ones. In Turkey the Mossafiri had a labor union and there was considerable honor connected with being a perfect Mossafir, as there should be in a world where nobody ever wanted to be alone. Tester, too, had a horror of solitude; the word privacy did not appear in his dictionary. Even while sleeping—which he did late in the day, as he never went to bed before 3 a.m., and mostly later—he liked the feeling that people were waiting for him in the next room.

At 6 p.m. in Tester's large salon at the Athene Palace there would be in one corner a card table with people playing belotte: a faded Rumanian princess who wanted to sell a house, a diamond bracelet, or a daughter to Tester; a vulgar, red-faced inspector of Moruzov's secret police who was on Tester's payroll because "one never knew"; a sad Jewish industrialist whose factory Tester was going to aryanize; and the "Colonel," an old Guardist, who had also entrée to General Antonescu and who sat on most of Tester's boards of directors. Another group would be formed by some pretty auburn-haired Tester daughters, a high official of the Ministry of Justice, an officer of the General Staff, a Hamburg businessman and a few members of Carol's first camarilla whom the Guardists had forgotten to put into jail. The door was open to a bedroom, where the still-beautiful Mrs. Tester talked to the wife of one of Carol's ministers who was in Vacaresti prison, and whom A. T. had promised to get out no matter what the difficulties.

"Lotti," as Mrs. Tester was called, for Charlotte, was German-born and in her middle thirties, a languidly beautiful blonde with long shadowed eyes, a lovely skin, and an enchantingly slow smile which wrinkled an other-wise classic nose such as one sees on children. Her small high head sat exquisitely on a slim neck and wide shoulders. Her hands, legs, and feet were of indestructible perfection. While to the Tester children, even the older daughters, who originated from an earlier marriage, she was "Mummy," to the Mossafiri she was "Madame Champagne."

For Lotti had an ice-cooled bottle of champagne at her elbow from the moment she woke up late in the morning to the moment she went to sleep at dawn the next morning. Empty and half-empty champagne bottles strewn over the tables, chests, and even chairs of the apartment were as much a feature of the Tester menage as A. T.'s plum-colored silk dressing gown or the Mossafiri. She drank her three or four bottles of champagne a day without any visible effect; it was just that champagne helped her stand life with the dynamic unexpectedness which was Dr. Tester. Some seventeen years of it had drained the beautiful creature of all personal initiative, of all desire to assert herself, of all wish for activity of her own. She had become the slender, silent shadow to this big, booming husband who at times took her for granted like a comfortable old shoe and at other times fussed about her like a college boy over his first love.

In the first years of her marriage, A. T. had been insanely jealous of Lotti, checking up on her every move, never allowing her to go to country clubs, beaches, or anywhere that she might meet other men; he even telephoned after her to dressmakers and milliners. In order to avoid scenes Lotti had resigned herself to an existence as hermetically shut off from the world as if she had been the favorite of some pasha. Though she had a car with two chauffeurs for her personal use waiting before the hotel day and night, Lotti never left the Athene Palace. Nor did she ever go down to the lobby or the restaurant. The hairdresser went up to her; she chose her clothes from collections which an endless stream of dressmakers brought up for inspection. It was the same with perfumes, shoes, lingerie, and everything else.

While Lotti wore clothes beautifully, she rarely seemed to get around to wearing them at all—she would say, "The bedroom is never free for me to dress"—and usually wore pajamas with a high Russian collar and over them a long tailored coat of the same. A. T. had his shirtmaker make her dozens of these outfits in every conceivable color and material. It was, I often thought, the perfect uniform for a modern harem.

On the other side of the salon was a little office where one could hear A. T. vituperating, cajoling, insulting, swearing and reasoning in English, French, and German. Tester had an office in his bank but did most of his work in the hotel. He was working now with his Rumanian lawyer and most intimate friend, a Jew who was the lawyer of the English legation, with his Rumanian son-in-law, and with his two secretaries, who were also Jewish. Now and then he would appear at the door, clad in a plum-silk dressing gown and smoking a gigantic cigar. There was a constant coming and going of more Guardists, more Jewish businessmen, more Tester children and their governesses, and more people who wanted to sell things.

Such a scene, with this or a similar cast, would continue until long after midnight. The business conference would go on; in between, A. T. would go off on a mysterious errand or would receive a mysterious telephone call and ask everyone to disappear into the bedroom because "someone wishes to see me who doesn't want to be seen." The someone might be Horia Sima or the Grand Rabbi of Bucharest or a special emissary of the Duce or an English Quisling. Around midnight Jews and Guardists and former Carol men and businessmen from the Rhineland sat down to dinner, and afterwards A. T. would play belotte unless he was called by the wife of a Jewish friend who was just fetched to the Prefecture. Tester's attitude toward terror and persecution was quite hardboiled as long as it was anonymous terror and persecution. But the moment he had any personal connection with the victim —even if the victim was the second cousin of his secretary whom the Guardists had robbed of his grocery shop— he would raise hell with his Guardist friends and go to all sorts of trouble to save the victim.

Rumor had it that Tester gave the Guardist party 25 percent of all his business deals and paid enormous bribes to high party members. In return, it was said, he had asked of Horia Sima and his boys that nothing happen to his two hundred best Jewish friends in Bucharest and to some members of the camarilla.

Such was the Englishman who could do business with the Guardists. Rumor had it that he acted only as a middleman for the Germans and with German funds, but this was hardly true. To my knowledge Tester made all his transactions on his own account and with his own funds and funds of a Rumanian friend. One of his business tricks was that officially he kept completely in the background, and put Guardists and friends of the General on the boards of directors of his various companies. In some cases he achieved with the Guardist government what the Germans never achieved: keeping the former Jewish owners on as managers. Some of the enterprises he certainly bought with an eye to selling them to German firms, but he rarely succeeded, owing to the Guardist resistance. Tester operated his enterprises in the spirit of collaboration with Germany. He also backed a new commercial firm which was part Rumanian and part German and concerned itself with the sale of goods to Germany.

In September, when the Guardists came to power, Tester made a bet that he would make a thousand million leis before Christmas. "Because," he said, "no matter how a revolution goes, one cannot help making a lot of money on it." I think Tester lost his bet, yet he ended up by controlling a string of the most valuable Aryanized enterprises in Rumania before the Guardists were through, which was more than any other foreigner could boast of. Though he was useful to them, the Germans never stopped being vexed that they needed an Englishman to do business with the Guardists. And the British were not amused.

"The trouble with the Guardist movement," the Germans would regretfully say, "is that they have only Horst Wessels, and not a single Wohltat, Funk, Schacht, Goering, or Hitler himself. They are a movement of martyrs."

Yet while they admitted that it might have been a mistake to have Carol go and bring the Guardists in, the Germans continued to feel that they could afford to keep to their do-nothing policy, and were rather Olympian about the growing danger to their much desired quiet in the raw-material sphere.

The new order, German economic experts quite reasonably insisted, could not be achieved as if by clockwork. In enterprises on such a large scale one had to allow for all sorts of human frailties, and the unexpected in all its forms, and for all kinds of setbacks. Planning was limited in every sphere of life. Exactly as one could not foresee every single move in crossing a street, but could only plan to cross the street, so too one could only plan the main lines of the new order but not every single phase of it. This did not mean that the Germans were inefficient, they pointed out. It would only be inefficient on their part if they forgot to include all the possibilities of failure and of the unexpected into their calculations, but this they never forgot. So they had included, they said, the possibilities of disturbances in the Rumanian raw-material sphere in their calculations and had not based their war-plans on Rumanian grain and oil. They did not have to close shop if they did not get it at all. Though there was no reason to think that they would not get it at all. Nothing had happened in the raw-material sphere which could not be repaired in a very short time, and this was all that mattered.

Temporary disturbances, they explained, did not count in their kind of enterprise. They took a very long view in these matters, and were apt to laugh at foreign correspondents who talked of the disruption of the Rumanian transportation system and of Rumanian business as if they were final and irretrievable. This was, they said, as dilettantish as the way foreign correspondents gloated over the busting-up of bridges in a campaign or over the burning up of oil wells. As if the most efficiently busted-up bridge could not be repaired in a few hours and any burnt-up oil well fixed within six months. It was the same thing with that much-advertised disruption of Rumanian economy: there was nothing, they said, that could not be fixed in a few months.

Thus, on the whole, German economists were not dissatisfied with their bloodless conquest of Rumania in spite of temporary difficulties which they considered of a passing and peculiarly Rumanian order. It was after all, they pointed out, the Germans who sat at the Rumanian oil wells and not the English. Also they had improved their strategic position toward the Balkans and Russia, which pleased the military authorities no end. Moreover, they said significantly, they were in a position to restore quiet in the raw-material sphere if and when things got really too troublesome.

This was, as future events showed, true. Still, one wondered if the Nazis could not even achieve their chief objective painlessly in a country which surrendered voluntarily, ranging itself with the Axis almost spontaneously, where then could they achieve their objectives painlessly?

//—MILITARY MISSION

On the thirteenth of Oc-
tober 1940, the much heralded German military mission
at last arrived in Bucharest: the military mission which
Carol had tried to get in July in order to frighten off the
Hungarians and Bulgarians, but which Hitler had then
refused. Even General Antonescu, breaking the news to
the public, modestly confessed that in inviting the military mission he only took up the "brilliant idea" of the
former government, thus putting the whole thing on the
doorstep of a regime which his revolution had over-
thrown.

The object of the military mission was, according to
General Antonescu, to give the Rumanian army first-
class training such as only the German army could provide, and to perfect air defenses in the oil region. But
it was evident that the Germans on their part did not go
to all this trouble for the beautiful eyes of the Rumanians,
but had a definite purpose of their own. Inasmuch as they

had a vital interest in the oil region, their purpose in perfecting air defenses was clear. But for the rest, did they wish to strengthen the Rumanian army in order to strengthen Antonescu's position against possible revolts? Or did they need Rumanian troops to fight their battles —and if so, which battles? In the Balkans? In the Near East? In Russia? Where? A year later the answer was clearer.

The coming of the German military mission was preceded by wild rumors about German divisions "pouring" into Rumania. In the lobby of the Athene Palace the number of these divisions mounted to thirty, fifty, seventy-five, before a single German lieutenant had passed the frontier. Nor did anyone call it a military mission. Everyone called it "German occupation force," despite the fact that here, for once, the Germans were going to great pains to practise restraint. But for all people believed them, they could as well have gone the whole hog and occupied the country. Being good *once* simply does not pay.

Actually the German military mission, for the time being at least, was just what the German and Rumanian authorities said it was—only more so. It was a high-powered military mission, led by a general of the air force and a general of the land force, with a staff of several hundred officers of both forces, and of several thousand men, nobody knew exactly how many, which formed the so-called "instruction cadres," units of the various branches of arms which were to instruct the Rumanian troops, plus the personnel to staff the air defense in the oil region. . . . That's how, on that October thirteenth the American military attaché, Colonel J. P. Ratay, explained

the German mission to American journalists who, fired by
the sight of hundreds of high officers, clung stubbornly
to the story of "German divisions pouring in."

"The trouble with you journalists," Ratay said, "is that
you haven't got the faintest idea of what a military mission looks like. That's why you imagine that every tzuyka-
drinking general has an army corps at his tail."

The Colonel looked like a Cossack chieftain out of a
legend of Boris Godunoff and blood-reddening-the-snow-
on-the-walls-of-the-Kremlin. He had the square head with
dark hair *en brosse*, the long mustache twirled up at the
end and rows of strong white teeth to go with such a picture. He was my favorite military attaché.

Life in Bucharest without Ratay would have been
plain miserable, for not only was the Colonel's house in
the Strada Q lovely and filled with the beautiful things
he had collected when stationed in Peking; not only did
he keep the best table in town, lend out books and even
the last issues of the *Saturday Evening Post* and *Time*,
nowhere else to be found in wartime Europe; but he
answered the most idiotic questions on military matters
with unfailing patience—and, what was even more important, his predictions about the course of the war had
proved so far uncannily right. When American diplomats
in Europe still faithfully repeated the Allied blah about
Hitler missing the bus, the impenetrability of the Maginot
Line, and the revolting German generals, Colonel Ratay
talked about the strength of the German army, the su-
periority of its command and prophesied the campaigns in
the order they came and the German victories in these
campaigns. It needed inner independence and pluck to

say such things at the time. Even a military attaché was not above the suspicion of being pro-Nazi.

Like everybody else, the Colonel, who generally shunned the lobby of the Athene Palace, had put in an appearance before luncheon this October thirteenth. It was a Saturday. In the morning the news had spread that the chief of the military mission, General Hansen, would arrive by train at noon and that the chief of the air mission, General Speidel, would arrive by plane later in the afternoon, and that both the Generals and their staffs would take up residence at the Athene Palace. A tall swastika flag had been hoisted right under my window, and the entire second and third floor of the hotel were hurriedly being evacuated for the officers, and the guests who had to move were furious. Some fifty swastikaed Messerschmitts and thirteen Henkel bombers in formation had roared over the city that morning, presumably on their way to Ploesti —a wonderful sight under the radiantly blue sky.

Never before had I perceived exactly this kind of excitement in the lobby of the Athene Palace. The air between the yellow marble pillars glimmered with it; it was visible in the wary way people sat forward in their chairs and in the absent-minded way they made small talk and drank their tzuyka. I had never seen the lobby so full for the luncheon apéritif as it was today. All the diplomats, military attachés, intelligence agents, oil men, and journalists had turned out in force. Demimondaines and femmes du monde had come, looking all ready for work in their new red fox coats and high caps decorated with red fox tails. People had spilled over to the bar, and some who could not find chairs leaned against the marble pillars or promenaded up and down the middle aisle.

Even the British journalists and diplomats could not forego the sensation of seeing the German military mission arrive. It was the last time that the English were to be seen, for a few days later they evacuated the English colony in Rumania and most of the legation staff. It was the last time, this Saturday noon, that the lobby of the Athene Palace held the excitement of war-in-the-making plus the international glamour connected with Grand Hotels.

In the big red and gold restaurant beyond the lobby, which had been closed during the summer season, one could see the long flower-covered table where the Rumanian generals were to lunch their German colleagues. Anton, the Austrian headwaiter who had spent a lifetime at the Athene Palace and was never astonished, stood at the open folding door. Nobody would go in to luncheon before the German generals arrived.

Presently there was a commotion in the entrance hall and people in the lobby paused in their talking and drinking. Everyone watched as the German officers made their entrance, and it became so quiet between the yellow marble pillars that one could hear the little metallic clankings which accompanied the officers at every step, as they made their way to the green salon reserved for them. Then for a few moments there was nothing but the sharp clicking of heels as they gave the Nazi salute to the assorted Axis diplomats and Rumanian officers and officials the German military attaché presented to them. The salute was a new custom with the German army, a concession to the Nazi era. They gave it only when bareheaded, but then they did not just flick the hand up in the casual manner of the Führer and his paladins, but brought their heels together and shot their arms high up and held the position, presumably while slowly counting one, two, three.

There were some eighty high German army officers, dressed in gray-green, some of them with red-lacquered collars and red-lacquered stripes down their trousers. Most of them wore the Iron Cross first-class and even higher decorations. Why their tunics were cut so short they made their behinds bulge out, not even Colonel Ratay knew—or at least he did not tell. Every eye was riveted on the Generals and everyone thought, so these are the samples of this irresistible army.

They were a dependable-looking lot; a few were handsome in a very masculine way. There were a few who looked like the late Herr von Seekt, the maker of the Reichswehr, which was the cadre of Hitler's army: dry, thin, intellectual aristocrats with monocles in the high arches of their cool eyes which seemed especially made for wearing monocles. These intellectual aristocrats came in all ages, but what struck me most was that the boyish type with clean-cut features and ruddy complexion prevailed up to the highest officers, showing up especially in comparison with the Rumanian officers and their pouchy, pasty faces. While the Rumanian soldiers looked excellent in a peasant-like way, the Rumanian officer somehow always succeeded in giving the impression that he had made too much love the night before and was very, very tired. This was the last thing you would suspect with the German officers. They looked wide awake, alert, agreeably martial and healthy.

General Hansen was very bald and had a narrow pink face. He looked young, and had, it seemed, directed operations in the Netherlands. Colonel Ratay said he was "a white man." Neither he nor any of the other high officers was arrogantly sinister in the way Eric von Stroheim plays German officers in American movies. They were too business-like to be sinister and too dignified to be arrogant. They were, I found, greatly different from the German officers under the Kaiser, who had been models for Stroheim and whom he stylized into the golem-like figure which moves over the screen with jagged, stiff, rattling, lifeless movements and an inexorable purpose. Somehow Hitler's high officers were less stiff and jagged and did much less rattling than the Kaiser's high officers. Also they did it in a more polite and subdued way. It seemed to me that the old Prussian tradition with its frugal simplicity, its contempt for wealth, its severe noblesse oblige had asserted itself in a new way. The German officer corps still felt itself the privileged caste, as it was in the scheme of modern Germany. But the consciousness of these privileges did not translate itself any more in an arrogant, world-is-mine attitude, but rather in the humbler pride of being the first servant of the nation. Sometimes when I saw them walking down the Calea Victoriei in their long gray coats, very upright, with slow measured steps, it struck me that there was more of the lonely dignity of priesthood about these men than of the martial arrogance generally connected with the idea of Prussian militarism. But these impressions came later.

First curiosity satisfied, the lobby of the Athene Palace found its voice again. "God," I heard an English diplomat sigh, "and they have told us that the German army was clad in papier-mâché. Why, they are simply reeking of the best wool and leather." The Old Rumanian Excellencies were not impressed by the performance: "All this, *chère amie*,"—Bratianu-beard waved his black-rimmed monocle in the direction of the green salon—"all this I saw in 1916. They came as conquerors then. Court and Government had fled to Yassy. It was even worse than now and one could not imagine that they could ever be beaten. Yet two years later they were through here and anywhere else. Such experiences make one philosophical."

As the procession of German and Rumanian officers crossed the lobby on the way to the restaurant, the voice of one of the demimondaines rose charmingly and throatily—in German. Until now she had never let anyone suspect that she could speak anything but French, and probably the last time she spoke German was when she said *"Ich liebe dich"* to one of General Mackensen's boys in 1917. But she clearly intended to adapt herself to this new emergency.

Everyone crowded into the red and gold restaurant after the officers. This was a big room in which guests usually lost themselves, but today it was filled to the last table. Even Princess Elisabeth Bibescu was there. Carefully she chose the table next to the officers and seated herself in such a way that her back was to them. It was a fine touch, but for all the effect it had she could as well have had luncheon in bed. For aside from a few English and Americans nobody noticed the brilliant Asquith daughter, least of all the Germans. "A new King ruled in Egypt and no one knew of Joseph any more."

I sat with a young American journalist who said it all reminded him of Oslo when the Germans came there in April. I wondered incredulously whether there had been the same pleasurable curiosity in Oslo, where the Germans had come as conquerors, while here they were at least nominally guests. "The same atmosphere," said the young American laconically. "That's how these Europeans are. Like little babies, who laugh happily at the kidnapers who take them for a ride." He ate a few spoonfuls of his Ciorba and added reflectively: "Of course, later they get frightened and cry, but chiefly because meanwhile we Americans have got hold of the case and raise hell about aggression and the wickedness of it all. Otherwise they might have lived happily ever after under the Germans, really like babies at the kidnapers."

The Rumanians were certainly not too depressed about the arrival of the German armored might. At the official reception they had given to General Hansen at the station, the Government, a Guardist detachment, and a military company turned out to greet him, singing *Capitano* and *Horst Wessel* in Rumanian, as well as the German and Rumanian national anthems. One could draw few conclusions from a formal reception, but in private conversations the Guardists seemed to think the German officers would help them to build up an army with which to beat the Hungarians, Bulgarians, and Russians, and get back everything they had lost, and they were quite pleased. Some, too, felt safer against an ever-possible Russian move, now that a token force of the irresistible German army was here. The crowd which gathered in the Square in the afternoon, gaping at the impressive gray motorcars and trucks of the German military mission parked before the hotel, and at the orderlies going to and fro carrying luggage, showed no emotion other than plain curiosity.

That same afternoon the chief of the German air mis-

sion and his staff arrived on the air field of Baneassa. He
was Lieutenant General Speidel, who up to now had held
a high position with the high command of the air force
in the West. In his early forties, looking like a slightly
damaged Rodin sculpture with a beautifully shaped head
with bits of nose knocked off, the young General's knightly
appearance was the answer to every woman's dream, but
he did not seem willing to acknowledge this fact. The
business of war seemed to absorb him in a truly infuriat-
ing fashion. When in the restaurant or the lobby of the
Athene Palace the Rumanian ladies stared too insistently
at him, his long eyelids went down over his gray with-
drawn eyes with the same finality that the iron curtain
goes down over a scene. It was fascinating to watch.
Otherwise Speidel was easy to talk to and friendly to
journalists.

Having been air attaché at the German Embassy in
Washington in 1931, Speidel talked tenderly of American
landscapes and of American flyers. Flyers all over the
world, he said, liked and understood each other, even
if they had to shoot each other down. There was a noble
sporting camaraderie which one did not find in any other
kind of arms. He said this strange "love between enemies"
remained very real even in the wildest air battle. There
was, he thought, a fundamental nearness between people
who shared spaces of such silent remoteness, so dream-
like, yet so filled with all the energies of our time, a life
of such fantastic intensity, and which was altogether beyond the experiences of other men.

I found this sense of apartness of the airman coming
out in many conversations I had with officers of General
Speidel's staff. These young men in gray-green, with white

collars and white stripes down their trousers, were good
company, representing a maximum of race in the sense
the French used the word, and a soldierliness enhanced
by an aristocratic lightness and aloneness.

Colonel Ratay said that both the air mission and the
military mission proper were staffed with the best people
of the German army, which showed that they must have
important plans for Rumania. In his opinion, this pointed
even then to the attack on Russia; he thought that for a
Balkan campaign the German army would not take the
trouble to send such outstanding officers. Events proved
that, as always, the Colonel was right.

For a day or two the German military mission was
dined and wined at the hotel and at the Axis legation
and at the Palace and at the Presidency. At lunch and
dinner time the orderlies of the generals and other high
officers stood in the entrance hall, waiting with big flower
bouquets in tissue paper, which their masters would bring
to the lady of the house: it was a picture of old-world
douceur de vivre.

Then the military mission got down to brass tacks,
and the first thing they did was to establish a brothel
for German soldiers. Well-organized brothels, it appeared,
were an achievement of modern civilization, and as important for an army as canteens. When the Japanese conquered Manchukuo, I saw the Korean girls who were sent
down to the halting places. There was nothing spectacular
about the fact in itself. Spectacular only was the way the
Germans did it, for the eighty girls wanted had to be
not only healthy but also Aryan. The "guaranteed Aryan
whorehouse," as the Old Excellencies put it, seemed to the
Rumanians the funniest thing that had ever happened

in Bucharest, and for the first time since the cession of
Bessarabia Rumanians laughed again. Not even the Guardists took seriously the perverse logic by which the Germans carried their ideas through to the point where they
become sheer farce.

In the last war Field Marshal Mackensen was quoted as
saying: "I came to Bucharest with a troupe of conquering
heroes and I leave here with a troupe of gigolos and racketeers." What had happened under these deep blue skies
and this violent sun to hard, disciplined German officers
was exactly what had happened here to the Hohenzollern
dynasty. Lacking the natural protective matter which
enabled the native Rumanian upper class to carry off the
life of debauchery and corruption with a certain saving
grace and sense of proportion, these Germans, who had
never experienced anything like it, forgot that there were
limits—even in Bucharest they out-grafted the Rumanians
and loved too well but not wisely, and some of them went
to the dogs—in a blaze of tragic love affairs and unsavory money scandals.

Determined to avoid such doings a second time, German
officers had been forewarned to be careful of society ladies
and demimondaines, especially as they were all considered
potential agents of one or the other secret service. They
had been warned, too, of the racial dangers in the shape
of pretty Jewish ladies lurking behind every yellow marble pillar in the lobby of the Athene Palace.

So the German officers kept very much to themselves,
and one could see groups of them roaming the good restaurants and night clubs in town. They wore mufti then.
Later, when the military mission had moved to the Am-
bassador, on Saturday nights one could see the young

officers, also in mufti, each with a girl, check in for the night at the Athene Palace. The girls these officers brought along looked like Volksdeutsche servant girls picked by Gauleiter Conradi, with the accent on the four Aryan grandparents and nothing else. In former times a German officer would never have showed himself in public with this type of girl, not even when he was in mufti. He would go out with a demimondaine or with some charming *petite amie*. The Count explained that the younger generation handled these things differently. "All these boys," he said, "are married well, I mean from a racial point of view, and would think it improper towards their wives at home to start here an affair which might engage them in any other than a functional way. With these Volksdeutsche girls such a danger does not exist."

I said: "How awfully dull!" He replied laconically: "This generation likes it dull."

As long as the military mission stayed there, the Athene Palace swarmed with agents of the military Gestapo, keeping track of every guest who might be a potential assassin of German generals. At night when one came home strange figures sat in the entrance hall, turned up at the landing of the staircase, or peeped through a hole in the door of the servants' pantry. As the military mission had arranged for the nightly blackout of all houses in Bucharest, and only scant violet bulbs lighted the corridors and stairs of the hotel after midnight, these oddly behaving figures were apt to give one the creeps.

On the other hand the Germans were rather careless. I for one could follow the private life of one of the high officers of the mission through an air-shaft which ran between his bathroom and mine. His existence, inasmuch as it unrolled in his bathroom and bedroom, was an open book to me. As he carried on lively conversations with his orderly while shaving and taking his bath there was never a dull moment in the morning and when he changed in the late afternoon. Unfortunately this big shot had a way of talking chiefly about wine, women, and song, while he whistled the *Liebestod*. If he talked about the war with his orderly it was reminiscences on the campaigns in France and Poland.

The nearest I ever came to learning military secrets through this air-shaft was when I heard him converse with his adjutant about the air bombardment of England. It was a great flop, the boss said, and would do no decisive harm to English industry, nor would it break British morale. It seemed he felt very gleeful about this. These Luftwaffe boys, he said in effect, had it coming to them. They had acted as if they alone had won the German campaigns, but now they were to see that air power without an invading land force was ineffective.

At the time—it was November 1940—this was an unorthodox opinion to come from the mouth of a high German officer and it was the first inkling I had that the German army doubted the effectiveness of the air bombardment of London. A few weeks later the officers spoke quite frankly. Air bombardment of such scope, they explained, had never been tried before and therefore they had only been able to guess its effect on civilian morale, industrial production, and military objectives. Their great raids over England in October and November had convinced them that air attacks alone would never be of any decisive value one way or the other. The Germans would not be able to bomb England off the map, still less could the

English do the same with Germany, even if the English should reach equality in the air, for the simple reason that Germany was farther away and spread out more.

There was much speculation as to what political position the German military mission would take in the Rumanian revolution, for every day the inner political situation deteriorated more. Horia Sima, under the pressure of the radical group of his party, began to veer towards a course of sheer terror. There was no night without the dreaded Guardist police rattling across the Square on their motorcycles on one of their raids on Jewish houses. People just disappeared; one did not know where. It was considered dangerous to go out alone. Business was dreadful. Antonescu was appalled. There were rumors of constant friction between the Conducatore and the Capitano's vicar-on-earth, and for days at a stretch Antonescu sulked in his tent in Predeal, and Horia Sima's Guardist friends boasted that in a very short time the Guardists would be able to rule without the General. But there was also friction between Horia Sima and Codreanu's father, and there was friction between Horia Sima and a third group in the Guardist movement thought to be communistic.

The whole Rumanian revolution depended on which of these factions the military mission would support, whether they would try to strengthen General Antonescu at the expense of Horia Sima or strengthen Horia Sima at the expense of General Antonescu. Or would try to reconcile these two forces. The Guardists themselves were convinced that the Nazis would stick to them through thick and thin even if they dropped Antonescu. Their reason was chiefly sentimental. The Guardist movement, they argued, was a younger brother who had always shown loyalty to the Nazis. Actually, as I learned very quickly, the question never posed itself to the Nazis in terms of little-brother-in-totalitarianism. Though they would have preferred to keep the two forces—General Antonescu and Horia Sima—together as a team there was never a doubt that the Nazis would throw their support to the one who proved strongest and gave the best guarantee of quiet and order. The presence of this important military mission proved that Rumania was not only important for raw materials, but also as the ground on which to draw up troops for a campaign in the Balkans, in Russia, or both. It was quite clear to neutral observers that, no matter how fond they were of their little fellow-totalitarians, the Germans would not stand for chaos in the back of their army.

Only Horia Sima and his boys refused to see it that way. Until their last hour in power they were convinced that they were favorites with Adolf Hitler and the Wilhelmstrasse, while the German military mission was playing single-handed political intrigue with General Antonescu.

They were all wrong. The German military mission was the most unpolitical lot to be found, at least as far as Rumanian politics were concerned. Its job was to give the Rumanian army and aviation the works for future reference and to build an air defense for the region of Ploesti and its precious oil wells. This was all that interested them about Rumania. Meanwhile they strove valiantly and successfully to preserve a total ignorance of Rumanian affairs.

When the military mission had been around for two months, I mentioned the name of Maniu once in the course of a conversation with General Speidel. "Who *is* Mr. Maniu?" the General asked. I first thought he was pulling my leg, as Maniu was about the best-known political figure on the Rumanian scene, but he reminded me gently that only a few weeks before he had been flying over England and had never heard of greenshirts or Maniu.

Whenever a German officer heard about some new Guardist killing or intrigue, the stock answer was, "Thank God I have nothing to do with this dirty business. I am a soldier."

Yet while the German military mission did not push any political scheme of its own, its sheer presence tended to strengthen the force of quiet and order, whoever it would be that would emerge as such a force. The frightened victims of the Guardist revolution looked to the German officers as to shimmering knights who would save them from the avidity and sadism of the Guardists. Harassed Jews gave their eyeteeth to have German officers requisition their villas or part of them. Then at least they were safe from the nightly raids of the Guardist police.

One story was significant in that it indicated the sort of legend which formed around the German military mission: One Saturday afternoon in the middle of a show in a big movie theatre on the Boulevard Bratianu, the lights went on suddenly and a Guardist told all Jews to leave the theatre immediately. Whereupon one of a group of German officers got up and made a speech to the effect that this was no way to handle such an affair. "These people have paid," he said, "exactly as we have and if they have to go, I and my comrades go, too." As Guardist thugs had been waiting on the street to beat up the Jews, the German officers had practically saved Jewish lives. I could never verify this story; the German officers I asked about it steadfastly denied it as running against their policy of aloofness. But no matter whether true or apocryphal, it showed that in the midst of the Guardist terror the German military mission was found somewhat restful by the Rumanian people.

*I add . . . that swift and cou-
rageous determination, that manly
and frank candor, the spice of
social life, can be found in our
age almost exclusively with educated officers.*

FICHTE

12—THE HOHE TIER

At the end of December
German troops and matériel really began to pour into
Rumania, as premature rumor had had it in October.
Between Budapest and Bucharest traffic was almost completely stopped for civilians, and American journalists said
twenty-two trains pushed into Bucharest every day, full
of men and machinery. The Square outside the Athene
Palace looked like a German field-camp with row on row
of dullish gray autocars and trucks parked on the thick
rug of snow.

There were also long dullish gray buses, in which groups
of German soldiers traveled around Bucharest and saw
the sights before they were shipped off to border villages
where there were no sights at all. The soldiers were young
and apple-cheeked and seemed to enjoy themselves very
much. These clearly were not instruction cadres any longer,
nor did they look to experts like an occupational army.
Even though the Guardists were making trouble, there
was no need for an occupational army of such scope. A

few tank units, one knew, could crush any possible Guardist revolt. To experts these looked like troops preparing
for some campaign. But which campaign did not seem too
important to the Rumanians at the time. For the Guardist
situation was coming to a head.

As the unending gray-green stream of German divisions
rolled south, little groups of generals appeared in the
Athene Palace, stayed there for a few days, and moved on
again. They had nothing to do with the German military
mission and no luncheons and dinners were given for
them. They looked all work and no play, and very important. They were from the General Staff, and where they
appeared things were sure to happen. These generals had
lacquer-red lapels on their long gray-green fur-lined coats
and lacquer-red stripes on their gray-green trousers and
their heads emerged from the high red-lacquered collars
of their gray-green tunics. There were very good heads
among them, sharp-featured, furrowed and with thoughtful
eyes. Some looked clean-shaven and healthy and a few
looked only clean-shaven.

The German generals would lunch at one of the corner
tables at the restaurant of the Athene Palace, arousing
a minimum of interest among the other guests, who were
now all Germans and Italians anyway, with a small sprinkling of Rumanians, who had lately seen too many generals
to get excited about new ones. The generals drank and ate
sparingly, and conversed in low voices. They were polite
with each other and with everybody else. Seeing them sit
there you would never believe that they were here to plan
a war. There was nothing tense or excited about them,
nothing that would indicate that they sat up all night

poring over their maps. They looked as cool and leisurely as a Chanel lace dress.

I remarked on this to Colonel Ratay, who laughed and said, "My dear girl, how do you expect the German General Staff to act? Shout at each other, pull their hair and go around with fatigue rings under their eyes? It's not their way of doing things."

There was one general, a fine-boned little man of fifty, whose face reminded me of Moltke's as I remembered it from a painting: a thin-lipped, very mobile face with a sharp nose and good gray eyes which looked at you in a serious appraising way, if they looked at you at all. They sat in a nest of little wrinkles, these eyes. One of the German officers of the military mission told me the name of this general who looked like Moltke, and it was a very important name. He was what the Germans call a *Hohe Tier*. In American this would be "Big Shot." This General had been a hero of the first world war and today he was close to the Führer. He wore the *Pour le Mérite*, the choicest German world-war decoration, and the *Ritterkreuz*, the choicest German decoration of this war—which were both decorations to wear *"Aus dem Halse heraus,"* on the throat, instead of on the breast, which made them the real thing.

From the table in the corner where he took his meals with the other generals or alone the Hohe Tier had frequently looked at me in that seriously appraising way of his. Then one night as I left the dining room he spoke to me politely, just as a respectable lonely gentleman anywhere in the world would pick up a respectable lonely lady.

I was standing at the table in the lobby where they

displayed the foreign papers, and the Hohe Tier strode over to my side and observed that the foreign papers were all old. I echoed that they were very old indeed. Then he mumbled his name and I mumbled mine. We walked to one of the little red sofas and sat down. We had dined early and there were still a few people left from the cocktail crowd, but the after-dinner crowd had not yet arrived. The Old Excellencies were sitting at their strategic table, missing nothing and sure to bombard me with questions afterward; and there, with a party of diplomats, was the beautiful Rumanian lady who was the friend of the German, Italian, and Hungarian ministers, just taking on the Spanish one too—the lady from whom Hitler must have had stolen the idea of the Tri-Partite pact.

Henry, the barman, stopped at our table, and the Hohe Tier ordered tzuyka for himself and Turkish coffee for me. How long had I been in Bucharest and what was I doing here, the Hohe Tier asked, and I told him. He asked me whether America was likely to enter the war, and I said "Yes," and he nodded gravely and said that he believed so, too. Then he said wistfully: "Isn't it a pity, though? The American entry will just make the war more terrible and prolong it." He said that the Americans' entry would not change the outcome of the war, though, he said, he was the last person to underestimate the immense production capacity of America.

"We have a long head start," he explained, "and I don't think we'll just hang around waiting for America to help England on a really large scale. We'll deal our decisive blow before."

I asked: "Wouldn't you have to try dealing a decisive

blow to England anyway, whether we come in on the war or not?" "No, we wouldn't," he said very firmly. "If the English didn't count on American support, they would make peace." I insisted that if their decisive blow on the British Isles were successful, the American war entry would not prolong the war. But the Hohe Tier said: "Oh, once America is in the war, it is conceivable that the British will fight on from Canada and Australia. We'll get a war of the new world against the old world. Though how the new world could get at the old one or vice versa, I can't see. Nor do I think such a war could effectively prevent Hitler from organizing Europe. But it would be a war all the same, and we want peace."

The Hohe Tier smacked expert little kisses off in the air and roused a piccolo languorously leaning against a marble column. We ordered another tzuyka and Turkish coffee.

Then the Hohe Tier leaned forward and turned around so that he faced me. "Tell me," he asked, "does your President really believe that Hitler might one day attack the United States?"—and he threw himself back in the cushions of his seat so violently that his *Pour le Mérite* clanked together with his *Ritterkreuz*, and he answered himself: "Good God, how could he get over to America when he can hardly get over to England?"

The Hohe Tier lifted his glass to me and gulped it down in one big gulp. And he said: "There are greater statesmen at the helm of great nations today than there were in the world war." I expected him to go on about Hitler and Mussolini, but instead he praised Churchill and Roosevelt. "You can't help admiring Churchill," and about Roosevelt, "What a superb politician! I used to listen to his fireside talks before the war."

The Hohe Tier paused for a moment, reminiscent, and then said: "It's a pity that a great statesman like Roosevelt misses his real historical opportunity. He could become the peacemaker of the world on a much larger scale than Wilson was. The tragedy of Wilson was that he wanted to save Germany while his partners Clemenceau and Lloyd George wanted to destroy Germany. But this time it's a different story altogether. Roosevelt wants to preserve the British Empire and the Führer wants to preserve the British Empire too."

I asked: "Does the Führer, really?" And he said: "Of course he does. The Führer realizes that of all the European people only England can manage the Empire. He knows that Germany can't, because Germany has neither the tradition nor the personnel. Nor does the Führer wish that the Empire, which he considers a great European patrimony, be lost to Europe by being divided among the Russians, the Japs and the Americans. The Führer does not like this idea at all."

"But," I said, "the American public does not believe a word Hitler says, and they would certainly not believe that Hitler would spare anything or anybody, least of all the British Empire." To this the Hohe Tier replied very gently: "It's very sad that the world always believes the wrong things about Hitler and never the right ones."

Before I could answer, a blond, blue-eyed officer came towards us, clicked his heels, and stood very still with his arm raised in the salute while he probably counted three. The Hohe Tier presented him as his nephew, and told me that he had fought in the campaigns in Poland and in France. Afterwards he said: "All these young heroes have no idea what a real war is like. They are used to the enemy throwing his hands up and running whenever they appear. One of these days they may have a different experience. They will come on an enemy who will fight. And then they will be able to prove their mettle." He went on talking about France, and how broken French spirit and morale had been before the battle even began. It was not so much the lack of machinery, he said, that defeated the French, but that they did not know what they were fighting for. "The Nazi revolution had already won the Battle of France before our first armored divisions went to work," and he grinned a little sheepishly. "Not that I like to admit this. It goes against my professional pride."

The Hohe Tier told me then that he came from an old Prussian family which for centuries had provided Germany with officers and diplomats, and that he himself had started his career as a page of the Kaiser. After the world war he decided to study law. He was not young any more and was married. He smiled reminiscently and said, "My wife and I were very poor, but we always had lots of books—they stuck out of all our pockets, and we were very happy." They never worried about money, because it always came to them in the most unexpected fashion. He said, "I've always been very lucky, quite beyond my merits." And he looked happy and humble. I decided that I really liked this man, aside from all curiosity.

Then he asked me how I managed to speak German so well, and when I told him, he wanted to know how I happened to live in America. And I replied that I came over eleven years ago and that I loved it and stayed on. I added that it was a lucky break for me. Being a non-Aryan I couldn't have worked in the Third Reich.

It always fascinated me to watch the reaction of well-bred Germans when I said this. Most of them looked pained and guilty and uncomfortable. I could see their faces tighten to sudden watchfulness and see the cautious thoughts that passed behind their clouding eyes. They tried to remember every word they had said to me and whether they had kissed my hand too long and whether there was anybody watching if they did kiss my hand too long. When they found that nothing compromising had happened so far, the naked relief on their faces made them resemble auto drivers who had succeeded in escaping the ditch in the nick of time. The *nazissime* Nazis, in the same spot, plainly looked their peeve at Nature who, they felt, owed a pure Nordic danger signals in the form of unmistakable Jewish noses, feet, eyes— or at least an infallible instinct. The Count once told me that it was a painful discovery for a pure Aryan not to be able to tell a non-Aryan when he saw one.

The Hohe Tier took my communication like a man and said that the treatment of the Jews was what he approved of the least in the National Socialist revolution. The injustice of it, he said, was difficult to bear.

"You mean difficult to bear for the victim!"

He replied, very gently: "Injustice is very hard to bear for the onlooker, too. Don't forget, I am a Prussian officer. Prussian officers don't like injustice."

"But Hitler needed his high officers. You could have made an effective stand against persecution."

He said very seriously: "It wouldn't have been of any use. It would only have created disunity, and we had to be united to be strong."

I told him that this point of view was very difficult for American public opinion to understand. The American public did not believe in the right of the strong to harm the weak, no matter how useful this might be for the welfare of the state. Whereupon he beamed at me: "I like to think that there is a rich and great people which can afford the luxury of being good."

We talked on about the war, and he answered most of my questions. To some of them he would say very patiently: "I am afraid, *meine gnädigste Frau,* that I can't answer that one," and he would smile, apologetically. He found the Polish campaign more interesting than the French, but said that so far the war had not produced one battle as interesting as one of the great battles in the world war. "Except the British retreat at Dunkirk, which really was a first-rate job."

But I did not learn a thing about the campaign which the Germans were planning for the Balkans and the Near East, or whether they planned such campaigns at all. The Hohe Tier said it seemed like a good idea to deploy a few of the many unemployed German divisions into Rumania, and he said that they might have to use these troops, if, as it looked now, Mussolini's defeats in Albania allowed the British army in North Africa, released as it was by Mussolini's defeats in Libya, to land in Greece. I asked whether the German troops in the Balkans were directed against Russia, and he said, "Maybe"—and added quickly, "only inasmuch as it is easier to negotiate with the Russians in the shadow of our divisions promenading in the Balkans."

I found that personally he very much approved of the German-Russian pact, and talked with great warmth about the traditional friendship of the Red Army and the Reichswehr. He told me that Molotov, when he came to Berlin in November, actually wanted to enter the Three Power Pact. But the Führer, he said, was apprehensive: "The Three Power Pact means that the Russians with their enormous appetite could make us fight for them long after this war is over, because the Russians want a new province every year. The Führer did not like this idea."

Molotov, the Hohe Tier hinted, was somewhat unhappy when he was in Berlin in November. The reason, he said, was that Hitler had refused to recognize Russian claims on Turkey, but declared that the Balkans, including Turkey, were a German zone of interest, and that Hitler had made certain demands on Russia concerning political and economic adjustments. There had been, he admitted, a cloud in German-Russian relations since then.

However, the Hohe Tier for one did not expect the Russians to double-cross the Germans in any serious way, because, he said, the Russians were too afraid of the German army. He thought that the presence of the German divisions in the Balkans and Poland would be sufficient to keep the friendship intact, but if it were not—"Would it not be interesting to have a war between the best army in the world and the second best army in the world?" he asked, and added meditatively: "And the army which wins would be the only army left in the world of today. I can't remember when in history there was only a single army in the world." There was no doubt which he considered the "best army," which would be the only army in the world.

The Hohe Tier smacked more kisses in the air and ordered more tzuyka and Turkish coffee. Still the Old Excellencies watched with the unrestrained curiosity which they reserve for bizarre romance.

The Hohe Tier told me that after Dunkirk the German army had planned to go right on invading Britain instead of mopping up the rest of France. On the twenty-eighth of May, he said, Ribbentrop came to lunch at headquarters somewhere in Flanders and told them that they were to force France into complete capitulation, and that the invasion of Britain was off. Ribbentrop explained that France would capitulate within the next few weeks and afterwards they would start a big peace offensive against Britain. Berlin, the Hohe Tier said, was convinced that England would be ready by then for a negotiated peace.

I asked: "Do you consider it a mistake that you didn't invade England last summer?" He pondered this for a moment and said: "Last summer we could have gone through England like a knife through cheese. The English would have been too surprised to defend themselves." He explained that now the possibility of surprising the British was gone, but that meanwhile the Germans had perfected their preparation in such a way that this was largely counteracted. He was not at all sure whether Germany would invade England, though. The Führer's guiding principle, he said, was economy of force, and while the General Staff believed that an invasion would succeed, he knew it would be extremely costly in lives.

Another reason he gave why the invasion of England was no certainty was that the Führer still had not given up hope of an early negotiated peace with England. Paradoxically enough, Hitler feared two results of this war: one was, of course, to be beaten, the other was to see the British Empire destroyed. Hitler, he thought, would only undertake the invasion of England if and when America's entry into the war canceled the last hope of a negotiated peace. Even then Hitler might wait until England's and America's combined power constituted a real danger for the European continent—which would be several years from now. The Führer, he insisted, was rather sentimental about England.

I purred, "The British must make Mr. Hitler very proud of the Nordic race."

The Hohe Tier beamed at me and said, "Believe it or not, he is!" And he said enthusiastically, "Aren't the British wonderful? The way they write in their bulletins: 'Cardiff is burning.' As if burning were just the thing for Cardiff to do." He said that the secret of British greatness was their stubbornness, and that the Germans were much less stubborn than the British. But then he said, "In a war it's not enough to take it. You must give it, too."

"You don't think that one day the British will be able to give it? Even with American support?" He shook his head. "They can't land anywhere in Europe."

I reminded him that he had spoken of the British-Egyptian army possibly landing in Greece. And he said, "Oh, that! That's not an army. That is a token force. We can get them out any time we want to." And he said, "My dear *gnädigste Frau*, you don't know much of military matters and why should you? But keep this in your mind: we can be everywhere in Europe 'firstest with the mostest.' Remember this and you will not make many mistakes."

I asked, "So you think you can defeat England?" And he replied very soberly, "I think we can." Then he added with a grin, "But, please, don't ask me how!" I said, "There is just one question I should like to ask. Do you think that you can decisively beat England on any battle-field outside of the Isles—I mean in the Mediterranean or in the Balkans or in Africa?" He said very firmly: "The war against England can only be decided on the British Isles and nowhere else." I asked: "But if you don't invade the British Isles? Then the war would keep on and on?"

"On and on," he agreed.

Did I know, he asked with a smile, the words of Frederick the Great during the Seven Years' War? "I am like someone who is looking for the end of an epigram but cannot find it. I don't see how I can ever find the end of my campaign." That's how it might well be with this second world war. Nobody would be able to find "an end to the epigram."

Not that a long war, the Hohe Tier went on, presented a pleasant outlook for Hitler. It would dash many of the Führer's hopes. It would cramp his style in building the new order. Still, he could organize Europe economically, war or no war.

I asked: "But how will the German people take a long war? Will it not lead to a revolt against the regime inside Germany?"

He laughed. True, he said, the German people were puzzling. Disgustingly indifferent to the victories—because they had so many, diplomatic and military, in these last seven years—one could not dazzle the German people with visions of world power and might tire them by a long war and its privations. But—the Hohe Tier jerked forward so that the *Pour le Mérite* clanked together with the *Ritterkreuz*—"Mark my word, *meine Gnädigste,* there is no German who does not fear defeat more than he likes peace or hates Hitler. Not even the German socialists and liberals want peace at any price. The Germans distrust any English propaganda which promises them an honorable peace provided they get rid of Hitler. They remember that one from 1918, and they wouldn't fall for it a second time. They realize that the peace of Versailles was heaven compared to what they would get this time. They know that the English not only want to destroy Hitler but any potential Hitlers of the future, which means they would try to destroy the German people. Our best German war propaganda is not victories but fear of defeat."

I found the Hohe Tier extremely well read in German and French, though not so much in English. At the time he was reading Bainville's *Histoire de France* which he enjoyed extremely and commented on shrewdly.

"The trouble with you and me is," he said, "that we are both such damn liberals. We always see the other fellow's point of view and don't hate anybody. This is very bad." Then he said in the tone of one conspirator talking to the other: "You know, I understand even Nazis. I mean the real ones, the ones who don't understand but *believe.*" And he told me about an adjutant of his who died of his wounds in Flanders. Throughout his last hours, which the Hohe Tier spent with him, he talked of his

Nazi belief. The Hohe Tier said, still puzzled: "He talked *Voelkische Beobachter* and Alfred Rosenberg. It all seemed the most god-awful bunk to me. But he believed in it, lived and died his belief. He was a wonderful soldier."

It was then that we got to talking about Hitler. What had been, I asked, the Führer's personal contribution to the success of the war so far? "Why, everything," the Hohe Tier said enthusiastically. Hitler's vision which, he said, was the vision of a revolutionary, had inspired German armament and the building of the air fleet and the concept of the campaigns. He said that Hitler was a genius in choosing his collaborators, and as never before in Germany the best men were on the top and everybody just in the place where he belonged. This went for the army, too. And this was what made the collaboration of all parts of the German machine so perfect. Also Hitler had succeeded in keeping everyone's personal initiative intact in spite of the totalitarian system.

Then he got really enthusiastic: "The Führer has been the one statesman in the world to grasp the essence of total warfare *and* to act accordingly. Hitler has understood that the whole country in each and every function must be geared for the war. That's what he has done."

Talking with the Hohe Tier, I was amazed at his emphasis on the word "revolutionary." It came all the time: "the revolutionary character of the German officer corps"; the *"élan révolutionaire,"* to which he ascribed German mechanical might and the miraculous coordination of all their forces, and the personification of the revolutionary élan was Adolf Hitler. His vision, his sense of timing, his daring had the revolutionary oomph, and that's why it was so successful. Hitler's practical contribution to the planning and execution of all their campaigns, was, the Hohe Tier said, much more decisive than the world knew.

But was Hitler a collaborator? From what I had read in the memoirs of foreign diplomats who met him, he seemed to shout everybody down or talk to them as to a mass meeting. The Hohe Tier said that Hitler might do that from time to time when he wanted to produce a certain impression. But with his co-workers Hitler was quite different, believing in experts and listening patiently to other people's opinions.

"You know," he said, "that's the funny thing about the Führer: though he is a revolutionary and a genius, he really is exceedingly rational."

"Do you like him?" I asked. "I don't mean admire him. I mean *like* him?" The Hohe Tier said he did, that for a genius Hitler was a very charming man. At first when he met him, he had many reservations against him because he could not get used to the Third Reich. But even before he admired Hitler, he liked him.

He told me that Hitler was now surrounded with a court ceremonial not unlike the ceremonial of the Kaiser's days. At the formal receptions in the Reichschancellery the old imperial lackeys passed champagne and caviar canapés, And he said that the Führer fitted perfectly into this pomp, being simple and unostentatious himself, but so dignified.

I said: "I often wonder how Hitler thinks about himself. Whether he marvels all the time at his own fairytale life. Whether he really believes that what he is building for Germany will be there forever or, as he says, for a thousand years. Whether he sometimes feels that the curses of the millions he makes suffer reach out to him. Whether he is afraid of the future. Or whether he says as Napoleon did: '*La vie, que m'importe! Mon nom vivra aussi longtemps que celui de Dieu.*' "

The Hohe Tier couldn't answer definitely. He said Hitler rarely talked in personal terms but gave the impression of a man who believed in what he was doing, and who believed that even the hard and cruel things were necessary. He didn't believe Hitler was afraid for himself. Sometimes he seemed very conscious of the fact that he was a Man of Destiny, but again he seemed to forget it entirely, and talked and laughed like somebody enjoying himself enormously. He was really a very unexpected person, this Adolf Hitler.

The Hohe Tier added that he personally had never found the Führer oppressive. On the contrary: whenever he was in his presence he felt more intelligent and brilliant than he really was.

The Hohe Tier scoffed at the idea that the German generals might revolt against Hitler. He said: "You might as well expect the New Dealers to shoot President Roosevelt. A movement to overthrow the regime, if it ever comes, will never come from the army." The army, he said, would not only never revolt against Hitler, but would hold on to him as to a mascot. Hitler and the Nazi revolution were fine for the war.

The Prussian officer caste and Nazism, the Hohe Tier insisted, understood each other perfectly. Contrary to the Anglo-Saxon myth of the conservative "Vons," he said, the Prussian officer caste was never identified with the aristocratic caste or with the capitalistic caste. Contemptuous of wealth and luxury, it was always by nature socialistic and nationalist. Of course, its socialism did not deal in the contrasts of Poor and Rich as Marxist socialism did. Prussian socialism defined itself in the contrast of Command and Obey. Individual freedom never meant much to the Prussian officer, he said. Instead discipline and the collectivism of All for One and One for All was his ideal.

Moreover, the Prussian officer caste had always been revolutionary when at its best, as in the wars of liberation of 1813. Blücher and York von Wartenburg and Clausewitz were the children of the French revolution, but the French idea of individual liberty had turned into the Prussian idea of national freedom.

Today, the new German officer caste did not recruit exclusively from the old Prussian families any longer but partly from the rank and file of the SS and other party organizations, and thus owed its very existence to the regime. These two strata, the old Prussian and the new Nazi, were so completely welded in one that it was hard to tell who was of the old Prussian caste and who rose from the ranks.

The Hohe Tier was slightly less skeptical about the possibility that the generals would win the ascendancy over the Nazi Party and set up a military dictatorship *with* Hitler but without the party. The Hohe Tier admitted that owing to the war the army, as the most important part of the machinery of the state, had naturally won the priority over the party. But this ascendancy, he felt, was merely of a technical nature and for the duration only. He did not think that any responsible figure in the army thought in terms of the elimination of the party, for the party was the broad basis on which the German revolution rested. To break up this basis meant to have the revolution hang in a void. And, unpolitical as it was, the German officer corps was for revolution—for revolution as atmosphere, without wishing to have anything to do with revolution as action—because revolution was good for war. Throughout history only revolutionary armies smashed their way through to victory. Military dictatorship was always oligarchic and counter-revolutionary. This stage was not reached yet in Germany. Germany needed her revolution in order to win the war.

The Hohe Tier and I passed several times in the Athene Palace lobby, after our talk. The last time I saw him he was in mufti, an ill-fitting brownish pepper-and-salt suit which he wore with an ugly necktie of brown and red. In these clothes the Hohe Tier was no longer the impressive general, but a mild little man who looked like a college professor, someone who made you wish to cut up his meat for him. Whenever I read about him in the news after seeing him this way, I remembered he had told me that after the campaign in France he had lived in a house on the French countryside and every morning early had picked flowers in the lovely garden, and put the flowers in vases all over the house.

Men reject their prophets and slay them, but they love their martyrs and honor those whom they have slain.

DOSTOEVSKY

13—NOVEMBER IN BUCHAREST

November 1940 was an exciting month in Bucharest. Everything happened: earthquakes and party purges and nights-of-the-long-knives and the belated State Funeral of the Capitano, to name just a few of the acts of God and men. There were also quite a few political events in November—political events which concerned Rumania directly, such as her entry into the Tri-Partite pact, and political events which happened farther away but which registered with violent repercussions in Bucharest as they did all over Europe. I mean the re-election of President Roosevelt and the first defeats of the Italian army in Greece.

Before November was over, Rumanians said, "The seven plagues have visited upon us: the Hungarians, the Russians, the Bulgarians, Lupescu, the Guardist regime, the German military mission, and the earthquake." And they would also say before this month was over, "Since we have entered the Tri-Partite pact, we eat like the Germans, we have an army like the Italians, we have a civil war like the Spaniards, and we have an earthquake like the Japanese."

Looking back to this crowded month I believe that the earthquake was the most important event. Perhaps without the earthquake the belated nights-of-the-long-knives would not have happened. To a deeply religious and superstitious people like the Rumanians this terrible earthquake seemed by way of divine reprisal for their failure to revenge their martyrs.

It was my first major earthquake. I found it very convincing in the sense that God in his ire can still do far better than man. In less than three minutes some ten thousand houses in Bucharest had become uninhabitable, and thousands more in the country itself. There were many dead. The damage achieved by nature in these short minutes could not be equaled by the RAF or the Luftwaffe in days and weeks.

There was something inexorable about the earthquake. In an air attack, you run for shelter and do all the right things prescribed by the authorities. The mortality is comparatively small. But you can't be smart in an earthquake. There are no right things to do; the house either holds together, in which case everything is fine, or the house crumples. Then one is buried underneath, no matter whether one is halfway down the staircase, or out of the house, or in bed. It happens that fast. The feeling of helplessness in an earthquake is something to remember. It frightened even hardened German soldiers. "Say," I heard a young officer say to his comrade, "did I have to come here to find certain death? In a storm attack a guy can at least run. But here? I saw those yellow marble pillars coming toward me and not a chance of an escape. Awful feeling!"

The earthquake came at 3:30 in the morning, when

most people were asleep. I awoke only when the stucco of
the ceiling began falling on my bed and the walls made
slow solemn curtsies over me. Through the window I saw
the houses around the Square waving to and fro like trees
in a wind-swept forest. This, I thought, must be the end,
and I put the pillow over my face: not because I thought
it was safer but because I thought it would hurt less, when
all this plaster that was the Athene Palace would come
down over me. I heard the noise of creaking wood, such
as one heard on boats, of tiles in the bathroom cracking
off, of glass breaking, of voices and shrieks outside in the
corridor. I saw no point in going downstairs; the hotel
would probably crash while I was on the stairs.

The earthquake lasted only two and a half minutes, it
was said later, but they seemed a very long two and a half
minutes and the suspense got terribly on one's nerves.
The walls bent at an ever steeper angle, tables tumbled
over, the wardrobe wobbled dangerously. . . . At the next
jerk it will crash, I thought time and again. But suddenly
the earth quieted down, and my small flashlight, for the
lights had gone out, showed me a room in shambles, with
fragments of bottles and pieces of stucco all over the floor
and deep cracks in the walls. The room looked as if it
could not hold together through one more shake. One of
the Tester children knocked at my door and called excitedly that more was coming and I had better come down
to the lobby. Putting on some clothes, I picked my way
downstairs.

The guests had already gathered in the entrance hall
and the passage, as far away from the yellow marble pillars
as possible—and also as near the door as possible. Most
of them looked disheveled and bewildered. A young Ger-

man woman was in hysterics and in her best fur coat.
Everyone was in negligee except for some German businessmen from Hamburg who had been celebrating in the
bar. I discovered that night that Italians wear their party
buttons even on their pajamas, and that they prefer violent, striped dressing gowns. The German Babbitts in negligee looked exactly as I had always suspected German
Babbitts of looking in negligee. This was a night rich in
confirmations and disappointments.

Princess Elisabeth Bibescu walked up and down the passage hall like a tigress in captivity—a tigress in trailing
rose crêpe de chine with laces, looking rather chilly on
this uncomfortable November night. She seemed resentful
that a major unpleasantness in the Balkans had happened
for which one could not blame Hitler. Someone heard her
mutter, "This earthquake makes me sick, but all the Huns
here make me sicker." The prospect of being buried rub-
bing shoulders with the Huns apparently worried her.

"Did you find anyone in this crowd with whom you
would like to die?" I asked Priscilla Bibescu, Elisabeth's
young daughter, an amusing mixture of the most civilized
West and the East at its most sophisticated, with large dark
liquid eyes and copper hair. Unlike Mama she was not
much given to political brooding and never discriminated
against any man on national grounds. "Don't you think
those little Italians are cute?" She gestured in the direction
of the violent, striped dressing gowns.

Otherwise the talk was mostly of the earthquake and
what everybody thought and did when it happened, and
what he was going to do when it came again, as everyone
seemed convinced it would.

The husband of the young woman in hysterics went for

his car; he thought it smart to get out of the city into the open where nothing could fall upon him. But Dr. Tester felt that so much might fall upon you while making for the open spaces that it was as well to stay here. Tester looked less than ever like a dashing revolutionary; draped in a raspberry-colored silk dressing gown and surrounded by his wife, children, sons-in-law, governesses and pet dogs, he was Abraham the patriarch.

News came that Carlton House had crashed, burying beneath it hundreds of its inhabitants, and some of us went out into the steady rain to see it. It was dark and very windy. Carlton House was an apartment house in the Avenue Bratianu less than five minutes from the Athene Palace. It was a skyscraper with a picture theatre and shops downstairs. When we came to where Carlton House had been, there was nothing but a heap of plaster and stones and twisted rods and wirework. The heap was not even very high, and the awful thing about it was that it was so very quiet. One knew that there were some three hundred people buried underneath this pile, and it was the quietness which made it all so horrible.

The architect and the contractors of Carlton House were later put in jail, for there was something seriously wrong about the construction. But they should not have built skyscrapers in Bucharest in the first place. "Never build in the principalities," one of the phanariotes once advised his son, thinking of the earthquakes and fires which periodically ravage Moldavian and Walachian cities; and until the beginning of the century Bucharest houses had been one-storied and many of them still were. These were very much in demand now.

A silent crowd gathered around the heap that had been

Carlton House, hopefully watching German soldiers, hundreds of them, who were frantically digging away. The German soldiers had been the first to arrive. Both the Generals and their staffs supervised the work, their long dark leather coats glistening in the light of the torches which were placed around the heap. There were, it appeared, people still alive in the basement of the Carlton. They had talked over the telephone. Could they be saved? One of the German officers shrugged his shoulders. The digging had to be done with the utmost care so as not to hurt anybody still alive in the heap. A few had been saved so far, people who lived in studios directly under the roof and had got away without a scratch by just sliding down. The Germans were trying to make the elevator shaft free to get down that way. There was great danger of fire.

Side by side with greenshirts and Rumanian soldiers, the Germans dug away for forty-eight hours, and though the people in the basement of the Carlton House were not saved, the Rumanians were touched by the efficient and matter-of-fact way the German soldiers had shared their national disaster. Like an individual—any of us knows the kind—who is no great shakes in the daily routine of friendship but knows how to make himself useful in emergencies, the Germans owed their short hour of popularity to an earthquake.

The earthquake, topping so many misfortunes, had an unsettling effect on Rumanian morale. And no wonder! Now Rumania had, aside from the refugees from Bessarabia and Transylvania, thousands of evacuees from houses which had crashed or were in danger of crashing. Prices rose by leaps and bounds, the maximum prices on foodstuffs which the Government set only resulting in an al-

most complete shortage of eggs and butter in the cities.
People said, of course, that everything was going to the
German troops, but this was not true at the time. The
chief reason was that the peasants had begun to hoard
their foodstuffs instead of selling them at prices which did
not cover costs. Another reason was the too-sudden elimination of the Jewish middleman, which had partially in-
terrupted marketing facilities. Half-starved dogs began
roaming the streets, for the first thing Rumanians did
when they felt the pinch was set loose their dogs. The
gypsy beggars told their story of "mama on her deathbed"
so convincingly that it nearly broke your heart.

In this atmosphere of gloom a shepherd to whom the
Rumanian people attributed great gifts of clairvoyance
prophesied a bigger and better earthquake on Saturday,
the twenty-third of November, saying that the earth would
swallow up Bucharest and especially that great house of
sin, the Athene Palace—a prophecy which resulted in an
exodus of the wealthier bourgeoisie and of many guests
of the Athene Palace to Sinaia and Brasov "for the week-
end." People had really grown nervous. Even I watched
out for marble pillars and glass chandeliers apt to crash
down in case of an earthquake.

The main thoroughfares of the city were still blocked
off, because of danger from stones falling from houses;
around the Carlton House was the smell of decaying
corpses, and the papers were full of reports of the *cutremur,*
which means earthquake, when suddenly General Antonescu went to Berlin and signed Rumania's entry into
the Tri-Partite pact. This pact was a typical diplomatic
instrument of Hitler's New Order in that here not even

a pretense was made that the minor powers enjoyed equal rights with the great powers. According to the stipulations of this pact Rumania had no say in the councils of the Big Three, but would only participate in deliberations of vital interest to herself. Yet while the entry meant only that the Guardist state officially recognized the domination of Europe by the Axis and the domination of the Far East by Japan, the Guardist press did its best to play up the event as a major success for the young state and the forerunner of more profitable events. It was strange to see how sanguine the Guardists were about the whole affair.

Because they had gotten rid of a regime which had double-crossed Hitler, Guardist Rumania felt entitled to a revision of the Vienna decision, caused, they were convinced, exclusively by the sins of the former people. It was, so they reasoned, all right for Hitler to punish Carol, but there was not the slightest reason to punish his loyal little brother fascists. The least Hitler "owed" them, they felt, was the immediate return of the region around Cluj in Transylvania. So when Antonescu came back from Berlin, the Guardists turned out for a big reception, then marched straight to the German and Italian legations, heartily cheering both Axis ministers, but finishing their ovations with shouts of "Revenge for Transylvania!"

While all this happened quite amiably, it worried thoughtful Axis diplomats, for the Guardist attitude indicated by such demonstrations was apt to conflict embarrassingly with the necessities of Axis policies. How could Hitler, even if he wanted to, give back Transylvania when Hungary was forever loyally linked to the Axis and her revisionist claims closely tied to all he stood for? It was completely unrealistic even to consider. What could one do with these Guardist-babies, with their unbroken record of loyalty towards the Third Reich, and so stupid and unrealistic at the same time?

Yet even though Antonescu did not bring Transylvania back from Berlin, he did not come home empty-handed. The success he scored, while it remained intangible then, and even something of a secret, was a very consequential success indeed. For Antonescu had made a quite amazing, quite unexpected personal hit with the Führer. I heard from German diplomatic sources that he spent several hours with the Führer in strict tête-à-tête, while even the German minister, Dr. Fabrizius, who chaperoned Antonescu around the Wilhelmstrasse, cooled his heels in the waiting room. Afterwards the Führer was reported to have told his entourage that, of all those "Latins"—and one surmised that he meant Pétain, Darlan, Laval and maybe even Mussolini—this Rumanian general was the only one with whom he could really work. There was little doubt that in this long heart-to-heart talk the General made a clean breast of his anti-German past and also of his present difficulties with Horia Sima, and that the Führer exhorted him to show his mettle and promised support.

To let the General go to Berlin without him was a terrible mistake for Sima. It showed that the long-haired revolutionary lacked the most elementary knowledge of human relations; he did not know that the absent ones are always in the wrong. Horia Sima had two reasons for staying in Bucharest. One was that he felt cocksure an old Guardist would always be nearer the heart of the Führer than a former chum of Gamelin—a notion which showed how little he knew about the political game as Hitler played it. The other reason was that Sima was afraid to turn his back on the mounting intrigues and unrest in his own party. This reason was valid.

The rank and file of the Guardist party was understandably sore that they got so little out of their revolution. After they had been fed for a while on beautiful but tiring demonstrations, they had been reduced during the last weeks to a series of funerals. The Rumanians have a passion for funerals, the longer the better, and it seemed a good idea to exhume the party martyrs and to bury them anew, with honors. Ordinarily this would have pleased the Guardists no end, but on an empty stomach the long marches which were connected with these ceremonies, and the standing around in the cold November air made the boys realize that they were very hungry. Even before the earthquake, it was evident that exhuming and burying corpses alone did not make little Guardists happy. They needed better circuses and, above all, they needed bread.

This growing discontent among the rank and file was, of course, taken up by Codreanu père, that wily old gentleman. Old Codreanu had successfully tried to harass Horia Sima all along. He put his protégés on the Party or on the Government's payroll, nobody knew on what right; he said mean things about Horia Sima, and finally ended up at one of the big Guardist meetings in Yassy making a public speech to the effect that if there was a vicar-on-earth of his son, it was certainly he, the father. This speech, hurriedly censored for publication, was heard by thousands of Guardists and duly increased dissatisfaction in the party. A radical group in the party, with a definite communist streak to it, ganged up with the old man for a common effort to wrench the power from Horia

Sima. One day a few hundred of these opposition Guardists invaded the Green House, Guardist replica of the Nazi Brown House and headquarters of the Guardist Party on the outskirts of Bucharest, and some shooting occurred. Horia Sima proceeded to a party purge the extent of which was never known. Several hundred Guardists were put in jail and some were shot. Codreanu père, was, of course, sacrosanct, but seemed to agree to an *arrêt de domicile*, at least for a few days. As he put it himself in his sly manner, "I like to stay home. I feel safer there from bullets—from communists, you know." It was clear that he did not mean communist bullets, but the bullets of the Sima crowd.

If Horia Sima thus had performed a minor party purge to rid himself of the articulate opposition within the party, much in the way Hitler did when he shot Roehm and his crowd in 1934, he followed his purge with actions very different from Hitler's. To Hitler the purge of the radical wing in his party was the means to reach an understanding with the conservative forces of the army, an understanding which was to form the real foundation of his power. Instead Horia Sima's game was to become the head of this radical group himself, after having eliminated its leadership.

I met frequently with Guardists close to Horia Sima and in high government positions. They said that it was necessary for Sima to cater to the radicals, for otherwise he could not hold his flock together. He had to suffer now for the tactical mistake he made at the beginning of the revolution, when he failed to permit a bloody holiday.

So at last, in November, Horia Sima, by way of catering to the radicals, let down the barriers and permitted his boys to have the kind of bloody revolution they were longing for. And because so much bitterness, hate, and lust for revenge had festered too long, the revolution degenerated into orgies of terror. First of all the Guardists got what amounted to a green light in persecuting the Jews. Two hundred squads of six men each were turned loose in Bucharest every night for raids on Jewish houses. Officially the purpose was to search for hidden money, but in reality these Guardists looted, terrorized, and blackmailed the Jews into giving up silver, jewels, money, whatever was in reach. The leather-clad figures of these boys with their high fur caps and their motorcycles became a nightly feature of Bucharest, the symbol of Guardist terror.

Jewish shops were confiscated openly by Guardists, without even the formalities of purchase, and the Jewish shop owners were robbed of their last farthing, in the smaller towns even more than in Bucharest. When decent party elements—because there were decent party elements—or the Nazis asked Horia Sima to do something about it, he shrugged his shoulder and said, "I can't. They would not stand for it." It had come to that.

Dr. Neubacher once said to Horia Sima, "Did your Capitano die so that the worst criminals should get the richest spoils?" Horia Sima had no answer to such questions any longer. He was now committed to giving his revolution a holiday.

Looting the Jews was only the first part of the program. The second was a night-of-the-long-knives, several nights-of-the-long-knives—revenge for the death of the Guardist martyrs.

Already, in the month before, the Rumanian Government, in order to appease the radical wing of the party, which had never forgiven their escape, had asked the Spanish Government to extradite Lupescu and Urdareanu. Actually nobody except the Guardists themselves ever believed that this extradition would take place, for there are immense formalities connected with the extradition of political refugees. Not even fascist countries stooped to extraditing political refugees until Marshal Pétain, probably under terrific pressure, admitted a clause to the Armistice treaty extraditing political refugees to Hitler. The Rumanians could not bring such pressure on Franco; it is a safe bet that they did not even try it, for two important people were certainly dead set against it. They were King Michael and Queen Helen. Also Antonescu himself, who had, after all, tried to preserve the dynasty, could not look forward to a trial which would compromise the dynasty hopelessly. As to the Germans, they were opposed to the idea because the Führer, having a weak spot in his heart for the Hohenzollern dynasty in Rumania, did not wish to involve it in a scandal of enormous proportions.

While fascist governments treat legality cavalierly if it suits them, they become sticklers for legality when it fits their plans. The legal point Axis diplomats made against Lupescu's extradition was that she was Carol's wife. A wife cannot be a witness against her husband, so, as a witness against Carol—and this was what Lupescu's part in the planned trial would amount to—she was out, which was why Axis diplomats proclaimed Lupescu could not be legally extradited. After a few weeks one heard no more of Lupescu's extradition, but the Guardists were still hopeful about the extradition of Urdareanu, thinking that because their men had fought and died for Franco his regime owed them a favor. In the lobby of the Athene Palace one could hear blood-curdling stories of Udurianu arriving at the Rumanian frontier, sewed in a sack, having made the entire trip from Seville in a cattle train. The Rumanians loved this story, even non-Guardists, but it was not true. The Spanish let Urdareanu slip out of Spain and over the Portuguese frontier, to the great relief of everybody but the Guardists.

With the extradition of the main villains a flop, a trial of Marinescu and his henchmen seemed to be the next best number on the Guardist program of revenge for the Guardist killings. A member of the camarilla, Gavrila Marinescu, Carol's Chief of Police, whose rackets would make Al Capone seem petty by comparison, was responsible for most of the bloody terror against the Iron Guard. Already foreign journalists were told that the writ against Marinescu was five hundred pages long, had been translated into four languages, and that in it we would get better reading than we had ever had in the worst dime novels. The trial was to be a grandiose affair that could not end otherwise than with a public hanging. Young Guardist officials told this as if it were something especially arranged for our benefit, something we could really look forward to.

Then one day came the news that there would be no public trial and no public hanging, as Marinescu and sixty-three other political prisoners had been killed at the military prison of Fort Jilava. Others killed were Moruzov, who was said to have worked up from a Russian spy to the all-powerful chief of Carol's secret police; General Argeseanu, former Prime Minister under whose Government the Guardist killings took place in 1939; all the officials, gendarmes, and the Minister of Justice involved in the killing of the Capitano. It was a tremendous story, but the censorship clamped down on foreign journalists. Only the German official agency could send the story, using the telephone of the German Legation which was uncensored.

Twenty-four hours later the Bureau de la Presse finally found a suitable version of the killings to give to the world. This was their version: A group of Guardists who were detailed to lift the slab of asbestos from over the grave of the Capitano and the ten "Decemvirii" and the three "Nicadorii" got so frenzied at the sight of the hideously mutilated bodies of their Capitano and his comrades that they stormed the prison and killed all those connected with the deed. The General and Horia Sima, the version went on, disapproved very much of the murder, and the guilty were in jail and would be punished.

The truth was essentially different. True, the mass murder was enacted after the exhumation of the fourteen corpses; so far the official version was correct. But—and this was important—the action was by no means spontaneous; rather it was planned and approved by the highest Guardist dignitaries. This does not mean that the murderers were not frenzied, for they certainly were. A communist who at the time was a prisoner at Jilava told later that the Guardists first killed everyone involved in the killing of their leaders, then when they were through, emptied their guns at everyone in sight. They could not stop, the communist said; it was a kind of madness which they had to get out of their systems.

The sight of the mutilated corpses alone could not have inspired the Guardists to this bloody deed, for they knew beforehand how they would find the corpses. It was rather that they were drunk with the lust for revenge-which-had-had-to-wait-too-long. The Guardist official who gave the story to the foreign press, a charming young man brought up in the United States, ended his report with a defiant statement of his own to the effect that every single Guardist approved of the Jilava mass murder, and this was so.

One of the highest Guardist dignitaries told me later that he had been in on the plans for the Jilava murder, and that Horia Sima had also been in on them. I have no reason to doubt the truth of this story. One of the bloodthirstiest, most sadistic men I ever met in my pursuit of reality, this man was proud of his own murder record. Nor did he wish to slander Horia Sima by pointing out that he too was a fellow who knew his way around. It had been agreed, so the Guardist dignitary explained to me, that Horia Sima would have an airtight alibi for the night of the murder and that he would play shocked surprise afterwards.

The only one who was really surprised and shocked, however, was Antonescu. The General took the murders very much to heart and was not fooled. He realized that Horia Sima was playing up to the radical rank and file of the Guardist party, possibly because he could not do otherwise. Detesting violence, Antonescu was reported anxious to resign, but Dr. Fabrizius, who since the happy encounter with the Führer, clucked over the General like a hen over her young, told him that he owed it to the Führer's friendship to stick it out. Also, the minister implied, the Führer was always with the strong. So Antonescu did not resign.

The day after the Jilava killings it came out that the Guardists had also killed Nicholas Jorga and Virgil Ma-

gearu, the latter one of the leaders of the Peasant Party
and Maniu's friend. I wept over the ghastly assassination
of Jorga. The Guardists kidnaped him from his country
house near Ploesti, took him to the forest and tore out his
long white beard before they killed him. I wept because
it was an unbearable thought that the last Goethean man
should be assassinated so ignobly. True, Professor Jorga
was only a Rumanian version of the Goethean man, but
there was genius about an erudition both encyclopaedic
and graceful and which, through his prodigious, never-
failing memory, he had always at his fingertips.

With Jorga it had also been a relief that for a change
a scholar lived in the princely style which elsewhere was
only affected by bankers, tycoons, and Hollywood pro-
ducers. Jorga had oscillated between the house in the
Chaussée Bonaparte in Bucharest, with its wonderful library of fifty thousand volumes, his summer university
near Ploesti, his house in Sinaia, his Rumanian school in
Fontenays-en-Roses in France, and his Palazzo in Venice
which housed his Byzantine school—teaching as he went,
telling his "Rabelaisian" stories, most of which were of his
own making but attributed to Rabelais because this made
them more respectable. Like many talented people he
changed his mind frequently and found nothing illogical
about it. He was curious about all kinds of political ideas
and able to make a good case for them, but people resented
his volatility.

From personal reaction to the Guardist killings I found
that it is one thing to talk nights-of-the-long-knives and
another thing to witness them. One's nerves are in no way
involved in theoretically acknowledging the necessity of a

bloody holiday for a revolution; but the real thing requires a strong stomach.

The Count, too, was disgusted when we met for the apéritif the day after the big killings.

"This is what comes from 'letting the revolution run hot,' " I heckled.

"Probably," he agreed meekly, "one should have let them have a go at it right in the beginning."

"Will the Germans do something about it now?"

"I don't think so," he answered vaguely. "It must get worse before it gets better."

To top off Rumania's gloomy week of mass murder, what was left of Corneliu Zelea Codreanu and the ten Decemvirii and three Nicadorii was laid in their last resting-place in the crypt of the Green House, on Saturday, November 30, 1940. In retrospect Codreanu's State Funeral was an apotheosis of the short-lived Guardist regime. On this occasion for the last time emissaries of the Axis turned out to honor a Guardist martyr. For the last time General Antonescu wore his green shirt, thus identifying himself with the Guardist revolution. And for the last time he and Horia Sima appeared together in public, thus representing a common front.

The day the Guardists chose for Codreanu's funeral was the anniversary of his assassination in 1938. Because everybody was jittery about the mass murders in the beginning of the week and the terror in their wake, one assumed that the funeral would be called off at the last moment. But the Guardists did not want to cancel the trip of Hitler's special envoys, Baldur von Schirach, former leader of the Hitler youth, now Gauleiter of Vienna, and Herr

Bohle, who handled the *Volksdeutsche* section in the Wilhelmstrasse. Moreover, the Guardists thought the funeral of their chief martyr a fitting finale for a week abundant in death: they liked it macabre. So they went through with the funeral of the Capitano according to plan.

Rumanians of all political colors are wonderful at funerals, and adore them, but the Guardists surpassed them all. No wonder theirs was called *"Le régime des pompes funèbres"* in Bucharest and people joked that in spite of their many martyrs there were not enough to satisfy the Guardist passion for exhumations and burials. The funeral of the Capitano was of course the biggest, beginning at 8:30 in the morning and ending around 4:30 in the afternoon. Except the dignitaries and the press most of the people who walked in the cortège covered some six miles on foot one way and six miles back.

The morning of the Capitano's funeral suited the occasion: the sky was gray, snow was in the air, and a Chicago-like blizzard blew cold. On the boulevards through which the cortège was to pass, all the street lamps were veiled in green, and large green posters carrying in big letters CORNELIU ZELEA CODREANU PRESENT were placed every few hundred yards. The cortège formed before the little church Ilie Gorgani, located on a side street off the Boulevard Elisabetha. All the outside of the church and the square before it were swathed in green drapes. Big woodcuts of the Capitano and the Archangel Michael hung on one wall, and on the other wall was again a huge sign CORNELIU ZELEA CODREANU PRESENT. Posted before the church was a battalion of Rumanian soldiers and troops of greenshirts, all shivering in the cold. Fourteen stands waited on the square for the fourteen caskets, and fourteen tables carried the "Coliva," the colored sugar bread which by custom was to be carried behind the coffins.

Following exhumation at the fort of Jilava the fourteen caskets had been placed in this little church and in spite of the sinister happenings—or because of them—people had streamed here to pray by the casket of the Capitano. Today only the family and dignitaries were admitted to the short religious service in the church, but it took some time to form the cortège before the church: it was such a long cortège. First came the relatives of the fourteen dead, then the envoy of the King, walking all by himself in a uniform which was practically all gold lace, followed by the General and Horia Sima in their simple green shirts. Then came the Tri-Partite ministers: German, Italian, Japanese, but not Hungarian though Hungary belonged to the Pact. Instead the Spanish minister marched, though Spain did not belong to the Pact. These ministers, in their diplomatic uniforms, were followed by Hitler's special envoys, wearing their SA uniforms, and behind them came General Speidel with a few high officers who were followed by the Tri-Partite military attachés, again minus the Hungarian but plus the Spanish one, followed by the press, the various Hitler youth and *Volksdeutsche* and Italian and Spanish delegations, and thousands and thousands of greenshirts.

The caskets were carried down the stairs of the little church, one after the other, decked out with the Rumanian flag. For each casket all hands went up in salute, except for the officers who gave the military salute. For each casket one could hear the mourners at the head of the procession bawling away as if their sorrow over the death was two days and not two years old. The last casket was the Capitano's, and here the bawling became a kind of howling, as I had heard the Arabs howl at Fantasias in Morocco. The clergy in gleaming brocade veiled in black ranged themselves behind the caskets, and the procession slowly set out through the silent green-veiled boulevards, lined with saluting greenshirts and other saluting citizens.

I walked next to the only English journalist left in Bucharest, a Mr. Clark, who must have had a tough and lonely time of it in Nazi-dominated, green-shirted Bucharest, but carried it off with great charm and dignity. Because it was a sad occasion the chef du protocole had forbidden us to talk or to laugh as the immense procession slowly wound up the boulevards, but we managed a whispered conversation, amusing ourselves in trying to find out who murdered whom. For word had got out that the assassins of the Jilava murder and of Nicholas Jorga and Magearu had not been put in prison, as had been officially announced, but were right in our midst. There were also some very tough-looking men in black leather coats and high gray fur caps walking beside the procession. They were the dreaded Guardist police, also officially said to be disbanded, but this was just one of the things "written on paper" which did not mean a thing in Rumanian reality.

The Green House was way out in the wilderness where there were not even cobblestones, only mud and dust. It had become icy cold. Even the German Generals had blue noses. The courtyard of the Green House was much too small to hold the thousands of greenshirts who had come all the way in the blizzard to see their Capitano buried. I felt sorry for them, they looked so hungry and cold, but their chiefs informed me that the Guardists were tough and that they were wearing jackets of cat's fur underneath their green shirts—and anyway: "These boys are happy to have been allowed to accompany the mortal remains of their Capitano, even if they can't attend the funeral."

Solemn snowflakes began to fall, as the gold brocaded clergy began intoning the litanies, and the caskets of the Capitano and the Decemvirii and the Nicadorii were let down into their grave. Rumanian and German army planes flew low over the yard, dropping their wreaths neatly into the crypt, before which older greenshirts stood as an honorary guard with the incense floating right by their faces and up into the gray afternoon sky. The officers gave the military salute to the grave and everybody else gave the fascist salute. It was almost intolerably cold. Some diplomats were shivering so much that their saluting hands looked as if they were winking. Again the mourners bawled away with the abandon of fresh sorrow. Old Codreanu cried very hard. He wore his white peasant costume and I hoped that he too had a cat's fur under his linen shirt; however, it was surprising that he was alive at all. Horia Sima stood on an elevation of the crypt, his small eyes darting quickly from the generals to the possible Guardist murderers and back to the Tri-Partite envoys and over to Codreanu père and back to General Antonescu. He did not miss a thing.

After the funeral one of the German generals said to Horia Sima by way of praise: "It was a lovely funeral." Whereas Horia looked him over severely and said: "You call this lovely? It was *sad*." The General, duly abashed, commented later that he had never realized how "awfully mystical" those Guardists were. But for once the General was wrong and Horia Sima was right. There was a melancholy grandeur to the burial of the Capitano: These high foreign dignitaries who represented the Powers with whom the Capitano vainly desired his country to ally eventually. Their gleaming uniforms contrasting strangely with the shabby mourning clothes of the mothers and widows of the dead they had come from afar to honor. The young Guardists lining the yard shivering in a cold as relentless as the fate which had robbed them of their real leaders. This bare hunted landscape. The slow solemn snowflakes. The sweet scent of incense mingling with the sour scent of terror. The tragedy or tragicomedy of mutual betrayal developing in the shadow of the Capitano's grave.

The sour smell of terror pervaded the air of Bucharest and the Athene Palace, shocking even the Old Excellencies into discreetly whispering atrocity stories instead of shouting amorous indiscretions, as they usually did. There seemed to be nobody who did not have a friend or relative among those killed, and now not only the Jews were thoroughly frightened, but also everybody else in Rumania.

Except that Dr. Fabrizius spirited out of the country some of the "former people" who sought the German legation for protection, among them Manoilescu, Gigurtu, and Tatarescu, the Germans did not interfere with the course of Guardist terror, one way or the other—an aloofness which gave rise to an outburst of vehement criticism. Juliu Maniu, the old liberal, sent off one of his letters to the Führer which, if it did not reach Hitler, at least reached everybody in the lobby of the Athene Palace. In this missive Maniu told Hitler how shocking it was that such awful things happened right under the nose of the

German military mission, which was costing the Rumanian people too much money anyway. (It had been one of Antonescu's minor successes in Berlin that he had considerably reduced the expenses for his military "guests," but this detail was by and large ignored.)

But on the whole the chief complaint of the Rumanian bourgeoisie was that the military mission was altogether too small. What with terror rampant the Rumanians now clamored for an honest to God occupation army to hold the Guardists in check. After all, they argued, Hitler owed them protection against the regime which he himself sponsored.

Moreover, the Rumanians felt that the terror was actually Hitler's fault, not only in that he had sponsored the Guardist regime, but even more so in that he had introduced the standards of lawlessness which now prevailed all over Europe. While in Germany, people pointed out, these standards were interpreted with more bureaucratic thoroughness than bloodthirsty zest—due to the fact that the Germans had no talent for hate and were deep down too disciplined to get a kick out of violence—the Rumanians could not be expected to interpret the lawlessness in any such disciplined terms. Rumanians, they said, were a sadistic lot, half oriental, savage, carrying in their subconscious memory the image of the bloody deeds which all kinds of foreign conquerors had perpetrated on them through the centuries, and also carrying in their conscious memory the picture of the murdered Guardists lying about in the streets. Give Rumanians half a chance for blood revenge and they take it in a big way.

This unrestrained Guardist interpretation of totalitarianism was bound to compromise the Nazis as advocates of totalitarianism. No doubt many more Rumanians thought the Germans wonderful, or at least tolerable, before the Guardist terror than afterwards.

"The Guardists are discrediting totalitarianism as such," I said to the Count. "Don't exaggerate!" he replied languidly, "the Guardists discredit totalitarianism about as much as a chimpanzee, taught the trick of using knife and fork, discredits good table manners." But the Count was wrong. The Guardist terror did hurt the Nazi prestige in Rumania.

Probably, Rumanian criticism of Nazism would not have dared to become so articulate that November had not the Axis for the first time suffered a setback of sorts. While, after the swift fall of France, Rumania, like the rest of the European continent, felt nobody had a chance to resist armed forces of the Axis, now the unexpected British resistance against German air bombardments, and also the Greek resistance against Italian aggression, buoyed European people up, especially the people in small countries. Possibly, they thought, the German army was not invincible. Possibly, they thought too, the Germans will lose the war, now that Mr. Roosevelt had been reelected and promised aid to the British. At that time everybody in Europe except the Germans and the French in Vichy believed that America could do military and industrial wonders on the spur of the moment—a belief which American diplomats and distinguished travelers fostered assiduously.

"I don't think that there is a single Rumanian today who believes that the Germans will win the war," the Count confided to me with a half-amused, half-annoyed frown one day that November.

"Maybe General Antonescu believes it," I suggested amiably.

"Maybe General Antonescu wishes to believe it," corrected the Count. "But does he really?" Then he added energetically, "They will snap out of this ridiculous mood, the Rumanians, the moment the Führer pulls a new rabbit out of his hat."

The Rumanians did snap out of it. Nobody who did not witness it himself can imagine the fickleness of European moods in this war. When, for a few months, Hitler suffered what looked like setbacks, people bet on a British victory, only to return violently to the belief that Hitler held all the cards once he reasserted his monopoly of military power on the Continent. Everything is fluid about the moods of the European people, and this the Germans realized only too well, and did not take seriously. As long as the war was on, and the Germans had their armies everywhere in Europe to enforce their will, they did not have to worry.

Still, it was fascinating to watch how, hardly five months after her abject surrender to life-with-Hitler, Europe began to put up some sort of opposition to Germany. For just as last summer Rumania's surrender was typical of what happened all over Europe, her opposition in November was the image of opposition all over Europe. This opposition, temporary as it was, proved an important fact: Hitler had not won the soul of the European Continent after the first exhausted surrender of the summer of 1940. Any slight weakness he showed anywhere became a signal for stiffening resistance against him. He had to say it with tanks and parachutists all the time. He had to prove his power over and over again, or, as the great German historian and sociologist Max Weber put it: "A ruler by charisma (the Greek for charm) must prove his charm all the time."

And the real point was: how long could Hitler, how long could anybody, keep up proving his charm? And how would he go about proving it after the war, once he could not say it with tanks and parachutists any longer? Could Hitler win the soul of Europe with his new order?

14—GERMAN ORDER

In the course of this autumn in Bucharest I saw the pattern of the new European order coming little by little into focus. This pattern made me wonder whether the Germans could ever make a go of their new order, even if they should win the war. It was not merely their diplomatic and political muddling through which cut scrawls of its own all across the design. This muddling through, astounding though it was because everyone attributed to the Nazis a superhuman efficiency, did little irreparable damage, one had to admit, and had merely slowed up the effectiveness of the German plans. But beyond this I detected intrinsic weaknesses and contradictions in the pattern itself which seemed to jeopardize the workability of the New Order and make for its own defeat. More often than not this muddling through came up against these intrinsic weaknesses and contradictions. Then the New Order did not seem to make any sense at all.

What the pattern showed unquestionably was that the
Nazis were good at conquering but deplorable at exploit-
ing their conquests, even for their own good, not to speak
of the good of the conquered. The Germans had been
quite smart in bringing about the Rumanian surrender,
what with their delightful fifth column doing a neat job
on Rumanian society and their barter and hardworking
thoroughness bringing undeniable advantages to Rumanian economy. But from the day the fall of France finally
catapulted Rumania, fifth richest oil land in the world and
second richest in Europe, right into Hitler's arms, their
policy became a succession of uninspired improvisations,
blundering along in a half-hearted fashion with no fore-
sight and a minimum of ideas. Which showed that also
in totalitarian politics genius does not work on a twenty-
four hour basis.

The Germans' first mistake was the unimaginative decision of Vienna, which created a new Rumanian revisionism without quite satisfying the old Hungarian one. Some
observers argued that this Vienna decision was a cleverly
devised instrument of Hitler's policy of "divide and rule"
in the Balkans—a way of perpetuating the enmity between Hungary and Rumania so that the two could not
unite against Germany. But as Hungary and Rumania
could not do anything to Germany, even if united, this
argument did not hold. What Hitler needed in his Southeastern Grossraum was not the tension which goes with
a policy of divide and rule, but a measure of quiet and
peace. Instead, with this new revisionism went all sorts
of potential disturbances in the Southeast, all undesirable to the Germans and all eventually directed against
their New Order.

The first consequence of the Vienna decision was Carol's abdication. Happy though the Rumanians were to get rid of Carol, it was not in German interest to let him go. In retrospect the German officials themselves admitted wistfully that it was easier to deal with a Balkan king than with these Guardists, who were corrupt too, but so many other things besides. Carol in the long run would have made a perfect tool in German hands, as only a man with a perpetually guilty conscience about perpetrated or planned sins against the Führer, a man detested by his people and dependent on outside support, could be.

These German officials also admitted that the cabinet of Gigurtu and Manoilescu, who in spite of their fascist tendencies were basically bourgeois and loath to disrupt Rumanian economy, had been much easier to work with than the present Guardist regime. Not only were they financial and economic experts, while the Guardists were experts only in revenge and destruction—they were also much more amenable than the Guardist regime to collaboration with Germany.

In the intricate pattern of the German conquest of Rumania nothing was more indicative than the fact that the Guardist Government, the Government of complete Rumanian totalitarianism, was less amenable to German collaboration than the Gigurtu Government, the sincere fascism of which the Nazis always rightly doubted.

This had little or nothing to do with German muddling-through or inefficiency, but was rather a matter of the intrinsic weaknesses and contradictions in the New Order. For by no means were the difficulties which the Germans experienced with the Guardists caused solely by a lack of Guardist experts or the revolutionary quality of the regime, or by the fact that the atrocities perpetrated by the Guardists compromised totalitarianism as such, thus alienating the good will which Germany had first enjoyed. The main reason why Rumanian fascism did not work into the hands of Germany was that, with the Guardist revolution, a wave of nationalist egoism such as a bourgeois regime could never conceive swept over Rumania. This sharp nationalist egoism, which was the raison d'être of the Guardist revolution, was bound to conflict with German interests. Nor was such sharp nationalist egoism limited to the Guardist revolution. It was what all fascist revolution is about, which was why the Nazis will be in trouble wherever in Europe they achieve fascist revolution. From the pattern, as I saw it in Rumania, it would seem that fascist revolution in subjected countries is actually more dangerous for Germany than the preservation of some kind of status quo.

In Rumania I saw it work this way: the Germans, while not overjoyed over the prospect of the Guardist revolution because of its lack of leadership, were nevertheless resigned to the idea. The Guardists, they figured, owed their very existence to Nazi Germany and would have a vested interest in the German victory. German welfare would be their prime consideration, and loyalty to Germany would exclude any other loyalty. But it did not work out this way. The Guardists were not disloyal to Germany, but their first loyalty belonged to Rumania—and their second loyalty, too, and their third and fourth. Then there came nothing for a long space and the next loyalty after this belonged to Germany. So the Guardists forgot most of the time that they owed their existence to the Nazis, and spent more time wondering what they could get out of them.

Collaboration with Germany interested the Guardists only inasmuch as it would help them strengthen their military and industrial machine for their own revisionist purposes. Their entire attitude towards Germany was on a strictly "Gimme"-basis, an attitude which Carol with his guilty conscience would have never dared to take, but which these virtuously fascist revolutionists thought quite natural. Their loyalty to Germany was chiefly linked with their belief that Hitler would make them a strong nation and that he would give them back the lost provinces.

First sign of the Guardists' sharpened nationalist egoism was the passive resistance to attempts at Germanizing the Rumanian economy, the Guardists' lack of collaboration with the German desire for quiet in the raw-material sphere. But in the last few weeks the crass nationalist egoism of the Guardists became even more pronounced. To the exasperation of the Nazis it became increasingly clear that the first aim of the Guardists was not German victory but the return of Rumania's lost provinces.

Guardist dignitaries expressed this hope in two ways. The more moderate ones would say, "We have to be armed to the teeth so as to fight the Hungarians and Bulgarians and Russians. That's why we tolerate the German military mission and the German experts meddling in our industry: they teach us a lot." The extreme Guardists, by far the majority, said that the Führer "owed" them the return of Transylvania at once, in appreciation of the fact that they had created a new Rumania altogether different from the double-crossing, unreliable Rumania of Carol.

It was fascinating to watch the nationalist egoism of Rumanian fascism clash with German interests, for on their part the Germans had no interest in a strong Rumania and it was out of the question that they would do anything about Transylvania, as the Rumanians hoped. After all, Hungary had the seniority of fascism over Rumania. Some Germans were sincere enough to make this clear to the Guardists. In my presence a hardboiled Nazi diplomat said to a Guardist leader that Rumania did not have a chance in a thousand of getting Transylvania back, and as for Bessarabia, the Germans, if they got it back from the Russians at all, might keep Bessarabia for themselves. The Guardist leader said savagely, "In this case, monsieur, we will fight against Germany together with the Russians." And he meant it.

That is what loyalty to Nazi Germany was like in a totalitarian country. Unbridled nationalist egoism being the very essence of totalitarianism, it was inevitable that every country which went fascist, no matter how spontaneously, had one aim: the preservation or restoration of its national independence and integrity, which was why it was bound to turn against German domination. This opened the unexpected vista of a totalitarian Europe, spelling the doom for the motherland of totalitarianism.

I discussed all this by the hour with the Count. In a half serious, half mocking way, he loved to discuss theories, even if they were not sanguine for the Third Reich. In the main points he thought, of course, that I was wrong. The Count, like most Nazi intellectuals, contended that European people might detest the Germans, but they took to the totalitarian revolution like ducks to water not only because eighty-five percent of the people had nothing to lose and much to gain by a change, but because the simple human being (and the vast majority of mankind were simple human beings) did not know what to do with freedom, had no use for it.

"It was evident from their performance that the European peoples did not wish to fight for freedom," the Count would say, and he was right so far. To the great majority of the European peoples freedom was about as necessary as a polo helmet to the occupant of a flophouse. But the same was not true for national independence. The European peoples were prepared to fight for their national independence. There was the one point which the Count overlooked. Why did the European peoples take to totalitarianism like ducks to water? Only a few did it because they loved Hitler and thought fascism wonderful. Most countries which went fascist did so only because they realized that in order to make a stand for their national independence they had to be strong and disciplined and united; that is, they had to take a leaf from Hitler's book, putting public welfare before the pursuit of happiness, national necessities before personal gain, preparedness before individual freedom. Nor would the people of Europe fight against Hitler because he was a Nazi. They would fight Hitler in order to throw off the Germanic domination.

Indeed, something like this had happened in the wake of the French Revolution in 1789. Then the cry for liberty swept the continent like wildfire. But when Bonaparte began to subjugate Europe in the name of the French revolution liberty to the European people did not mean individual liberty any longer but became national independence. And with the cry for national independence fired by the élan of the Revolution, Prussia and Austria and Russia turned against France, motherland of the French revolution, and defeated Napoleon. Hitler, like Napoleon, might be beaten by a totalitarian Europe of his own making rather than by a democratic Europe.

The comparison of Hitler with Napoleon was one of the few things which made Nazi intellectuals nervous. I was entirely wrong, protested the Count heatedly: Totalitarian Europe would not want to fight Nazi Germany because they would be quite satisfied with the new European order Hitler would establish. Nazis, he insisted, were not quite as lacking in ideas as I made them out, and they did something for their people. As an example, he held up the organization in Galatz of a camp for German refugees in from Bessarabia. It really was one of the better German jobs, the Count insisted.

"Why not have a look at Galatz," the Count suggested, "you will change your opinion about our capacity of building a European order after seeing it."

A few days later I stood on the bank of the Pruth River, near Galatz. The cold wind that blew around me seemed to belong far more to the Russian plains than to Rumania. It *was* from the Russian plains, all right, at least for the time being, for across the narrow brown river bayonetted Russian soldiers were pacing up and down. Across the Pruth was Bessarabia, once more a Russian province.

This was a sullen border. Two bridges, blown up by the Rumanians on the eve of the cession four months ago, reared their desolate iron bridgeheads to the gray sky. Bayonetted Rumanian soldiers guarded one end of the pontoon bridge built expressly for the passing of the Bessarabian Germans from Russian to Rumanian territory, and bayonetted Russian soldiers stood at the other end. Between them in the middle of the bridge were two unarmed SS-men guards. Each night the Rumanian soldiers cautiously took the pontoon bridge apart, though why was difficult to see, as the Pruth was shallow and narrow at this spot. It was more in the nature of a gesture.

For several days now the Bessarabian Germans, thousands of them, had passed over this pontoon bridge on the way to the Fatherland. In the camp in Galatz they would stay only for a few days and then be shipped on Danube boats to Austria where they would be put in camps again until spring, when the Führer would decide what should be done about them.

When the Russians took Bessarabia, the German authorities had told the 100,000-odd German settlers to stay on their farms until further notice and not to be afraid of the Russians: the Führer would protect them. The idea was to effect this mass evacuation only after sufficient preparations. And really the Russians left the German peasants strictly alone and, ever cautious, put posters on the German farms, reading "German Property." At the time at least the German authorities praised the "correct" behavior of the Russian conquerors terming the arrangements concerning compensation for the values the German emigrants would leave, as quite satisfactory.

The evacuation of these 100,000-odd people, and their transportation to Germany was handled by the so-called Resettlement Command, an organization created by the Nazi Party and formed by SS-men, doctors, nurses, and

girls of the Nazi women's organizations in Rumania and
Jugoslavia.

As I stood there in the sharp Russian wind, a young
Austrian SS-man, a Ph.D. from Graz University who was
the Press chief of the Resettlement Command, told me
that the agents of their organization had been all over
Bessarabia, helping the *Volksdeutsche* to pack up, advising
them as to what to take along and what to leave, assisting
them with every conceivable support. It took, he said,
more time to get these people on their way than to create
the camp in Galatz that was to receive them. They were
not the traveling kind, these Bessarabian Germans whose
ancestors came from Wuerttemberg as early as 1775, yet
had kept their German language and their German customs, as had the German settlers in Transylvania and on
the Volga and wherever else they sat among foreign nations in Europe.

There was only a small group of Germans waiting for
the arrivals from Bessarabia; the big reception had taken
place on the first day. Some SS-men, who were to precede
the refugees on motorcycles to the camp were there, and
talking with some visiting firemen from Bucharest and
Berlin was the Gauleiter who headed the Resettlement
Command, one of the most competent organizers in
the Nazi Party, a good-looking, middle-aged man with a
peculiar habit of nervously turning his neck that was
reminiscent of the Duke of Windsor in the pre-Simpson
days. Beside the Gauleiter were his two daughters, roaring,
long-legged beauties who worked as nurses in the camp.
Not even the drab uniforms could hide their radiant
youth. Favorites with the Reichskanzlei and the outstanding debutantes of all German-dominated Europe,

these beautiful spoiled kids were to spend the fall and winter season of 1940 in the hard service of the Resettle‧ ment Command, in camps and on boats as part of their labor service, which was certainly no picnic.

"They are coming," somebody in our little group said now, and far away on the flat horizon of the other shore the first wagon appeared. Someone gave me a Zeissglass, and I saw a spectacle which reminded me of engravings of the American frontier era: a long line of wagons, covered with white canvas, oxen drawn, sometimes with a colt or a horse running alongside. It was strange to find the covered wagon, America's symbol of individual pioneering, become Europe's symbol of the totally protective state.

The Bessarabian Germans did not stop on the Russian side of the Pruth before leaving the land to which they were bound by every memory and tradition. The first wagon came lumbering steadily over the pontoon bridge. As it arrived in the middle where the SS-men were standing, the arrivals gave a hearty "Heil Hitler." There were several generations in the first two wagons, and the crying of little children mixed with the jabbering of feathered animals. As they stopped on the Rumanian shore the Gauleiter made a welcome speech, punctuated by his little Prince of Wales ticks—a warm friendly talk calculated to make these refugees feel at home and secure. He stressed that the Führer would look out for them, and they looked happy and confident.

The organization of the Galatz camp itself was a top achievement of German efficiency, and evidence of the considerate friendly way the Third Reich took its sons to its heart. Formerly a military airport, the camp slept 16,000 people in hangars comfortably arranged with straw-covered bunks and blankets. These hangars had names—they were called "Flanders House," "Dunkirk House"—reminiscent of victories, and also "Stuttgart House" and "Schwarzwald House" after the refugees' erstwhile Fatherland. There were very good sanitary arrangements, all new (with the implements brought from Germany), and in a state of cleanliness that was certainly rare in and around Galatz.

Teeming life filled the camp. Horse dealers and cattle dealers were busy buying up the animals which would not be taken on the Danube boat. There were the gray motorcars of the Command and the gray Red Cross motorcars driving in and out of the camp, and large trucks full of foodstuffs which came from all parts of Rumania, Jugoslavia, and Hungary, so as not to deplete the county of Galatz of its supplies.

Old people sat peacefully in the sun on benches arranged on a patch of grass as on a village green. Women with the headcloth of the Germans in these parts of the world gossiped as they did their washing on troughs along the hangars. There were porches, overgrown with green, where other women did their pressing and washing. The youngsters marched and sang and heiled under the supervision of SS-men and *Volksdeutsche* in the black chauffeur's outfit I had seen in Transylvania. There were more babies and little children here than in French Canada, so it seemed, playing in the care of kindergarten teachers, chiefly young German girls from Rumania and Jugoslavia who thus were doing their voluntary labor service. Now and then a young SS-man fondly picked up a child and carried it around on his shoulders or held it on his lap. No matter what

SS-men were elsewhere, I thought amusedly, here they were a gentle, baby-kissing lot.

In the wide kitchens of the canteens girls were at work on enormous shiny new kettles and other kitchen gadgets, the most modern kettles and gadgets imaginable, brought all the way from Germany. Which showed that German industry of consumers' goods was going strong in spite of the war. Food was good and rich, taking account of the way the Bessarabian Germans were used to eating, a way the German dieticians who worked in the kitchens heartily disapproved of. They thought it awfully heavy, especially for children.

The refugees ate at long tables under trees in the nice midday sun. It could have been any popular open-air restaurant. There was even someone playing on an accordion, and what must have struck these people as especially pleasant was that none of it cost them a penny. It was all on the Führer.

I talked with a lot of the refugees, picking them out at random as I walked around, since the German authorities did not bother to come along. It was amazing to listen to these refugees. According to all standards they had suffered a major catastrophe in being forced to leave the lands of their ancestors. Nor did they know yet where and when they would find new homes. Their immediate prospect was other camps, as their final destination had not yet been determined. Yet old and young, rich and poor, expressed a minimum of regret and a boundless confidence in their future in the Führer's Germany. These prolific descendants of prolific colonists, who spoke the antiquated German of the Wuerttemberg at the time of Schiller, were returning to Hitler's Germany as to the Promised

Land. Every German a man of destiny—that's how these people felt. To have inspired them with such fervent belief was, one had to admit, a great triumph for Hitler.

You could not help being impressed with this triumph. Here the protective state acted really protective in a grandiose manner.

But as always when one was struck with a more humane aspect of the Third Reich such as the camp at Galatz, a shock followed that obliterated the favorable impression.

The Rumanians had an express train between Galatz and Bucharest, rather a fancy affair, all white and terribly fast and one of the sights in this part of the world. I took a seat in the Pullman car, a Pullman to end all Pullmans, with every conceivable gadget in it. Facing me sat a couple of SS-men and a dark-haired Rumanian lady with a dark-haired little boy. The boy ran excitedly around the car, looking at all the gadgets. He bumped into one of the SS-men.

"If that's not a Jewish mama with her little Moritz, I'll be hanged," one SS-man said in German loudly enough to be heard, if not understood.

"He's a Rumanian," the other SS-man corrected him. "His father saw him off—an officer."

"A Rumanian is he?" said the first. "Just wait until we are masters here, then Rumanian boys will travel in cattle trains and not in Pullmans."

So this, I thought, was the new European Order. It was nothing of the sort—it was a German order. The Nazis, I saw in the Galatz camp, did beautifully by the Germans, gave them a sense of security and pride and closeness to each other which had never existed before among them. But clearly this new order benefited only Germans. The same SS-men who were gentle baby-kissers with little Germans from Bessarabia were savages with a Rumanian or a Jewish boy. It was an order in which only the Germans partake of mercy and salvation, and almost everyone else is condemned to everlasting doom. Yet, I knew one could never organize Europe on *"Deutschland, Deutschland über alles."*

Hours later I sat with the Count at the bar of the Athene Palace. It had been a long day for me, but I was not tired. In fact, I felt immensely pepped up, because of "Pervitin," the new German stimulant, which the Count had given me because he wanted me to tell him what I thought of the Galatz camp.

The Germans began by giving Pervitin to pilots and soldiers who had strenuous tasks before them, which may account for the stories from France about the fighting "ecstasy" of the Nazi soldiers. Now Pervitin was taken by everyone in Germany who wished to keep going on little sleep, and this meant practically the whole upper stratum of the German nation which, yoked to the Nazi machine of conquest, had little time left for recreation or even for sleep.

"Pervertin," as I got to call it, to the irritation of my Nazi acquaintances, could be bought over the counters of drug stores in all Nazi-dominated Europe. It is an inexpensive drug, and also, I was told, harmless. Its pepping-up effect was produced by a very high vitamin B-1 content. Much later a German army doctor warned me against its use "in excess," as the Nazis had begun to feel unsure of its after effects, having noticed that regular users of Pervitin were given to nightmares and depression.

"Let's talk all night!" the Count suggested, when he met me at my return from Galatz. His face was as eager as the face of a severe young sixteenth-century Cardinal can ever look. It was not love with the Count, to sacrifice his night's sleep for me, but curiosity. To him I was, as he put it, "the last Kiebitz" in the gigantic struggle between two worlds—a skeptical, tolerant onlooker. That's how the Count saw me, and I never tried to change his picture, though of course I did not feel tolerant all the time. But most of the time I felt skeptical.

I took the Count to the bar, because I knew Henry could be persuaded to keep it open until morning. Aside from an American oilman who sat at a small bar table with an Austrian cutie, and a bunch of Nazi youngsters, officials of the German Ministry of Economics, newly arrived to prepare the forthcoming German-Rumanian trade treaty, the bar was empty. The Nazi boys exchanged casual salutes with the Count. None of them was older than thirty. Blond, sharp-eyed, hard-jawed, they were fair samples of the Nazi generation of German officialdom, which in some German ministries, especially Economics and Agriculture, already formed up to forty percent of the entire officialdom. I wondered vaguely whether they had inherited the Prussian genius for bureaucracy which so often had saved the day for Germany.

Settling in the far corner of the bar I asked the Count for the xth time whether it would not get him into trouble to sit around with a non-Aryan lady. The thought that I might cause the abrupt end of a promising Nazi career worried me sporadically. But the Count just laughed

about my concern and assured me that all these regula-
tions were merely for the common people. In the complicated hierarchy of the Nazi Party, he insisted, much
was permissible to the "initiated" which was heresy to the
masses. It was, I understood, very much the way the
Church in the Renaissance handled the law of celibacy,
when Princes of the Church could sleep with girls but
low priests could not. The higher one got up in the
hierarchy, the fewer were the rules—provided, of course,
one believed in the main principles of National Socialism.
Even if some enemy would try to frame him, the Count
thought, it would not lead to anything much. The Nazis
were terribly short of good people and very careful not to
throw them to the dogs without urgent reasons. This was
one of the differences between the Führer and Stalin,
who had shot so many managers of his revolution.

Henry brought two bottles of Ruedesheimer in an ice-
filled bucket and took his leave. Soon the American oilman and his cutie went out, and then the youngsters
of the Ministry of Economics departed, flicking their
salutes. From time to time a late-comer hopefully looked
in but, as no one was there to serve a drink, would take
himself away.

Sitting there in the still dark bar of the Athene Palace
it was as if we were alone in the world. A dim light shone
on the table before us, making us almost invisible for each
other. Soothed by the gloom and the quiet and stimulated
by the wine and the Pervitin I told the Count that the
Galatz camp was all he made me expect it to be and even
more. It was an impressive job. But then there was also
the snatch of dialogue between the two SS-men that I had
overheard in the train, and I told him that the entire

Galatz experience had finally convinced me that the Nazis could never organize Europe, that Hitler, even if he won the war, could never win the peace. The reason being that Hitler's new order was an exclusively German, not a European order.

I said: "Let's assume you have an economic plan for Europe and are even able to carry it through. So what? It's not enough to organize Europe on."

"Have the democracies more of a plan for Europe?" asked the Count politely. They had less, I admitted, nor did I feel convinced that they would be able to organize Europe. However, history proved that the status quo could get along on comparatively few ideas, while the usurping force had to show something striking.

"We show the totalitarian order," said the Count. What man needed and what democracy did not give him, he went on, was an order—an order that contained everything simple human beings had known and understood from the beginning of time: a hierarchically organized society instead of fraternité; leadership instead of égalité; sacrifice and discipline instead of liberté, and an absolute truth, around which a system of sin and expiation, of paradise and hell, was centered.

Like all intellectual Nazis the Count was cheerfully convinced that practically any order would do, provided people recognize it as such. Whoever could get across to the masses that thirty knee-crookings every morning would get a man into paradise, while to skip those knee-crookings got him into hell, created, he thought, the categorical imperative, the prerequisite to any order. However, this was not quite enough. The order must impose itself on every sphere of human existence, as the Church had so well succeeded in imposing its order.

The Nazi order rested on the trinity of race, nation, and state. Their church was the Party hierarchy; the Gestapo was their Holy Inquisition; the French revolution was their original sin; Dachau was their purgatory for the sinners against the trinity of nation, state, and race. Heretics were everyone who was neither Nordic nor German.

On first sight it looked like a complete order, though on a low spiritual level. But on second sight one found that the most important element indispensable to any order was lacking, and this element was universal mercy. And this was why the German order was no good.

The Church lets any heretic who repents and sees the light partake of its mercy; but in the Nazi new order only the Germans could hope for salvation. In fact, paradise was practically granted to them because they were Germans. But the Pole and the Czech, and even the Latin, could pray and do good work, yet he was still dirt to the Herrenvolk. There was no mercy for the Jew in the Nazi universe, only everlasting doom. Not even one of their field marshals could find mercy for his percentage of Jewish blood, but had to make himself out a bastard and his mother an adulteress.

Hitler in building up his order with the mercy strictly limited to the German people—or to the Nordic race— was like an architect in whose skyscraper the stairs and elevator led only to the first floor. One could not get anywhere.

This absence of mercy in the totalitarian order robbed it of the universal, all-embracing character which any real religion had and which any revolution that became a world revolution had, too. The French revolution of 1789 had this inclusive mercy and conquered the world—or almost. And the Russian revolution of 1917 was inclusive and still had quite a good chance to conquer the world.

This universal mercy was the imperialistic element in any order, for no order could hope to conquer the world by condemning *a priori* entire races and nations to everlasting doom. Their avowed doctrine of the Herrenvolk, of the chosen people, had been all right for the German revolution proper, but for world revolution or domination of Europe it was entirely wrong. By excluding the Poles and Czechs and God knows who from the sweepstakes for paradise, Hitler's totalitarian order was essentially anti-imperialistic.

An order might conceivably relegate freedom to the small circle of the initiated: that had been done by every Church. Even justice in every order was dependent on what was good for the order itself. But there was one thing that must be inclusive and universal, and this was mercy. Without one principle admitting all the people of Europe to the sweepstakes for paradise, the Germans could never hope to organize Europe.

To this the Count reacted with the indignant question as to whether I shared the silly democratic notion, especially dear to Americans, of putting practically all European nations on a footing of equality—a Serb equal to a Frenchman equal to a Lithuanian equal to a German. This, he insisted, was utter nonsense. Why, of the powers on the European continent which had had a decisive effect on the history of Europe, only France and Italy and Germany—and if you counted her as a European

power, Russia—were still great powers! It was inconceiva-
ble, therefore, that in the new order of Europe all the
small nations should be allowed to have a say about the
concerns of the great nations, as they had in the League,
or to upset the entire European applecart for their own
minority problems or frontier questions.

I had to admit the Count had something there. Those
League of Nations meetings in the twenties, where whole
sessions were taken up by a shyster politician representing
some Baltic country, were aggravating; and so were the
pompous Balkan politicians, inflated by the fact of being
on the side of the angels, sitting in judgment on whether
Germany should conclude a customs union with Austria
and other matters of life and death for a great nation. I
always felt that there was something wrong with an order
that kept up the fiction of small nations, full of ambitions
but lacking the physical strength as well as the creative
force to fulfill these ambitions on their own steam, playing
at being Great Powers and cluttering up the international
scene with their intrigues and grievances.

Some kind of hierarchical organization of the European
countries, giving only the real Powers a say on the great
European issues and calling the small nations in only to
discuss matters which really concerned them had seemed
quite desirable to me back in the twenties, as I watched
Briand's lion's head bobbing up and down in his sleep
over the Geneva Council table and Sir Austen Chamber-
lain's monocle glittering through long empty hours. But
this was a matter of equality and not of universal mercy.
An order might be recognized by a nation, though the
order denies her equality, but no order could be acceptable to a nation which extirpates her intelligentsia and

treats her people as slaves. Yet the Germans were admittedly extirpating the intelligentsia and by and large the whole upper class of Poles and Czechs, liable to oppose German domination; and before they were through with Europe, they would do the same with other subjugated nations.

This the Count did not deny. "One generation," he said, "has to be sacrificed to make Europe reasonable"—reasonable, he meant, to the acceptance of German domination—and afterwards everybody would be ever so much happier. Any fundamental revolution, any establishment of a new order, he pointed out, cost a generation and more.

Perhaps, but the point was: would Europe stand for such enormous sacrifices for the establishment of an order which so far had produced only one European idea—and this idea not genuine but a loan from Soviet Russia and bound to perish with the end of the German-Russian friendship. It was the idea of the "young revolutionary nations against the old plutocratic nations" and it had produced the most dynamic war slogan the Germans had in world-war-two. It was also the only idea yet produced by the German revolution which had overtones of the universal mercy inherent in world revolutions, and the inclusiveness which could make an order appeal to Europe.

Still, even while it was smeared at the time all over the *Voelkische Beobachter*, very few Nazi leaders were sincere about it. Hitler most of all mistrusted an idea which put the Nazis together with the Bolsheviks and always believed in the Nordic race ideology as an integral part of the national socialist revolution, which had done all right for the German people. He did not seem to see that there was little dynamism to the idea of a Nordic race the chief nations of which were just trying to bomb each other off the map. And especially he did not seem to see that the same ideology which had been all right for the German revolution was all wrong for a European revolution because it frightened, discouraged, and infuriated the European people and put them against the German domination.

It was clear to me that the Germans could dominate Europe only as long as they could say it with tanks. There was already evidence that the resignation of the conquered people was waning, but as long as the emergencies of the war lasted the pattern of force was plausible. The war spared the Nazis the trouble of having to whip up any ideas for the organization of Europe other than economic. The Nazis might even enjoy the benefits of the doubt about actually having ideas of a European order, but were prevented by the war from carrying them out. The war was a godsend for Hitler. With the coming of peace his lack of a European idea would be found out. With the coming of peace he would have to take his armies away from the European continent—or it would not be peace!—and then the European people would begin to revolt in earnest against the German domination. Hitler's German order, such as it was, did not have a chance to survive very long in peace-time Europe.

Possibly this order would develop, broaden, and take a European complexion. But then it would not be Hitler's order any longer. For Hitler's genius and weakness, the source of his immense successes and also the source of his potential downfall was that he could and would not think as a European—but only as a German.

A little terror overexcites minds; much terror calms them. I use this word on purpose: they are not only subjugated, they are calm.

TOCQUEVILLE

15—RUMANIAN FINALE

Never did Bucharest seem as real to me as it did in December, as irresistibly between East and West, between ancient and modern, between rustic and metropolitan. In spite of the memory of nights-of-the-long-knives still alive and terror going on in a subdued fashion, December was almost gay. The snow made it so and the Christmas spirit and events happening so fast in Europe. In December all comings and goings of German diplomats seemed to center around Bucharest. Everybody sat in the lobby of the Athene Palace at one time or other between trains or planes, as if attracted by the intense and colorful life which Bucharest splurged for all comers the way a beautiful woman, who knows she is to die soon, splurges her possessions on all and sundry. But actually people came to Bucharest because it was the terminal of all traffic between Europe and the Orient, and a stop here was necessary on the way to and from more or less mysterious missions. And while at last the Great Guardist revolt erupted in a finale furioso, its prelude was so fantastic, with plot and counterplot, intrigue and double-cross, that it too held an irresistible fascination.

Winter became Bucharest. Suddenly, overnight, all noises of the city were suspended and there was a new sound: the little bells of sleighs. A thick fur of white, the blue and absolute white of pure diamonds, padded everything, lying in luscious cushions on the cupolas of the hundred-odd byzantine churches. Except on the boulevards, where street cars pushed the snow away by using an inefficient contraption of wood, nobody touched the snow in Bucharest and thus it retained its noble freshness. Most of the time the air was calm; around noontime it was warm, with the sun bursting from a clear blue sky. At times a severe wind coming from Russia, the *crivetz*, which the Bucharestians say "has teeth," drew tears from your eyes.

Then rich and poor pulled their high bonnets of black or gray astrakhan or white lamb over bluish ears. Rich men wore long coats lined with mink or sealskin almost down to their feet. Poor men wore short coats, lined with lamb, with vertical pockets in the stomachs. The gypsies wore newspapers. Snowboots and high galoshes of rubber piled up in the waiting rooms of offices, in the cloakrooms of hotels, in the entrance halls of private houses, in the portals of churches, making a complicated ceremony of comings and goings, for you had to sit down while your escort or a servant helped you to put these on and take them off.

On the streets, so silent that one got alarmed at one's own steps crunching on the snow, gypsy children sold paper flowers, huge red and white roses and daisies, and threw corn at you while shouting that they hoped you would grow old, "wrinkled like an apple."

In the dusk, prolonged by all the whiteness around, Bucharestians exposed themselves to the temptations of the Calea Victoriei—the last Paris perfumes, English woolens, Vienna leather goods, and mountains of salami, candies, and marron glacés. Baby-faced German soldiers stamped through the snow carrying candy boxes with painted golden angels on them, instead of guns. Scholarly German officers shopped for the beautiful Rumanian peasant embroideries which are made into blouses and for the thinnest of nighties, and lingered in the "Cartea Romaneasca," the Brentanos of Bucharest, where you could get books in every language, even the ones which were burnt in Germany. On the way back to the Athene Palace was Lucchiano's, a tiny shop, which sold the best caviar from Bessarabia.

The cold made everyone appreciate Rumanian food, which really was Russian, Hungarian, Turkish, Greek, Viennese, and Polish—only more so. You ate Ciorba, a sour soup seasoned with lemon, with fowl or game or boiled beef in it, and a dab of sour cream; chopped meats, rolled in vine leaves, served in double cream; warm patés; pilafs of shrimp and chicken livers; immense grillades. You ate parts of animals you never thought of eating, such as cow's udders done in a red wine sauce, or—a special delicacy—the testicles of ram, which in Rumanian are called "the pride" of the ram, done in a sauce which has everything in it. And you polished off your meal by very sweet confitures of fruit with a touch of maraschino. From all this you put on two pounds every day and got the gout. Every respectable Rumanian had the gout—that is, the few hundred thousand Rumanians who could afford such meals. The vast majority of the people ate "Mamaliga," day in day out, cornmeal boiled in water, which they ate without butter, meat, or even salt because they were too poor.

At first, after the bloody last week of November was over, it looked as if everybody had had enough of terror. Terror went on, but in a slowed-up, discreet fashion, partly due to the silencing quality of the snow, which made the nightly motorcycles of Guardist raiders inaudible, partly to new legislation by which Antonescu decreed death penalty for practically anything, partly to preoccupation with Christmas. The forces of law and order—General Antonescu, the Germans, the Church, and the army—one felt for a few weeks were drawing together, and had the situation well in hand. The Guardists would not get away with things any longer.

There was, for instance, the Guardist campaign "Codreanu for Saint," which flopped lamentably. The Guardists, it appeared, had approached the Holy Synod, supreme council of the Orthodox Church in Rumania, with the demand that the Church make a saint of the Capitano. At which the Synod politely said to come back in two hundred years, as it took that long to create a saint.

In other respects, too, the Guardists seemed to be condemned to second place. The Germans, at last awake to the fact that the Guardist terror was harmful not only to the quiet in the raw-material sphere but to their own prestige, made a few timely gestures which showed that while they did not wish to be mixed up in Rumanian affairs, they were still there.

The first German gesture was a parade, in which the military mission showed the Rumanians part of their gadgets and men. On a beautiful calm sunny day, a grandstand was set up on the Chaussée, from where the King and Antonescu, both in uniform, together with the two German generals of the mission, watched the spectacle. Young Michael looked less sullen than usual, asked the generals questions, and seemed interested. There were lots of pretty women bundled in furs on the grandstand and Axis diplomats in their uniforms, and much gold lace gleamed in the wintry sun. It looked a little like old times in Europe—the times before the first world war, when the accent was unabashedly on the military.

All Bucharest lined the Chaussée, and as German tanks and men went by, and airplanes flew overhead in formation, the Rumanians cried, *"Formidabile,"* and were delighted. It was a lovely parade but, as Colonel Ratay said, all parades are. This one was small, comprising not more than 6000 men and little machinery. Still, to the people it was part of the magic German army.

I was with two young American journalists who swore under their breath all during the parade at this display of Germany military might, and did not seem to enjoy its chamber-music precision and elegance. They really detested militarism as such, an attitude I met in many young Americans and which was somewhat disturbing because at the same time they felt America should have an army to lick Hitler. But how could America ever get an army to lick the best army in the world if young Americans detested militarism? Soldiering is like making love: in order to do it properly, you must put your heart in it.

A few days later the German military mission held maneuvers outside Bucharest, which were also attended by the King and Antonescu. "We thought it would make a nice change after so many funerals," one of the German generals said gently.

At the same time the German economic experts went into action. They sent to Rumania two thousand German-made tractors and established schools for tractor drivers all over the country. The idea was to train five to six tractor drivers for every tractor, who next spring would cultivate every foot of arable land in day and night shifts so as to make up, partly at least, for Rumania's territorial losses. This was one of the astonishing and inimitable feats of German organization in the middle of the war, and was not diminished by the fact that the Germans did not do it so much for the Rumanians as for their own benefit.

Tractors and tractor-driver schools were samples of what the Germans were to do for Rumania in the framework of the new German-Rumanian trade treaty, just signed in Berlin. This trade treaty took the form of a ten-year plan and was, the German economists themselves said, a blue-print of a system of trade treaties meant to form the backbone of the new European economy, in that these treaties aimed at cultivating the natural wealth of each country and building up its natural resources and industries. In Rumania, a predominantly agricultural country, the trade treaty emphasized the intensification of industrial production, and with this in mind the Germans were to furnish agricultural machinery and machinery for great projects of drainage and irrigation and improvement of roads and communications, on which plans German and Rumanian technicians would collaborate.

This was an ambitious treaty, but there was no reason to doubt that the Germans could carry it out, in spite of the war, once the Rumanian revolution had got over its terrorist stage. The Germans from a purely economic point of view had done in one year everything for Polish agriculture that the Polish republic had failed to do in twenty years. And the Germans were doing amazing things in France. Nor was there any doubt that eighty-five per cent of the Rumanian people would benefit immensely from such a plan. Germany alone of all world powers had the imagination and the direct interest to take the trouble to make and carry out such a plan which for any other Great Power would be a charity project and, as such, make no sense. This had been proven in twenty years of unproductive effort on the part of France and England toward eliminating German influence in the Balkans, efforts which resulted in the impoverishment of Eastern Europe and in the restoration of the German influence with a vengeance, even before Hitler came to power. Unfortunately no economic plan for Rumania anywhere nearly as constructive as this German ten-year plan was ever produced by another Power. Which showed that it was a mistake to imagine Germany as not being in the future Europe. Only Germany as a Great Power could do for the East what needed to be done. Though emphatically convinced that an economic plan was not enough to organize Europe on, I realized that it was nothing to sneeze at, and that for large parts of the European people it might have a more vital importance than Union Now and even the Eight Points.

It would be silly not to face this fact. Even the objection that Hitler did it by imposing "slave labor" was not valid. From what I had seen in the Balkans and in Poland in the last twenty years, I knew that slave labor was just a phrase, in that these people had never known conditions appreciably different from what Hitler imposed upon them, and it was conceivable that, in the long run, they would get better conditions under Hitler than they knew under the status quo, provided of course that he did not decide to exterminate them as an inferior race or dangerous to the German Herrenvolk. But this is another story.

The greatest obstacle to the accomplishment of Germany's economic plans in Europe was not the war and not their political and diplomatic muddling through, but a scarcity of experts. Acknowledged by all Germans, the problem was where to get the experts who were needed in the various countries. Of course not all countries were as badly in need of imported experts as Rumania, but still local talent was scarce or politically unreliable everywhere. The Germans were hard pressed for specialists in practically every field, and an improvement in this situation was not expected in the near future. Consequently everybody had to double and triple effort and work.

I never saw anybody work as hard, for instance, as the present prima donna of German economics, Dr. Carl Clodius, who, as chief of Section "W" (Economics) in the Wilhelmstrasse, dashed all over Europe making trade treaties. He came frequently to Bucharest that December, getting in a twenty-hour working day between two airplane trips. Having known him well from more leisurely times, when he was third secretary at the German Embassy in Paris fifteen years ago, I found his new tempo staggering, but he seemed to like it.

Clodius was always one of the most suave and charming men any diplomatic service could produce. Tall, forty-fivish, heavily built, with a fleshy face, nice eyes and a light voice, Dr. Clodius would be a gentleman under any regime. He had studied economics in Heidelberg and Berlin, and I remember that we discussed National Socialism to gether as early as 1926, though in a theoretical vein. A few years later it became evident that he leaned toward the Nazis. Being a most unfanatical and gentle person, this would have been strange had it not been for two factors. Clodius had always believed in Anschluss with Austria and had always been deeply concerned with the problem of the German minorities in the Balkans. On both these questions he found that the Nazis had a most reasonable approach. Hitler's most useful followers, I found later, were not the ones who stupidly swallowed Nazism hook, line, and sinker, but the ones who liked his approach to one or another question. Clodius was this kind of follower. Nor did he throw his critical faculties completely overboard. He and people like him found many things in the Third Reich objectionable, but weighed against the things they found worthwhile, the objectionable ones did not seem of great consequence.

Clodius was an interesting case in that he would probably hold the same position today under the Weimar Republic or any other regime in Germany, and thus he was not a profiteer of Nazism. The typical German official who does not serve a regime but serves Germany always, Clodius was fired with the dynamism of the National Socialist revolution, the dynamism which went through the entire military and bureaucratic machine of Hitler's Germany. In all the high officials—many of whom I had known all my life—and whom I met again this December at the Athene Palace, I found this élan, even with the ones who had been much more hesitant in accepting the Third Reich than Clodius had been. It was like an intoxication. All said that they never felt as free in their work as they did now with no Reichstag to interfere at the wrong moments, and that never had they been allowed to develop so much personal initiative as now, or received such unstinted recognition from above.

I thought at first that this was just a case of liking to be in with the winning side, but it was not that alone. These men were not all so sure that they were in on the winning side. I got the impression that most of them thought the war would end with a compromise between the revolution and the status quo, as most revolutions end. All of them were convinced that National Socialism, no matter how the war ended, or whether it ended at all, was in for great modifications resulting only partly from outside pressure, but to a larger extent resulting from the impatience of the young generation with an existence that narrowed down the sphere of personal and private life to a minimum.

"Come to think of it," a high German official said, "the people who take best to totalitarianism are the middle-aged, who are too old to be excited about themselves any more and young enough to get excited about something impersonal."

There was, I was told by these men, most of whom had children in their teens, a growing resistance to the encroachment of the state and the party on personal lives among the more intellectually minded of the Hitler youth. Such resistance, they thought, could not go unheeded forever. But this too was in the day's work, for in revolution everything is fluid and change is its very essence. Nor did this knowledge diminish the kick these men got out of their work.

For a time nobody discussed the situation in Rumania.

The Germans now talked about the Italians, and I found that since the capitulation of France nothing had given the Germans such a kick as the Italian failures. All the good jokes about the Italians were invented by the Germans and altogether there was little love lost, for fundamentally the Germans seemed to resent that the Italians had created fascism and not they. But this they did not admit. What they did admit was that they had been mad at Italian arrogance all along. They said that the Italians were the cause of everything that had gone diplomatically wrong in this war: the enormous claims which Italy made on France had prevented a German arrangement with Pétain, and Ciano's pressure had made for the unfortunate Vienna verdict—all of which was certainly exaggerated or even untrue. Anyway, they hoped the military disasters would make Mussolini quiet down a little.

The Italians were no less dissatisfied with the Germans. There were a lot of Italian businessmen in Bucharest these days, most of them connected with the Brahova, an oil company said to be the property of Edda Ciano. All of them wore party buttons, but they were unenthusiastic fascists and severe on the Duce. The trouble with Italy, they said, was that the ignorance in which the nation had been kept so long was now infecting the Government. These men believed in the German victory, and thought that while it was bad to be on the winning side as a loser, it was still better than not to be on the winning side at all. Here in Rumania they had lots of grievances against the Germans, one of them being that the Germans had put moral pressure on the Italians to fire their Jewish employees, who immediately were hired by the German companies. This charge the Germans denied vehemently, but it was true.

Italians and Germans spoke about Molotov's visit in Berlin, strange reports about which were just leaking out. Molotov, it seemed, angered the Führer with claims on the Dardanelles and Moldavia and would not listen at all to Hitler's request for drastic reduction of the Red Army, the calling off of the Comintern in Europe, and an adjustment of the regime for the purpose of guaranteeing full economic cooperation. From the Molotov visit on, the Russo-German crisis entered its acute phase. This did not mean that the Germans had already decided upon the Russian war. Most of the military men were for it on the grounds that, as the final settlement was inevitable anyway, it was better to have it done with now, when they had a gigantic army and no place to go. It was, they hinted, very difficult to keep up the morale of such a gigantic army when it was unemployed for an indefinite period.

An important group of diplomats and economists centering around Ribbentrop advocated a peaceful settlement with Russia. Their chief reason was that even after a victory it would be terribly difficult to organize a country full of spiteful Russians who for twenty years had sabotaged their own government. These economists and diplomats did not take Stalin's blackmailing or double-crossing too seriously. They said fondly, "Oh, he will try it, of course, but what of it? He is such a smart guy. He does not really want to fight us." They also had ideological reasons for wanting a peaceful settlement: they thought their present slogan of "Young Socialist Nations against the Old Plutocratic Nations" the most dynamic war slogan anybody could have, and realized that it was their only slogan which had a universal European appeal. They feared that a campaign against Russia would not only alienate labor in Germany proper and all over Europe from the German revolution, but would weaken the dynamism of the German revolution itself. The European appeal of a Holy Crusade against Russia seemed doubtful from the start.

A hard battle was fought between these pro-war and anti-war factions in Germany. Hitler at the time had not committed himself, but while both sides thought he was still trying for a peaceful solution, they were nevertheless convinced that a campaign against Russia was the one campaign in which Hitler would put his whole heart. Hitler—this was no secret—was not happy about the English campaign. For Hitler sincerely believed in the excellence of the Nordic race, and admired the English; while he had never stopped considering the pact with Russia one of the grimmer necessities of the war, or stopped loathing the Russians and communism. The German military men were pretty sure that in time they could win Hitler over for their campaign in Russia.

The German diplomats, at the Athene Palace between trains, would say to me, "What are you hanging around Bucharest for? Nothing will happen here any more. The story is dying under your feet." But this was not true. While we were preoccupied with the winter and Christmas preparations and the future European campaigns, the big story in Rumania had moved forward, but like a swimmer under water, so that when it came up again, it had gone a long way unobserved, and Rumania had moved toward the final reckoning between General Antonescu and Horia Sima, between Rumanian Government and Guardist Party.

The military demonstrations of the last few weeks had quite naturally centered around Antonescu and left Horia Sima out of the picture, for they were calculated to show the Guardists that the forces of quiet and order were rallying closely around the General. This Horia Sima understood and did not like.

Moreover, the apparent friendship of the German generals and Dr. Fabrizius for Antonescu, and the stronger, surer tone the latter had adopted since his return from the visit with the Führer, got on Horia Sima's nerves. The General, following Hitler's severe admonitions to restore at least a moderate measure of quiet in the raw-material sphere, and to crush the communist influence in the Guardist party, showed his determination to crack down on terrorists. Moreover, Antonescu had agreed with Hitler that German economic and political "commissars" and Gestapo agents should be installed in every Rumanian ministry, in the National Bank and the Prefecture, to guarantee reasonable working conditions. Horia Sima clearly understood that counter-revolution was already on the way and that its success meant the end of his own leadership. Stupidly he blamed the General for going back on the Guardists who had brought him to power, instead of blaming himself for having so little hold over his party that he had to cater to its most terroristic tastes at a moment when the Germans at last had to insure quiet here for economic, and still more for strategic, reasons.

Sima decided to break Antonescu before it was too late. His method was to sour the Germans on the General.

After all, Sima reasoned, Hitler could never trust an opportunist newcomer like the General to collaborate with Germany, and it would not be difficult to play on Hitler's latent distrust. Sima went to work on this in the devious Byzantine fashion which characterized all regimes in Rumania.

One of the top men in the Guardist hierarchy said to me one night at a dinner party, "This will interest you as a journalist. General Antonescu tolerates a secret radio station to England."

In revolutionary countries it is dangerous for any foreigner to get involved in the confidences of a revolutionary party. Still, I was curious, and asked why the General should do such a thing. The Guardist said that the General did not believe in German final victory and played along with the English this way, so that in case of a British victory he could say that he had been pro-British all along. The Guardist said quickly that the General did not do this for his own advancement, but for what he considered his patriotic duty. Then he added that the Germans could trust only one man in Rumania and this was Horia Sima.

The next day this story of the secret radio station to England was all over Bucharest; the Guardists had made a good job of their whispering campaign against the General, for whispering campaign it was. From then on new stories of this kind, the only purpose of which was to undermine German confidence in Antonescu, were floated every day. The leader of this whispering campaign was a former Prefect of the Police whom Antonescu had forced to resign. According to legend this officer had smuggled Carol back to the country from Paris, and later became a Guardist. I certainly never met a man so eaten up by hate; he thought and spoke only in terms of terror.

When this man ran out of material against the General himself, he turned against the General's friends, his pet hate being General Rioseanu, Undersecretary of State in the Ministry of Interior, who was devoted to Antonescu. The Guardists spread a story that he was a Mason, used to visit Sir Reginald Hoare secretly at night, and that his wife was a Jewess, none of which was a recommendation with the Nazis.

This same Guardist officer not only had his hand in the whispering campaign against Antonescu, but had, to say the least, knowledge of several plots to murder him. The plots, it must be admitted, looked like opéra bouffe plots, but this was the way murder was carried out in this part of the world, and I myself still cannot understand how Antonescu is still alive. Rioseanu, it is true, has since "died" in the Rumanian-Russian campaign, and maybe we will hear one of these days that he was killed by a Guardist.

The main plotter against Antonescu's life was a lady. One day over the apéritif, the Count made me laugh with the words, "I have the assassin of the General lined up for you. Want to meet her?" But it was no joke. A Rumanian lady had made up her mind to murder the General or have somebody else murder him. She lived, the Count told me, in an elegant apartment house and, except that she was determined to save the Guardist revolution by liquidating the General, led quite a normal life. The lady, it appeared, had made herself leader of a Guardist cell of thirteen, all of whom she had chosen for toughness and fearlessness, taxi-drivers, butchers, teamsters, and such. These men, tied to her by all the oaths of their Guardist order and by personal devotion, were ready to commit any murder she asked them to commit.

The initiation of a new member of her cell was an extraordinary ceremony, a mixture of ancient Thracian customs and Sicilian Vendetta and Black Mass, with the lady officiating as High Priestess. She wore a clinging green gown, something between the Guardist green shirt and a hostess gown which showed everything. She was very thin but had good shoulders and breasts. After the ceremony she always retained one of the guests and swooned in his arms under the pretext that the initiation ceremony took everything out of her and left her all empty and terribly, terribly lonely inside—which was, one had to admit, a rather banal line compared to the elaborate build-up. But it became even worse when the lady bragged that she was a virgin, as if a virgin of forty was an attractive aim for anything but a panzer destroyer.

However that may be, this remarkable lady meant business about killing the General and Rioseanu, and her little organization of toughs was ideally suited for the purpose. I never took her as lightly as the Germans did; they laughed their heads off about her. But I never took her as seriously as the Guardists, who were in great awe of her. The funny part about the lady was that her sinister plans were not treated as a secret. Even the Guardist themselves were quite voluble about them.

Christmas Day in Bucharest was fresh gleaming whiteness all around, a deep silence broken only by the little bells of sledges and the big bells of churches. Christmas in Bucharest was excited German soldiers carrying fir trees; mountains of food; dull gray cars and trucks of the German Wehrmacht squatting in the snow before the Athene

Palace on their way South. Christmas in Bucharest was Midnight Mass in a small dark chapel, with the trembling lights of candles on golden ikons and the ceremony proceeding mysteriously behind the fumes of incense.

Christmas in Bucharest was a party for the German military mission, attended by the young King and Queen Helen, and a magician pulling doves from his hat, one of the doves settling on the pink bald head of General Hansen, while the Queen saved the situation by saying, "How charming, the dove of peace on the head of the General."

Christmas in Bucharest made for a temporary lull in Guardist terror but it did not make for truce in the struggle for power between General Antonescu and Horia Sima.

Antonescu, on Christmas, made one of his superbly direct and moving proclamations, which sounded right out of Tolstoy's peasant stories, and as far removed from politics as a mother's consoling words for her crying child. He said in effect: I know this year has been a great trial for all of you. You, rich man, are afraid of getting poor and you, poor man, are afraid of getting poorer. I am sorry for every single one of you and beg you to have patience and courage, and with God's help we will pull through somehow.

In this proclamation Antonescu did not mention the Iron Guard once, which enraged Horia Sima and his boys, who were enraged further when the General retired to his villa in Predeal, a winter sport resort near Bucharest, and celebrated the holidays in the chummiest intimacy with Dr. Fabrizius. The Guardists wasted no love on Hitler's minister, who, they said, could have prevented the assassination of the Capitano if he had wanted to; and now they suspected he was the chief wire-puller against Horia Sima.

The Guardists were delighted when, just before Christmas, a new German minister was appointed: Manfred von Killinger, once Consul General in San Francisco. Killinger, the Guardists thought, would have more tolerance for good clean terror than stuffed-shirtish Fabrizius, for Killinger himself had been up to the neck in the doings of the various "Freicorps" which fought the forces of Versailles in Silesia and the Rhineland in the 1920's and had even called his autobiography *Froehliches aus dem Leben eines Putschisten*—meaning, Gay Memories from the Life of a Putschist.

Sima and his boys looked at this change of diplomats as a clear victory for the cause of Horia Sima *vs.* the General, and there was great rejoicing in Guardist circles. In reality it was an accident caused by circumstances outside of the realm of the Sima-Antonescu struggle and was meant by Hitler in a way vastly different from Sima's wishful interpretation.

The story behind Fabrizius' recall threw a significant light on Hitler's manner of making clear-cut decisions. As explained to me at the time by a reliable German source, a difference of opinion had come up between Fabrizius and Gauleiter Conradi about who should have the authority over the German commissars to be placed in the various Rumanian ministries. The Gauleiter felt that the commissars should be subordinated to him as the representative of the Nazi party in Bucharest, while the Minister felt that the commissars should be under his authority as the representative of the State. The question was referred to Berlin, but the Wilhelmstrasse and the Party could not agree who should boss it over the commissars. Finally, the question was put to Hitler himself, who listened, thought for a moment, and announced calmly: "Fabrizius is quite right: the commissars should be subordinated to the minister. Only Fabrizius is not the right minister for the commissars to be subordinated to. So we'll have to have another minister."

While Fabrizius' recall, which almost broke the latter's heart, had nothing to do with the Antonescu-Horia Sima matter, the nomination of Killinger had, for Killinger was not chosen by Hitler for his gay memories of putschism but rather for the tough efficiency by which he had just shown what's what in Hitler's Europe to the Slovaks. Killinger would not stand for any nonsense detrimental to German interests, which is why Hitler sent him to Bucharest. So actually Killinger was bad news for Horia Sima, though Sima did not know it yet. Nor did he know that when Killinger made his entry into Bucharest at the end of January, everything was over for him, Sima.

When as a child seeing *Hamlet* for the first time, I was so carried away by the plot that at the duel scene I disgraced my father by shouting angrily at Hamlet, "Stop, you fool, his sword is poisonous!" I felt the same way watching Horia Sima blindly running into his fate, only I knew better than to shout at him. Instead I followed in fascinated and polite silence as he entangled himself with his every action deeper and deeper in the web which was to destroy him.

Until as late as the middle of January, 1941, the Nazis did not dream of eliminating Sima and the Guardist Party

altogether. The *nazissime* Nazis preferred him to Antonescu because they still considered him a little-brother
fascist, while Antonescu was to them an opportunist general. The other Germans, even the most conservative diplomats around Dr. Fabrizius, all saw an independent Rumania only in terms of a party dictatorship, since a military
dictatorship, they felt, would have no prestige in the
country. If they threw their backing to Antonescu, they
did so because they saw in him a strong man to restore a
measure of quiet and order indispensable for their military and economic objectives. But they never intended
him to rule without the Guardist Party or without Sima
and his influence with the Guardist masses.

If Sima had compromised on loyal collaboration with
Antonescu for the purpose of suppressing the activist and
terrorist groups in the party instead of plotting against
Antonescu and double-crossing him, he could have lived
happily ever after as far as the Germans were concerned.
But there was one thing the Germans would not tolerate,
and that was the elimination of Antonescu. Here the
German military mission, which otherwise did not bother
about politics, came in. Antonescu was clearly their man,
and they needed him now more than ever. With war in
the Balkans a certainty and a war in Russia a possibility,
they could not stand for any nonsense at the back of their
armies. All this made it evident that the Germans were
practically forced to throw their support to Antonescu if
a show-down came between him and Horia Sima. Though
this was quite plain, Sima only stiffened his attitude toward
Antonescu.

Never before had I seen as clearly that even shrewd and
hard-boiled men judge political personages and situations

in sentimental, storybook clichés, instead of the necessities of *Realpolitik*. Thus a man like Malaxa bet on Sima, because, he argued, Sima was necessarily "nearer to Hitler's heart" as a fascist revolutionary, and also because Hitler could not afford to betray a fascist revolution anywhere in the world—plausible arguments under ordinary circumstances but definitely unimportant with Hitler in an emergency where a measure of quiet and order in Rumania had to be the first consideration. Yet on the strength of these arguments, and also because he had a personal interest in getting rid of Antonescu who hated him, Malaxa was said to have furnished Sima and his boys with arms. There were quite a few influential people who thought like Malaxa and strengthened Sima in his dangerous course.

Two actions precipitated Horia Sima's fall and the first break-up of a totalitarian regime in Europe. One was of the cherchez-la-femme variety and the other political. One was a prank and the other was high treason. Together they convinced the Germans it was impossible to work with Sima.

One day in the middle of January an attaché of the German Legation told me gleefully that the Guardist police the night before had raided the house of the beautiful Rumanian who was the friend of the German, Hungarian, and Italian ministers. "Pappi"—he meant Dr. Fabrizius—was furious, recognizing Horia's fine hand behind the raid. It was only a few days before Pappi's departure from Bucharest, with dinners and luncheons in his honor every day, and Pappi guessed that the raid on the beautiful lady's house was by way of Horia's Bronx cheer for him.

What was more—the lady was convinced that she would be shot the moment Pappi turned his back on Bucharest.

"This is all that was needed to persuade Pappi that we will have to get rid of Sima," said the attaché.

I objected that, since His Excellency had been aware of the Guardist habit of raiding houses, why should he get into a political stew over this raid on his lady friend's house? How about matters like the Nicholas Jorga murder, which was so much more terrible? But the attaché insisted that only today Pappi had discovered the whole horror of the Guardist regime, because it had, so to speak, struck close to home—which made me remember Fritz Thyssen who, after seven years of Nazi atrocities, suddenly got excited about a man dying in a concentration camp, because the man was his nephew. The imagination of unimaginative people apparently needed very immediate stimuli to get going. Anyway, the attaché had begun to feel very pessimistic about Horia Sima and advised me to do the same.

I heard of the political action which precipitated Sima's fall the same evening. It was Tester who told me, as a big piece of news, that Horia Sima had sent a special courier to Berlin, carrying a personal letter to the Führer—a very curious letter. For it was written by Antonescu to his young friend Corneliu Codreanu in 1937. In this letter Antonescu told Codreanu that he agreed with him in most points, but that there was one point on which he could never agree with him, and this was the matter of collaboration with the Germans. In his, Antonescu's, opinion there was only one course for Rumania and this was collaboration with France. Sima, Dr. Tester explained, expected great things from the effect of this letter on the Führer, hoping it would finally open Hitler's eyes to the General's real feelings.

I gasped. Like the famous Berlin banker who was asked, "Guess who died tonight?" and answered cheerfully, "Everybody is all right with me," it was all right with me that Horia Sima should destroy himself. Still, the enormity of his *gaffe* took my breath away.

"You don't think it's such a good idea?" A. T. asked with some concern.

I answered, "Hitler will never forgive Sima." For Hitler had known all along that Antonescu had been pro-French and not pro-German. Neubacher had told me all about this in June; one could suppose that the Chancellery in Berlin had been informed about this interesting bit of news long before. So the Führer would resent Sima's presumption that he and his staff did not know what they were doing. Moreover, in November Hitler had had that heart-to-heart talk with the General during which they had probably mentioned Antonescu's past convictions, yet Hitler, as everybody knew, had emerged from the tête-à-tête delighted with the General. So the Führer would resent Horia Sima's action as an attempt to cast doubt on his, the Führer's, judgment. But above all, Horia Sima had committed treason in selling out the chief of a Rumanian Government which Hitler had sanctioned. There is treason and treason: Sima's was the cheapest brand, and it showed him up as a totally untrustworthy, unreliable fellow. The Count, sharing my view, summed up the situation by saying severely, "These Guardist babies can't last. They have no savoir-vivre."

A few days later Hitler's private plane picked up Antonescu and the still-acting German minister, Dr. Fabrizius, and took them to the Führer. I could never find out whether Hitler had invited Antonescu as a result of the Sima letter, or whether Antonescu asked for a meeting because of it or for some reason of his own. However, Antonescu again was received by the Führer alone and Sima was again the absent-one-who-was-always-wrong. For two days during Antonescu's absence the Guardists around Sima were slightly disturbed, as if they had a premonition but, with the return of Antonescu, rumor had it that the Führer had endorsed Horia Sima and raised hell with the General, a rumor put out by the *nazissime* Nazis in the German Legation and, of course, by exultant Guardist circles. But it did not make sense. For confirmation or denial of it I tried a bluff on the Count.

"Well," I said with false assurance, "you got it all wrong. The Führer did not endorse Sima. He promised to go the whole way with Antonescu."

The Count, taken off guard, snapped, "Who told you?" Then he added thoughtfully: "It's fortunate that we have a censorship here and that you can't use your information."

"So it is information?" I answered.

"Sure," grinned the Count, loath to show himself less well informed than I, "God told his little Jon to be strong and good and he would be with him. But who told you really?"

I confessed nobody had told me, but that I had figured out Hitler's attitude in the way the village idiot found the monkey: by wondering where would I hide if I were a monkey. A way which, I had found during twenty years of watching politics develop, led frequently to more correct conclusions than most so-called information.

Still some Nazis continued to spread the story that Hit-

ler had endorsed Horia Sima. Was it wishful thinking by
those who found it hard to believe that Hitler was letting
down a fascist movement, or was it that they did not wish
to precipitate a desperate action by Horia Sima? Or was it
both?

Before I could decide, the great duel between General
Antonescu and Horia Sima, the struggle for power between the Rumanian State and the Guardist Party, entered with unexpected swiftness its final phase.

Rumania says it with murder. So it was only right that
the Guardist rebellion was set off by a murder, the victim
of which was Major Doering, a member of the German
military mission. He was shot on the night of January 18,
1941, in the Bucaresti Restaurant, a sort of Lindy's on the
Boulevard Bratianu. The Major was a specialist on Rumanian railway communications in the last war, which
was why he was taken along again. He was one of the older
mission members, an unostentatious, anonymous man:
but if one of the top generals had been killed, it could
not have made more of a sensation.

Rumanian police captured the murderer, allegedly a
Greek who carried English money and a check book on
the National City Bank. Accordingly the official version
was that the murder had been instigated by the British
Secret Service. A less official but equally plausible version
was that the murder was planned and instigated by Horia
Sima and his crowd as part of their campaign to sour
Hitler on Antonescu's administration.

One interpretation of Major Doering's murder was almost as good as the next. There was only one that was
nonsense: the one which made the foreign press a few days

later. This interpretation had it that the murder was the signal for an armed revolt against Antonescu's pro-German policy and especially against the presence of the military mission. There was no doubt that at this juncture questions of friendship with Germany in no way entered the discussion, and that there was no difference of opinion between Sima and Antonescu as to the course of foreign policy. Even the activist group of the Party, with their pro-communist leanings, and the group around the Codreanu family to whose terrorist tastes Sima catered in order to keep them in line, did not dream of disavowing the basic principle of Codreanu's testament: friendship with Germany. The struggle between Antonescu and Sima, or between State and Party, was exclusively determined by differences of opinion on inner policy, which meant on the tempo and intensity of the revolution, and by the ambitions of Sima and his friends.

On the Sunday after the Doering murder other significant events took place. Fifty-four mass demonstrations of Guardists were held in all big Rumanian cities, which were evidently meant by Sima as a review of the Party forces before the great battle and as propagandistic preparation for a coup d'état. The murder of Major Doering and the Guardist demonstrations were certainly connected with each other, and both influenced future events.

For, if the Guardists tried to pin the murder on Antonescu, the General made a neat job of pinning it back on the Guardists. On Monday Antonescu fired the Guardist Minister of the Interior, General Petrovicescu; the Guardist director of the state police, Prince Alexander Ghyka; the Guardist Prefect of Police, Mironovici; and replaced all three with military men. In the official report he ascribed this action to a lack of efficiency on the part of the three Guardist officials in their efforts to solve the murder of Major Doering and to protect the German military mission.

On the same day Antonescu sprang a decree on the Guardists which abolished the Guardist commissars who had been put into Jewish and other enterprises and had ruined the Rumanian economy by their ineptness and corruption. This decree had been ready for weeks, chiefly at the instigation of the German economists, but its publication on this day completed the impression of a full-dress Guardist Brumaire. In one day the Guardists had lost most of the gains of their revolution—key positions in the government and financial spoils. And it was clear that they would not take counter-revolution lying down.

There could be no doubt that Antonescu did all of this with the blessing and the full support of the German legations, both in the Strada Victor Emmanuel III and in the Strada Wilson, and especially of the military mission, all thoroughly aroused by the murder of a German officer and determined now to have order at any costs. Yet from a series of conversations I had with close friends of Horia Sima on the evening of this fateful day—the last time I ever laid eye on them—I gathered that the Guardist leaders still believed in German support against the General. They even went so far as to believe that the German troops would eventually fight with them against Antonescu's troops, once bad came to worse. I felt almost sorry for these men, blinded as they were by their wishful thinking which centered entirely around their hopes for Hitler's loyalty to any fascist movement, right or wrong.

Throughout Monday afternoon radio calls went out to

the Guardists to meet at their various centers immediately. There was a thick fog that night, but from my window at the Athene Palace I could see troops of Guardists, silent and shadowy as an army of ghosts, run at the double over the snow-covered Square. A few hours later they staged a demonstration of protest before the Presidency demanding the dismissal of General Rioseanu, Antonescu's friend and Undersecretary of the Interior, whom they called a Mason and responsible for the murder of Major Doering. They also demanded the formation of an exclusively Guardist government. Strangely enough, they cheered Antonescu, who did not appear. Whereupon the demonstration broke up.

But the same night the Guardists started a pogrom, partly as gesture of protest, partly because they always wanted a pogrom, partly from the determination that if they had to go down, they would do so in a blaze of red-hot terror, dragging as many people along as they possibly could. That Monday, before the dismissal of the Guardist officials had gone through, the Guardist police had made several hundred arrests, chiefly of wealthy Jews, under the pretext that these Jews were in on the British Secret Service plot to murder Doering. They were brought to the Prefecture and now many of them were tortured in a fashion so inconceivably cruel that some committed suicide. Many were dragged to a slaughterhouse where they were mutilated, killed, and then hung up like hogs, while a large sign marked them "Kosher Meat." Some escaped death at Guardist hands by sheer accident and were saved when Antonescu's forces "conquered" the Prefecture on Wednesday.

To get killed on the Brumaire of a revolution seems

like being killed in action on the day armistice is declared, when everything is over. On the other hand the Brumaire lent zest to the bloodlust of the Guardists, for fury with the present and despair of the future, added to the frustration of the past, made beasts of the Guardist mob. For two days and nights they robbed, raped, killed in the Jewish quarter around the famous Strada Lipscani, Bucharest's colorful, noisy, oriental, lower Broadway. Synagogues were burnt, husbands were forced to watch the dishonor of their wives and daughters before they themselves were put to death in such hideous fashion that the only escape for their women was to go insane. No revolution or pogrom of the twentieth century, not even the terrible one of Kishinev, though larger in scope, held horrors comparable to the ones which took place in Bucharest during these two days, except the Turkish slaughter of the Armenians. The Guardists were in a frenzy of blood, horrible beyond description since it had nothing personal any more. A young green-shirted boy on the Calea Victoriei was seen madly emptying his gun at the passers-by, laughing as if the detonation and the sight of the men toppling over gave him exquisite joy.

On Tuesday the revolt gathered momentum. The Guardist Prefect Mironovici refused to give up his office to his military successor and barricaded himself with a garrison of Guardist rebels in the Prefecture. It was evident that the Guardists had prepared the coup for weeks. They were excellently armed, presumably by Malaxa, and proceeded quickly to occupy all strategically important points. By Tuesday night the best part of Bucharest was in their hands. Only the barracks, railway stations, and ministries were still held by Antonescu.

The General, wary of bloodshed, was reluctant to use troops against the Guardists. After an armed assault on the Prefecture resulted in the death of two Guardists, the troops retired so that the Guardists could lay out the bodies on the spot. This reluctance to use his troops was falsely attributed to Antonescu's fear that the troops might go over to the Guardists. Though over the radio, controlled by the Guardists, every effort was made to get the army to go over, and rumor had it that the Generals in the province were with the rebels, the army stuck to Antonescu—and this sealed the fate of the Guardists.

On Wednesday Bucharest echoed to the flickering of gunfire, the rat-a-tat of machine guns, the dull discharges of Panzer cannon. The Guardists were brave. The army blocked them in various sections where they had barricaded themselves, and ordered them to give up their arms, but the Guardists opened fire though they knew that they had no chance. In some sections they defended every house, set fire to their barricades and threw burning bottles of benzine, sparing themselves as little as they did the "enemy." Yet stubbornness, courage, rage, and even machine guns, could achieve nothing against a few real tanks. A few tanks can mow any rebellion over, which seems to debunk any hopes that anti-German revolts in the dominated countries may annihilate Hitler. Such a thing is sheer wishful thinking. Revolts may become troublesome, but as long as Hitler has a few armored companies, they can do no serious harm. Here the Germans did not interfere at all. They once paraded an infantry company and a few tank units, muzzles directed up to the windows of the houses, down the Calea Victoriei to show that they were still there and ready for action if need be. But Rumanian troops managed nicely alone.

Antonescu could have quelled the revolt in a few hours, but in his attempt to shed as little blood as possible, gave the rebels frequent chances to put down their arms and interrupt the fighting to negotiate. But the Guardists always attacked anew without waiting for the end of these armistices, fighting with Turkish ferocity and Russian contempt for death. Once, in their attack on the Telephone Building, a skyscraper on the Calea, the Guardists forced women and children with guns to lead their attack, and several got killed when the army finally opened fire.

For two days the face of Bucharest was convulsed with pain. Cars and buses were abandoned in the middle of the boulevards for lack of gas. Tramways stopped functioning, the city smelled of smoldering houses and people suffering fear and pain. Then Horia Sima emerged from hiding. There had been much guessing about Sima's whereabouts during these last few days. At the Athene Palace they said alternately that he was hiding at the German Legation and that he had become reconciled with the General and was working with him against the rebels. Actually, it appeared that he was all over Bucharest exhorting his boys in their last desperate stand, which, as he must have known, was doomed. Now, on Thursday, January 23rd, he ordered his Guardists to stop fighting and to "return to normalcy" immediately. This order, Antonescu said in his official declaration, proved that Sima himself was the author of the rebellion. While this was so, it is also true that the rebellion got out of hand, for in spite of Horia Sima's order the rebels went on fighting. And now the army went into action in earnest and in a few hours all resistance was mopped up. That night the shooting subsided; the shoutings and the demonstrations died down; the cries of battle, cries of fear, cries of death, so weird and terrible that one never knew whether they were dreamed or whether they were real, still sounded through the night, but spaced at long intervals of silence. The good white snow was very dirty, and the fires of the synagogues burned low.

Horia Sima had fled, nobody knew where. Even as this is written, his whereabouts are unknown. Rumor has it alternately that he fled to Russia to work with the communists against Germany or that the Nazis spirited him away to Germany where they held him like a Damocles sword over Antonescu. Thousands in Bucharest and in the country were in jail, among them the lady who planned to kill the General. And at last Max Ausschnitt's wish was fulfilled: a cell, a not too comfortable one, was prepared for Malaxa, who for once had bet on the wrong horse. He was condemned to ten years of hard labor. The Guardist Party was ordered dissolved; Rumania was a Guardist state no longer, and as if by magic the pictures of the Capitano disappeared from desks of offices. But people still whistled the song of the *Capitano*; you could not get rid of this insistent melody.

Antonescu was now the sole master of Rumania. He announced that he would form a government on a military foundation as "the expression of the unity and discipline such as the circumstances demand." He said in this proclamation that, once everything was under control, "I shall proceed to the political reorganization of the State. For it is I who on September 6, 1940, decided upon the establishment of a National Socialist state." This was the

new self-assured language of General Antonescu, the Conducatore of Rumania.

A coma engulfed Bucharest and the whole country. The
Rumanians were terrified of their capacity for excess, and
too tired to move a finger or to think. Everything, they
felt, was better than the Guardist nightmare of the last
few days and weeks. The General would rule with the
army, which had not fought? Let him! It did not matter,
as the Germans were behind him with their army, too.
The Germans had more or less been behind everything
all along, hadn't they? They had given the Guardists to
Rumania and now they had taken them away. It was difficult to understand, but the Rumanians were too tired
to bother.

The Guardists, too, were tired and disgusted with themselves. After holding power for five months, they had returned to the dust, the first fascist regime which went to
pieces in Europe, and this in a country under German
protection. Once more, the Guardists were without leadership, and there were those who thought that Rumania
was forever fed up with the Guardist experience. I did
not believe this was so. Nobody was free from guilt about
the miscarriage of the Guardist regime. General Antonescu caused it by miscalculating the revolutionary dynamism of a movement surging to power straight out of
the night of persecution; Horia Sima caused it by his
weak catering to the activists of the Party, his lack of political and revolutionary experience, which did not war-
rant his enormous ambitions; the Nazis caused it because
they never took a strong hand, but kept everybody guessing. Yet, in spite of this failure in leadership the Guard,

as a movement and idea, belonged to the series of revolutionary movements which today determine the face of Europe. As long as fascism rules in Europe, the Guardist Party would be the only possible national movement in Rumania. Even if Antonescu tried to take over the ideas of Codreanu, he would need the Guardist Party as the broad basis on which to rest his revolution. The Guardist Party was down but not out.

The Germans knew this. On the thirtieth of January the newly arrived German Minister, Herr Von Killinger, declared in his first speech that while the Führer recognized General Antonescu as the leader of the Rumanian State, it was hoped that the "national groups and healthy forces of Rumania which ideologically are very near to us find the way back to their Fatherland."

The Germans now had what they needed all along: their strong man, Antonescu; quiet in the raw-material sphere; and a country too tired to move a finger and the ideal halting place for an army. But the Germans had paid an extremely high price for what they got. They had paid with the betrayal of a fascist regime in Rumania which they themselves had sponsored, a feat which would lower their prestige with all existing and would-be Quislings and fascist regimes all over Europe. True, economic and military necessities made this betrayal imperative, but it was chiefly Germany's own fault that this was the case. It had been their own muddling through which had led to an untenable situation. By their atrocious policy in Rumania the Germans had lost the good will of a nation which was only too ready to love and admire them. In a scant five months they had robbed Rumania of her King, her best provinces, her revolution, and had made the Rumanians indulge in such orgies of terror that they left marks like a terrible disease. You can't organize Europe that way.

On one of the days of terror, I sat in the lobby of the Athene Palace with a young Rumanian prince. Machine guns stood in the entrance hall and soldiers stood guard. It was before luncheon and the few people in the lobby carried on whispered, listless conversations which at intervals were drowned out by the sound of guns. Presently a group of German officers approached, walking between the yellow marble pillars with their slow measured steps, clanking a little, looking unmoved and polite. They went to the restaurant where all the other guests huddled as close to the German officers' table as they could, for to be near the German army made them feel safer that day. But the young prince looked after the Germans with hatred in his handsome face and said, "What they do to us and what they make us do to each other, the beasts!" And he threw his hands before his face and sobbed.

No, this kind of New Order would never do.

—EPILOGUE

I left the Athene Palace at the end of January 1941, knowing that Germany's blood- less conquest of Rumania was as complete as if her armies had trampled the land underfoot and her airplanes bom- barded the cities from the skies. Uninspired as German diplomacy was in Rumania, and wasteful as were her methods, they had given the desired result: Bucharest, the last capital of international glamour on the European con- tinent, was now nothing but a halting place for German troops sweeping South.

The wind from Russia blew sharply the day I drove to the Bucharest station and a new layer of snow covered the ground, very white and pure. It was early in the morning and, as I glanced back at the Athene Palace from the Square, I saw the crack which crisscrossed its white façade, a reminder of the earthquake, showing as clearly as does a scar on a face asleep. This scar had done no damage to the structure of the Athene Palace but had only marred the whiteness, and thus seemed to fit in with what was my strongest impression of Rumania in these seven months: the indestructible quality of this flexible, realistic, fatal- istic people whom destiny had established on the frontier between Orient and Occident. Two thousand years of se- vere foreign masters, barbarian invasions, rapacious conquerors, wicked princes, cholera, and earthquakes have given Rumanians a superb sense of the temporary and transitory quality of everything.

Here nobody complained about the "end of civilization" just because Hitler tried to set up a mere one-thousand-year Empire. A people that saw the Roman Empire come and go and saw all sorts of barbarians invade their country, and still survived, does not believe that there is a definite end to anything. Such people are instinctively wise in the strange ways of history, which invariably seems to run into compromise, and so they are less afraid than many great nations of the West. The Rumanians possess to the highest degree the capacity of receiving the blows of destiny while relaxed. They fall artfully, soft and loose in every joint and muscle as only those trained in falling can be. The secret of the art of falling is, of course, not to be afraid of falling and the Rumanians are not afraid, as Western people are. Long experience in survival has taught them that each fall may result in unforeseen opportunities and that somehow they always get on their feet again.

And, as this is written, it appears that Rumania has fared better under German domination than anyone expected. Rumanian divisions under the leadership of General—or, according to latest war bulletins, Marshal—Antonescu have retaken Bessarabia and Bukovina, hardly a year after they were lost, and have announced the conquest of Odessa and her incorporation in a new Rumanian administered province which they named "Trans-Istria." Probably Hitler told the carrot-haired, freckled-faced General, whom he appreciated so much, that there was no way of undoing the Vienna decision and handing back Transylvania, but that if Antonescu could help himself to some territory in the East, he would be welcome to it. So Antonescu went ahead and helped himself to Trans-Istria, thus conquering new territory for Rumania. And aside from these territorial gains, the fact that the Rumanian army fought at last, blots out Rumania's deepest humiliation of the last year: having the country torn to pieces without fighting.

Because victory and sacrifice give the Rumanian army the prestige which it lacked last year, some observers think a victorious and tried army might completely eliminate and replace the Iron Guard as a popular movement. I don't share this opinion. While Antonescu may rule Rumania for an indefinite period as a military dictator backed up by Germany, the Iron Guard cannot be eliminated as the most powerful single factor in Rumanian politics as long as fascist movements determine the fate of Europe— and whoever rules Rumania must reckon with the innumerable cells of thirteen devised by Corneliu Zelea Codreanu.

Juliu Maniu, eternal hope of the liberals, wrote a letter—this time to Antonescu—saying that, now Bessarabia and Bukovina were back with Rumania, Rumanian troops had no business fighting on for the greater glory of Hitler. No doubt many Rumanians feel the way Maniu does, but unfortunately Hitler's wars are not conducted like climbing parties in the Swiss mountains, where those who get dizzy can wait in a rest house halfway up, while the tough people climb to the peak.

The whereabouts of the long-haired revolutionary, Horia Sima, are still unknown. As to King Michael, a recent story from London has it that he wishes to abdicate in order to marry Malaxa's daughter—whose father is still in prison—which, if true, shows that it really is the destiny of this family to take their love affairs seriously. Latest reports have it that Michael, involved in a plot against the Nazis, was forcibly removed from the Rumanian scene by the Gestapo. This highly improbable interpretation of Michael's little holiday trip away from General Antonescu's severe regime to the milder and more anonymous climate of Florence, Italy, has its origin mainly in Mexico City where Carol, Lupescu and Urdareanu have found a temporary haven. Carol's friends in the United States and England are very active on behalf of their exiled King. The State Department in Washington and the Foreign Office in London are swamped with lobbyists trying to win the powers-that-be to the idea that only Carol's return can save Rumanian democracy. A great amount of whitewashing is being undertaken by expert hands. Before me I have a column by Elsa Maxwell all about Madame and what a lovely woman she is, the great benefactress of the Rumanians, which makes me wonder what would have happened if Elsa Maxwell had been around to promote Lupescu in Rumania for the last ten years. Maybe it would have kept Carol on the throne. Incidentally, detested as Carol was by his people, the possibility of his return to the throne of his fathers should not be ruled out. For this, too, I learned at the Athene Palace: nobody is so detested that a few years later someone else is not detested more, and the old hate falls into oblivion before the new fresh one.